Praise for *Growing Up Empty*
by Loretta Schwartz-Nobel

"*Growing Up Empty* is a chilling account of the struggle to get enough to eat that confronts far too many people in the wealthiest country in the world. Loretta Schwartz-Nobel . . . tells the stories of men, women, and children who are confronted with the tragedy of hunger in America. . . . *Growing Up Empty* is a long-overdue and necessary contribution to the fight to build the political will to end hunger in the United States."

—CONGRESSMAN TONY P. HALL, chairman, Democratic Task Force on Hunger

"Seven thousand years after the first civilizations formed to alleviate hunger, the world's wealthiest nation leaves millions of its children without enough to eat. Now Loretta Nobel peels away the patina of compassion to reveal that most national leaders simply don't care enough to prevent this man-made tragedy."

—DR. J. LARRY BROWN, director, National Center on Hunger and Poverty

"After a decade of unprecedented economic growth, far too many Americans, especially children, still live such impoverished lives that they often are not sure where their next meal is coming from. Schwartz-Nobel's penetrating journalistic study explores the personal dimension of hunger in the United States today, putting a human face on a social issue that is too often expressed in dry statistics. This book should serve as a wake-up call to policy makers."

—KENNETH KUSMER, author of *Down and Out, On the Road:
The Homeless in American History*

"In a country where dieting is an art form, people still have difficulty believing that there are people who cannot afford to eat. From the military bases to the backroads of the rural South to the tony suburbs of Philadelphia, Loretta Schwartz-Nobel has captured the many faces of hunger in America and shown us our own reflection. *Growing Up Empty* should be required reading for every elected official, who, without a doubt, would finally be moved to use his or her power to end the needless tragedy of hunger in America."

—JOAN MINTZ ULMER, director, Greater Philadelphia Food Bank

"Once in a while a book comes along that stops us in our tracks and forever changes our vision. *Growing Up Empty* is such a book. A deft blend of tough investigative reporting and deep compassion, it combines the politics of hunger in America with the heartbreaking stories of its victims. We watch hunger ebb as (social) programs expand, and explode when they are contracted. But what sets this book apart is that, in the end, we come to know the victims of these policies the way Loretta Schwartz-Nobel came to know them—as if they were our sisters and brothers and children. This is an unforgettable exploration of public policy, its failures and its victims."

—WILLIAM RASPBERRY, Pulitzer Prize–winning columnist, *Washington Post*

"Loretta Schwartz-Nobel's *Growing Up Empty* is a forceful reminder of the great shame in our society that hunger still plagues millions of Americans. She puts a human face on hunger around us, and shines a moral spotlight on a problem that is largely ignored. She reminds us that the issue has been swept from the headlines, but not from the streets. More than just a forceful call to action, Schwartz-Nobel has issued a mandate for reform."

—SENATOR EDWARD M. KENNEDY

"This is a well-written, well-researched book that every thoughtful American should read. The paradox of millions of underfed people in the world's most richly endowed nation offends not only this author, it should offend all of us."

—GEORGE MCGOVERN, U.S. senator and author of *The Third Freedom: Ending Hunger in Our Time*

"Loretta Schwartz-Nobel offers a very personal look at hunger among diverse groups of Americans, including the working poor, immigrants and refugees, the middle class, and, shockingly, the military. *Growing Up Empty* will not only elicit understanding and compassion, it should also evoke outrage, a quality we need in our country if we are ever going to eliminate hunger."

—BILL AYRES, founder and executive director, World Hunger Year

"It's not possible to read *Growing Up Empty* without feeling like something is terribly wrong in our great nation. Hardworking parents and their children shouldn't go without food in a prosperous democracy, and we all need to pull together to make sure that everyone has a place at the table."

—JEFF BRIDGES, actor and chairman, Hunger Free America; founder, End Hunger Network

Growing Up Empty

ALSO BY LORETTA SCHWARTZ-NOBEL

Starving in the Shadow of Plenty
Engaged to Murder
A Mother's Story
The Baby Swap Conspiracy
Forsaking All Others

Growing Up Empty

The Hunger Epidemic in America

Loretta Schwartz-Nobel

HarperCollins*Publishers*

HarperCollins books may be purchased for educational, business, or sales promotional use. For information, please write: Special Markets Department, HarperCollins Publishers Inc., 10 East 53rd Street, New York, NY 10022.

FIRST EDITION

Designed by Nancy B. Field

Library of Congress Cataloging-in-Publication Data
Schwartz-Nobel, Loretta.
Growing up empty : the hunger epidemic in America / by Loretta Schwartz-Nobel.
p. cm.
ISBN 0-06-019563-0 (alk. paper)
1. Poverty—United States. 2. Hunger—United States. 3. Malnutrition—United States. 4. Hunger—Government policy—United States. I. Title.

HC110.P6 S327 2002
363.8'2'0973—dc21   2002020737

02 03 04 05 06 ❖ /RRD 10 9 8 7 6 5 4 3 2 1

*This book was written for all the
hungry children I met on my journey
and all those I never met.*

"We do not want to quibble over words but malnutrition is not quite what we found. . . . They are suffering from hunger and disease and, directly or indirectly, they are dying from them—which is exactly what 'starvation' means."

HUNGER, U.S.A.,
*Citizens' Board of Inquiry into Hunger
and Malnutrition in the United States,
Beacon Press, 1968*

Acknowledgments

Although the final responsibility for this book's shortcomings rests with me, more people than I can name here contributed to it.

First, I would like to thank all of the hungry men, women, and children I interviewed, for trusting me enough to let me into their homes and lives. Their hope, friendship, and generosity never ceased to amaze me.

I would also like to thank Dr. J. Larry Brown of the Center on Hunger and Poverty; Caridad Asensio of the Caridad Clinic; John Moore, director of volunteers at St. Vincent's; Dr. Debbie Frank of the Boston Grow Clinic; Toni Graff, director of the Light House; Lisa Joels, founder of H.E.L.P.; Pat Kellenbarger, director of the Military Parish Visitors; Pam Lawler, founder of Philabundance; Elaine Michelini, senior case manager for WINGS; Bill Radatz of the Presbyterian Ministries; Kallyane Sok of the Southeast Asian Mutual Assistance Coalition and Rita Ungaro Schiavone, founder of Aide for Friends. Claire Cooper, Joan Mintz Ulmer, and Rosemary Gross also provided invaluable help.

I want to express my appreciation to my husband, Joel Nobel, for his emotional and economic support, to my sister, Helen Driscoll, for reading early drafts and to my children, Adam, Rebecca, and Ruth, for their continuing belief and encouragement.

This book would not have been published without the persever-
ance of my literary agent, Ellen Levine, and the fine judgment of my
editor, Mauro DiPreta, and his assistant, Joelle Yudin.

I especially want to acknowledge the inspirational memory of
my beloved mother, Fay Rosenberg, who died before this book was
published, and the guardian angel who was always there helping and
guiding me through every aspect of the project.

Contents

Author's Note

The hungry people in this book are not identified by their real names. This decision was made for several reasons. Some of the mothers that I interviewed feared punishment by the authorities for stealing food to feed their children, others worried that the food stamp office or other federal programs would cut off their aid. A few also asked that I change exact addresses and other identifying details in order to assure their anonymity and protect their children from embarrassment or humiliation. Any similarity between the fictitious names used and those of living people is, of course, purely coincidental. Dialogue is transcribed from tapes or edited from notes. Conversations that took place over several days were occasionally resequenced and restructured for clarity. In some cases I have added descriptive details in order to convey more effectively the personalities and lives of the people.

All of the families I spoke to live in the towns, cities, or villages I described. The names of all food pantries, homeless shelters, food banks, soup kitchens, perishable food distribution centers, and academic organizations remain unchanged, as do the names of all employees, experts in the field, and volunteers.

Growing Up Empty

Preface

"I am not writing, after all, about numbers, trends, units or theories. This book is about humans, poor humans, and it is unashamedly on their side. These are my friends, you see. We have looked into each other's eyes. We have tasted each others lips."

LUIS ALBERTO URREA
By the Lake of Sleeping Children

There is a road near my house called Haverford Road. I have driven on it often but I never really knew where it led. One day last summer when the expressway was closed, I checked my map and decided to follow the road as an alternate route to the center of Philadelphia. After about fifteen minutes, my familiar-looking neighborhood began to change into a distinctly poorer one. Ten minutes later, it looked as if I had entered a third world country. Some of the stores had rusted iron bars across their windows, others had been closed down altogether and their doors were nailed shut. Many of the houses still appeared lived in but most had boarded-up windows. There was graffiti, broken glass and trash everywhere.

I stopped at a red light and instinctively turned to lock my doors, then I saw two young girls and a boy standing next to a large dark green trash Dumpster at the side of the road.

I watched the older girl, who was about six and rail thin, climb onto the boy's shoulders. She leaned forward and grabbed a white paper bag. Ignoring the flies that circled the bin, she jumped off the boy's shoulders, opened the bag and tore a leg from the carcass of a partly eaten chicken. She solemnly handed the leg to the littler girl, then, without speaking, the older girl and the boy began devouring the rest.

The younger girl, who was only about two, stepped off the curb and toddled toward me wearing a dirty yellow dress and carrying the chicken leg. There was a cross around her neck and desperation in her large, almond-shaped brown eyes. She pressed her sticky fingers against my car door then opened her mouth and smiled. As I smiled back, I looked at her more closely and saw something black moving across her tongue. Then I looked down at her hand and saw that there were ants, dozens of ants, on the chicken leg.

The driver behind me beeped his horn. The boy looked up and saw me. He shouted something I couldn't understand, then frantically grabbed the little girl.

"Wait," I called, forgetting the neighborhood, forgetting the car behind me, forgetting everything. But all three children had already flown out of sight and disappeared like fireflies into a dark, narrow alley, leaving only the iridescent magic of their life spark indelibly etched in my mind. They ran because they thought that they had done something wrong. They ran because they believed that they were the criminals instead of the victims. They ran because they did not know that there is a Haverford Road and children as desperately hungry as they are in every city, town and village in America.

Like many of us, they did not know that there is a hidden epidemic in this country. Sometimes it strikes children suddenly and without warning. At other times it starts before their birth and lasts an entire lifetime. Often, it is passed from one generation to the next, damaging not only the spirits of its young victims but their immune systems, physical strength and intelligence as well. Now and then there is a remission and occasionally there is a long-term cure, but it can also be fatal or permanently damaging, especially for the very young.

A young child's brain grows so rapidly that, by the age of two it has achieved 80 percent of its full development. If adequate nutrients are not available during this critical period, the brain's weight and size may be irreversibly compromised. The result may be a child who is mildly to moderately retarded for the rest of his or her life.

As the Harvard Physicians Task Force pointed out, in the end it all comes down to food. In its mildest form, and for short periods, all children have known hunger. But for most of them that uncomfortable craving is a symptom, not a disease. Hunger that continues because there is no food to eat becomes malnutrition, a torturous physiological experience that affects all of the body's most important functions and makes children desperate enough to eat anything they can find.

Malnutrition is a disease. If a growing child cannot get the food he needs, his body will soon begin to waste. Over a longer period the child's growth will be permanently stunted.

In advanced malnutrition, a child's hands and feet lack warmth and color; the muscles weaken and the subcutaneous fat wastes away. Both children and adults take on a puffy look; in very advanced cases, the abdomen and extremities become swollen, as we've seen in the photographs of African famine. Severe malnutrition devastates the nervous system, the mind loses its ability to reason and the child withdraws. As the condition worsens, the body becomes unable to maintain normal temperature, blood pressure or pulse rate. The heartbeat becomes faint. Sores appear that do not heal, bones break that do not mend and extremities swell noticeably. Diarrhea, generally accompanied by bleeding from the intestines, appears. These are signs of the advanced protein deficiency called kwashiorkor.

In the state known as marasmus, the body devours its own tissues. The internal organs atrophy, leaving only the brain at its customary weight. The cause of death, more often than not, is overwhelming infection that occurs when the immune system fails.

Tragically, after the Harvard Physicians Task Force traveled across America in 1985, they wrote, "We verified reports of Americans suffering from severe malnutrition: children diagnosed with kwashiorkor, marasmus or cavitary tuberculosis; adults and children literally dying from starvation, suffering from severe wasting or contracting serious infectious diseases."

The hidden epidemic in America is hunger. Now, in the new millennium, once again it is running rampant through urban, rural and suburban communities. It is affecting blacks, whites, Asians, Christians, Jews, and nonbelievers alike.

The physical suffering and the losses it causes to the bodies, spirits and brains of children are as debilitating and potentially fatal as the most serious diseases. But hunger is not caused by a virus or a bacteria. This silent American epidemic is caused by people, by acts of man, not acts of God or nature.

Countless millions of federal dollars and many of our country's most successful efforts to halt the spread of childhood hunger and starvation have recently been withdrawn. As a result, it is getting worse. The most recent estimates compiled by the USDA in 1999 indicate that 36.2 million Americans live in food-insecure households, which means that their access to adequate and safe food is limited or uncertain.

The cure is easily within our reach. We have the money and we have the food. We need only the courage to see, the compassion to respond and the leadership to change our course.

If any other rapidly spreading epidemic was weakening the health, minds and spirits of 36.2 million Americans and keeping 12.1 million children under the age of twelve from growing up healthy or growing up at all, there would be headlines in every major newspaper about it every day. But hunger is America's silent and hidden disease. More than 36 million Americans are suffering from an epidemic that still remains largely unacknowledged at the highest political levels. Our leaders often speak of poverty, but "hunger" is a word that is almost never publicly mentioned. Even in President Bush's inaugural address in 2001, the word "hunger" was never spoken.

Perhaps that is because, as George McGovern pointed out back in 1972, "To admit the existence of hunger in America is to confess that we have failed in meeting the most sensitive and painful of human needs. To admit the existence of widespread hunger is to cast doubt on the efficacy of our whole system."

Hunger in America was "officially" discovered and brought to public attention in April of 1967. Senators Joseph Clark and Robert Kennedy had traveled to the Mississippi Delta to study poverty programs, but when they stopped at the home of Annie White and her five children they found something they had not expected to see.

As Nick Kotz reported in *Let Them Eat Promises*, Senator Clark had gone on ahead of Robert Kennedy and had felt his way through a dark, tumbledown windowless shack. Fighting nausea at the strong smell of aging mildew, sickness and urine in the early afternoon shadows, he saw a child sitting on the floor of a tiny back room. She was barely two years old and was wearing only a filthy undershirt. She sat rubbing several grains of rice round and round on the floor. The senator knelt beside her.

"Hello. . . . Hi. . . . Hi, baby," he mumbled, touching her cheeks and her hair as he would his own child. As he sat on the dirty floor, he placed his hand gently on the child's swollen stomach. The little girl just sat there as if in a trance. Her sad eyes were turned downward as she rubbed the gritty rice.

For five minutes he tried talking, caressing, tickling, poking, demanding that the child respond. The baby never looked up.

Finally Senator Clark made his way back to the front yard, where Annie White stood talking to Robert Kennedy as she washed the family's clothes in a zinc tub. She told the senators she had no money and she was feeding her family nothing but rice and biscuits made from leftover surplus commodities.

Then Robert Kennedy went back and saw the child for himself. He stood alone for a few minutes, controlling his feelings before whispering to a companion, "I've seen bad things in West Virginia but I've never seen anything like this anywhere in the United States."

In the days that followed, the senators drove along the muddy roads and stopped at shack after shack, seeing with their own eyes hungry diseased children and hearing with their own ears the poor describe their struggle to survive.

The day after they returned to Washington, Clark and Kennedy went directly to agriculture secretary Orville Freeman to seek emergency help for the hungry children and families of Mississippi. They urgently described what they had seen. Freeman seemed concerned, and before the meeting was over he ordered two of his top aides to leave immediately for Mississippi to investigate the hunger problem. That meeting in Freeman's lavish office on April 12, 1967, began a Washington battle for food aid reform that is still raging today.

Robert Kennedy was so moved by what he saw that he underwent a political and emotional evolution. Urged on by his aides, he visited Indian reservations, Appalachia and a New York City ghetto.

"There are millions of Americans living in hidden places whose faces and names we never know," he said when he returned. "I have seen children starving in Mississippi, idling away their lives in the urban ghetto, living without hope or future amid the despair of Indian reservations. These conditions will change. Those children will live only if we dissent."

But even after Kennedy's reports were confirmed and supplemented by both a Hunger Task Force and a Field Foundation report, President Lyndon Johnson resisted food aid reform. Finally, after five years of trying to build a Great Society without addressing the problem of hunger, he relented. Food programs for the hungry increased from $173 million in the last year of the Eisenhower administration to $655 million in the last year of the Johnson administration.

Now, more than thirty-five years later, after all the political efforts and counter-efforts, all the years of funding and then dismantling of food aid programs, once again public denial and silence have returned. Most Americans still don't fully realize that today, more than ever, children and adults are still hungry or starving in all those "hidden places" that Robert Kennedy spoke of.

I didn't either until about twenty-five years ago. On October 10, 1974, just a few blocks from my house, I noticed a badly crippled old woman trying to crawl down some broken concrete steps. When I stopped to help her she told me that her name was Martha Roca. She was eighty-four years old and had almost starved to death.

I half carried her back into what looked like an abandoned, roach-infested brownstone and promised to return with food. Then I raced to the day-care center where my small daughter, Rebecca, was waiting. Together we brought groceries to Mrs. Roca. In the months that followed, it became our habit to take several bags of food to her each Saturday afternoon. Rebecca thought it was the best part of our week. Young as she was, the experience of giving moved and delighted her. When Martha Roca laughed with tears streaming down her face, saying, "Thank you. Thank you, darling dear. When I feel better, I'll crochet." Rebecca felt her joy and thought we were solving the problem. But by then, I felt certain that there were other people in Philadelphia who were desperate for food.

I went to the editor of *Philadelphia* magazine, where I was volunteering as a college intern, and told him I wanted to write an article on hunger in Philadelphia. But, like so many Americans, he was unfamiliar with the problem that had briefly been brought to public attention seven years earlier. He laughed and said that there was no hunger in our city, that the only problem people in Philadelphia had was eating too much. When I insisted that he was wrong, just to humor me he told me to take a few days and see what I could find.

Everyone I contacted during the first two days seemed to be as unaware of hunger as my editor was. Then, near the end of the third day, I reached the public relations director at the Philadelphia

Corporation for Aging. After I explained why I was calling, she sighed deeply and said, "You've come to the right place."

The next morning, I rode in the van that delivered one meal a day, five days a week to the homebound elderly. Soon I learned that many hundreds of people, who had worked all their lives, were surviving on only one meal a day, five days a week, and saving part of it for weekends. Even worse, thousands of others languished on waiting lists, barely getting by from day to day. In the weeks that followed, I visited the tenements and back alleys of Philadelphia and discovered small children and their mothers living with almost no food and sometimes with no heat or electricity.

When I told my editor what I had found, he was stunned. He praised me for my research but then said that he'd have to assign the piece to a real writer, someone with the experience to handle the subject. Ironically, the senior editor he chose was busy writing about a marriage-encounter weekend and let the hunger assignment slide. I quietly continued my research then assembled my notes. I was just a kid with no journalism experience, but somehow, when I sat down to write, the words and the images of the people I had seen and spoken to poured out. It was almost as if they were telling their own stories, as if my hand was simply the link between their lives and the empty page.

I can still remember my heart pounding when I handed my editor the first twelve pages and waited as he read them. When he finally looked up from the last page, he just stared at me for a long while.

I finished the piece and it was published in the Christmas 1974 issue of *Philadelphia* magazine. The stories of the people I had found shocked the city. From its first day on the newsstands, readers not only believed there was hunger, they began to think of the poor and the hungry as neighbors and friends. Offers of money, food and clothing flooded the magazine's switchboard. People began showing up in the slick Center City lobby carrying brown bags overflowing with groceries, clothing, blankets and toys. Some families donated their own brand-new Christmas gifts. They filled the place with bags and boxes and envelopes full of cash then left, still anxiously searching for more ways to help.

A few months later, I went to Washington to accept the Robert F. Kennedy Journalism Award for the article. The award program had been established to honor the slain senator's memory and recognize ongoing efforts to help the disadvantaged. In an experience that seemed almost unreal to an inexperienced young journalist, I sat eating lunch between Ted and Rose Kennedy, then I was called to a stage, where Ethel Kennedy handed me a bronze bust of her husband inscribed *For outstanding coverage of the problems of the disadvantaged.* But when I saw the audience filled with important senators, congressmen and journalists, I felt I should tell them that I hadn't "covered" the problem, that I had just barely begun to *uncover* it. I wanted them to know what I now knew and what Robert Kennedy had known eight years earlier, that there were hungry people and starving people of all ages, races and religions, not just in Philadelphia but all over America.

"May I say something?" I asked Ethel Kennedy very timidly. "Just say thank you," she whispered.

When I returned home, I was contacted by other magazine editors who asked me if I thought there was hunger in their area. I spent several weeks in each city then published investigative reports in Boston, Washington, and Chicago, and nationally in *Ms.* magazine, *Redbook,* and *Mother Jones.* As word of hunger spread, Dan Rather sent a news crew to Philadelphia. The Pew Foundation contributed $1.5 million to an emergency food fund, and I presided over the opening of several of the first food banks in the country, including one in Philadelphia. I went to Washington twice and testified before the Senate Select Committee on Hunger and Nutrition.

As one thing led to another, I spent much of the next seven years quietly exploring the lives of the hungry and researching what was to become my first book. I retraced some of Kennedy's steps traveling the muddy back roads of Mississippi. I spoke to the hungry in rural shacks and urban ghettos, on Indian reservations and in previously middle-class homes.

In 1981, when my book *Starving in the Shadow of Plenty* was published, 30 million Americans were living below the federally established poverty level and statistics indicated that their numbers were growing. But many of the programs that had been established to help them were now being eliminated or cut back by the Reagan administration. We were the richest nation in the world. Our food stockpiles cost half a billion dollars a year to maintain. We were actually exporting rice, wheat and corn out of America at an average rate of 70 million pounds a day. On top of that, there was enough food thrown into garbage cans every day to feed all the hungry people in the country.

Pam Lawler was working as an executive in marketing and communications at the Hays Group in Philadelphia when she read *Starving in the Shadow of Plenty.* She was struck by the irony of federal cuts, excess supply and ever-increasing hunger. Pam was living in a newly renovated Victorian house and eating in a lot of good restaurants. Now, for the first time, she was also thinking about the perishable food that they were throwing away at the end of each day.

One night in 1981, as she sat at the side of her young son's bed, thinking of how many children like him were hungry, an idea struck her. She reasoned that all that was really missing, between the food that was being thrown away and the people who desperately needed it, was a link. As she kissed her son good night, Pam decided right then and there that she would become that link. She quit her job as a well-paid executive and designed some business cards and a leaflet. First, she traveled to the social service agencies and churches in her area, then to the restaurants, hotels and supermarkets. She handed out her material and said, "If you have any leftover food, don't throw it away, call me, I'll come and get it." Whenever someone called, Pam just put her son in the back of her blue Subaru, picked up the food, then delivered it wherever it was needed.

The first call came from Superfresh; they had some fruit, mostly apples. The next was from the Hershey Hotel—a hundred leftover boxed lunches. Initially, it was just Pam Lawler, her baby and the blue Subaru, but as people began to hear about her work, they volunteered both time and money. The organization that she had named Philabundance began expanding. When it could no longer be run from her house, she rented an office and applied for funding. Today Philabundance provides the food for more than thirty-three thousand meals a day.

In New York City, a woman named Helen Palit established another perishable food rescue program called City Harvest. It too attracted considerable attention and, as it mounted resources, Palit began to take full-page ads in the *New York Times*. Other food programs followed. Pam Lawler and Helen Palit didn't know it at the time, but Philabundance and City Harvest were the beginning of a food rescue network that now spans the nation. These independent groups became officially linked by a central national organization called Food Chain that ultimately became the nation's leading food rescue program. It provided more than 150 million pounds of good salvageable food to more than twelve thousand social service agencies each year before finally merging with Second Harvest in April of 2000.

By 1982, hunger had burst into America's consciousness in a way that had not been seen since the late 1960s. Several factors were responsible for the change. First, the recession that began during the Carter administration caused widespread unemployment even among the middle class. Second, the Reagan White House and a Democratic Congress cut billions of dollars from the housing subsidies for the poor, which ultimately became a major factor in the growth of homelessness. At the same time, they also cut more than $12 billion from the food stamp and child nutrition programs that Senators Kennedy, Clark and others had fought so hard to start in the late '60s.

Suddenly, people in many parts of the country were not only talking about hunger, they were experiencing it firsthand. At the same time that Pam Lawler, Helen Palit and others had begun to mobilize perishable-food rescue missions, neighborhood churches had also started to notice that more and more of the people they were seeing each Sunday didn't have enough food for their families. Then doctors in various parts of the nation began to observe that many of their patients were hungry. They started seeing more hunger-related illnesses in their practices. But the first "official" recognition of America's hunger crisis came when a report was issued by the U.S. Conference of Mayors in October 1982. A national survey they conducted concluded that hunger in America represented "a most serious emergency." A number of the mayors actually requested emergency federal relief just as they would if their communities were hit by floods or tornadoes. Coleman Young, the mayor of Detroit, spoke of an urgent need to help the residents of his city "avoid starvation." Between October of 1982 and November of 1984, a total of fifteen major studies of hunger in America were produced. Even the U.S. Department of Agriculture concluded that "Hunger is increasing at a frenetic pace and the emergency food available for distribution is quickly depleted."

My own small, individual efforts had come at the start of a rising tide of hunger and of public consciousness about it.

With the common agreement that something needed to be done and a new awareness that hunger was in the hands of so many skilled experts and professionals, I believed that my own work in the field was complete. I told myself that I was a journalist, not a religious leader, a scholar or an activist. After eight years, I thought I had taken hunger as far as I could. I also believed that once public awareness and concern had risen to this level, solutions would be sought, found, implemented and maintained.

So, in an effort to support my children after my husband unexpectedly left, I did what most journalists do, I turned to different subjects. In the years that followed, I wrote and published four other nonfiction books on "more commercial" subjects. Eventually, I remarried, gave birth to a son and took great pleasure in watching him grow.

I was wrong about hunger, of course. The political struggle and the suffering of the hungry not only went on, it escalated.

By 1983, officials in Washington were once again trying to downplay the issue of hunger in America. It seemed as if their concern was not to find out how much hunger there was or how to solve the problem; instead it was to silence and discredit the people who did.

One of those people was Dr. Larry Brown, an idealistic young faculty member at the Harvard School of Public Health and the director of the school's community health program. With the support of the Field Foundation, Larry Brown gathered together and led a team of some of the finest and best-known physicians in America. Beginning in the last months of 1983, they traveled to twenty-five states and the District of Columbia. In each state, small teams of doctors and other professionals visited hospitals, day-care centers, schools, welfare offices, food stamp offices and especially homes. They spoke to people who had little or nothing to eat.

They were moved, just as I had been in the previous decade and as Kennedy had been in the decade before that, by the kindness, openness and decency they found. They were also angered by the policies that caused parents to become desperate and children to starve.

Finally, on February 12, 1985, the task force presented their findings before fifteen television crews and one hundred members of the press. National news carried the story at the start of the hour. Once again, the American public was shocked and eager to learn more, but the official response was an attempt to downplay or discredit the results. First, a Reagan spokesman refused to comment. Later, another spokesman for the Department of Agriculture flatly denied the validity of the findings. "The problem of hunger is not widespread," he declared. "The Federal Government is doing more to end hunger than any administration in history."

Even as word of hunger continued to spread and the public became increasingly involved, the White House kept on denying its existence and defending their position. Then, in 1986, Reagan told a young student from a Midwestern high school that there was plenty of food in America and added that "the hungry are too igno-rant to know where to get it." Within minutes, the comment had been picked up by newspapers and news broadcasters all across the country. The public outrage was strong enough to cause Reagan to eat his words. Just days later, he joined hands with Mrs. Reagan and the White House staff and participated in Hands Across America, an extraordinary human chain of six million people holding hands from New York to Los Angeles to protest hunger in America.

After several more months of escalating public outcry and diffi-cult political lobbying, legislation was finally shepherded through the House to increase nutrition programs by $5 billion. It was only a fraction of the $12 billion that had been cut from food programs by the Reagan administration, but it was a victory and it was a start.

During the mid to latter part of the 1980s, the partially re-funded programs led to a predictable reduction of about a million children living with hunger. But, once again, it was not nearly enough.

According to a 1995 study by the Center on Budget and Policy Priorities, 27.3 million people were being kept from hunger and poverty by existing government programs but 30.3 million more were still hungry and still needed help.

But instead of responding to the center's findings by increasing federal aid, in 1996 American politicians chose instead to implement the Contract with America, or Welfare to Work law, which included an additional $27 billion in cuts to the food stamp program alone.

Shortly before President Clinton signed the new law, the Physicians Committee on Childhood Hunger realized what was going to happen and issued a direct and powerful plea.

"The Contract with America will cut or cripple the very anti-hunger programs that Republicans and Democrats in Congress developed. . . . For the richest nation on earth to deny food to its own children is a shortsighted betrayal of our values and our future. It is also unnecessary. In the name of our nation and its children, we call upon reason to prevail in Congress." But the plea that was signed by hundreds of well-respected physicians from every state in the Union fell, like many other pleas before it, on deaf political ears.

As part of that plea, Dr. Ernesto Pollett, professor of pediatrics at the University of California at Davis, who had traveled the world in his research on hunger, issued his own unequivocal statement: ". . . our country is heading for a crisis of enormous proportions."

On March 10, 1998, an *All Things Considered* newscast on National Public Radio reported the early signs of that crisis. Host Robert Siegel announced that "Hunger in America has reached a point where one in ten Americans now regularly use a neighborhood food bank or soup kitchen in order to eat." I still remember pulling my car over to the side of the road so I could fully absorb the concept.

The new national survey was conducted by Second Harvest, the country's largest hunger relief organization. It reported that in 1997, 26 million people had requested and received food through their services alone.. More than a third were families where at least one adult was working and 38 percent of the hungry were children.

I think it was the magnitude of that 38 percent—the vast, blurred, incomprehensible images of millions of children suffering from hunger—that kept me awake that night and forced me to admit to myself that I had not found deep meaning in any of the other work I had done.

Early the next morning, I called NPR and had them fax me the transcript. When I returned home that night, I saw a front-page headline in the *Philadelphia Inquirer* that read, "New Hunger Report Shatters Stereotypes."

I was riveted. Eighteen years suddenly vanished, and like Fitzgerald's Gatsby I was born back ceaselessly into the past, back to Washington ghettos, Boston tenements, South Dakota Indian reservations, Philadelphia back alleys and rural shacks in the Mississippi Delta.

Five days later I flew to Seattle to attend the National Food Chain Conference. It was there that I began my second odyssey into the world of hunger and poverty. The large meeting room was filled to capacity. I could hardly believe how huge the volunteer hunger network had grown. There were hundreds of people in the room and none of them looked even vaguely familiar.

It wasn't just Dr. Brown's group at Harvard that had awakened people. World Hunger Year was also committed to the fight. They believed that the long-term solutions to hunger and poverty, both here and around the world, would come primarily through grassroots efforts, self-reliance and empowering the individual. Countless others, including Bread for the World and the Children's Defense Fund, had labored tirelessly on behalf of growing hunger among children. A Congressional Hunger Center had been established to train a new generation of young leaders. The center was led by congressional representative Tony Hall, who chaired the House Select Committee on Hunger and fasted for three weeks when it was dismantled in 1993. It was not a hunger strike. There were no demands attached to his action, it was a fast of prayer. Another remarkable organization called Share Our Strength had been set up to collect funds from the rich to redistribute to the poor.

A seemingly endless list of large corporations including UPS, Kraft Foods, Philip Morris, American Express, Coca Cola, Delta Airlines, Barnes and Noble and many more were now heavily involved. In addition Taco Bell, Pizza Hut, KFC and dozens of other well-known restaurants had all become regular contributors of food. At first I couldn't imagine what I could possibly hope to add to such an organized, well-funded, large-scale private-sector and corporate attack on hunger in America.

But then I realized that, despite all the effort and progress in the public response to hunger, there was still another story, a story of indifference and denial, a story so powerful that it overshadowed the first and resulted in the number of hungry people in America being even greater than it had been before the charitable efforts began twenty-five years earlier.

The political problem still had nothing to do with supply or capacity. We had not been caught between a poor economy and an inadequate food supply. In fact 27 percent of the food produced in the United States was still being wasted. One hundred billion pounds of safe, usable food was still being thrown away by food stores, restaurants and farmers while one in ten Americans now went to bed hungry. Worst of all, somewhere between 12.1 million and 14.5 million of them (depending on the source and date of the study) were children under the age of twelve.

I knew that, despite all the pleas of all the experts and all the efforts of all the individual citizens, our political leaders had, once again, turned a blind eye and a smooth tongue on the suffering of hungry children and their parents. Perhaps, most frightening of all, they had moved from the Johnson administration's stated drive "to end poverty in America," to the Nixon administration's unmet pledge "to put an end to hunger in America itself for all time," to a new level of political rhetoric, a rhetoric of public denial. "The rising tide of the economy is lifting all boats," President Clinton said in 1999. "Every income group is seeing economic growth, with the greatest gains, in percentage terms, being made by the hardest pressed Americans."

In his reference to the booming economy, President Clinton did not acknowledge that millions of people across the country were losing desperately needed food, medical assistance and cash. He did not mention that while the main intent of this law was to move people from welfare to work, many people were in fact being moved to increased poverty, homelessness, hunger and even death.

Nor did President George Bush mention these facts in his speech to Notre Dame University in May of 2001. Instead, he called for a new faith-based assault on poverty, claiming, "Much of today's poverty has more to do with troubled lives than a troubled economy." He added that the average American could help end poverty by meeting the emotional and spiritual needs of poor people. He described his vision of a faith-based social safety net as the third stage in a war on poverty that began with Lyndon Johnson's Great Society welfare programs in the 1960s. Bush said the second stage came in 1996 when Congress approved the Welfare to Work law and dismantled much of Johnson's legacy. He called the legislation a tribute to Congress "and to the president who signed it, President Bill Clinton."

When Bush praised the new Welfare to Work legislation, he was clearly looking at the dollars saved rather than the lives damaged by hunger or starvation.

That is not to say that meaningful work for just wages should not be the final goal for all who can achieve it. Self-reliance is in everyone's interest, especially the interests of the poor. It is simply to say that we must start by providing adequate food for our families, because without it nothing else can really succeed.

Most Americans have heard the official reports declaring Welfare to Work legislation a great success with reductions in welfare rolls, an increase in welfare recipients finding employment and a slight decline in overall child poverty. But the Children's Defense Fund took a deeper, closer look and found a far more troubling picture. They discovered an increase in extreme child poverty and hunger nationwide, a proliferation of inadequately paid employees and signs of rising hardship for many families leaving welfare. Disturbing findings in their study *Welfare to What?* also pointed out that only a small fraction of welfare recipient's new jobs actually paid above poverty-level wages. Most paid far below the poverty line. In addition, they found that many families who left welfare for work actually lost income or failed to find steady jobs at all, and that extreme poverty was growing more common for children, especially those in female-headed and working families.

The Children's Defense Fund's 1998 study also made it clear that, two years after the welfare experiment began, about half of the families who had been forced to leave welfare had still not found work at all. The number of children living in "extreme" poverty had increased from 6 million in 1995 to 6.3 million in 1996 and nearly 6.4 million in 1997. Most of the parents who left the welfare rolls and found full-time jobs were still not earning enough to support and feed their families. They concluded the only thing they could conclude, that the political goal of moving people off welfare had taken precedence over the desire to actually move them out of poverty or see them succeed at work. Politicians had simply dismantled a program that had been in place for sixty years, apparently on the assumption that former welfare recipients would somehow find adequate jobs.

But the reality is that since success at work can't be separated from training and preparation for work, many were doomed from the start to fail. Inexperienced people were simply being set out on their own at the worst possible time, a time when corporate America was downsizing.

In their eagerness to arrive at a quick fix, American politicians of the '90s had apparently forgotten that the true hallmark of an admirable society is not how it helps the rich but how it defends the poor; not how it advances the powerful but how it protects the vulnerable, especially the children.

Letting more American children go hungry was clearly not the intent of the 1996 Welfare to Work law; it was, however, an entirely predictable outcome, an outcome that added to the legislative errors of the past and to the rapidly expanding underclass of American children imperiled by hunger in the twenty-first century.

Introduction

"This story concerns the politics of hunger in affluent America. It is the story of how some leaders left their air-conditioned sanctuaries, discovered hunger among the poor, and determined to make it into a national issue; of other men who knew about hunger but lied; of still others who learned about hunger but voted for fiscal economy at the expense of the hungry poor."

NICK KOTZ
Let Them Eat Promises

When *Starving in the Shadow of Plenty* was published in 1981 there were very few charitable groups to help the hungry. Today, there are more than 140,000 hunger organizations. It is difficult to imagine the proportions that the hunger epidemic in America would have reached without them. But, even with them, cuts in welfare, food stamps and other government programs are creating a whole new generation of children reminiscent of the little match girl in Hans Christian Andersen's fairy tale. Unfortunately, these are real children locked just outside our mainstream world of food, warmth, light and abundance. With empty hands pressed against the window of prosperity, they can see it all, they can smell it, they can almost taste it and yet they have no way to reach it—*Growing Up Empty* is their story.

But it is also your story and my story and our children's story, for we stand, each of us, on our parents' and leaders' shoulders, and together we create one huge pillar of humanity with one collective story linked together through all the fragments, all the hope and all the sorrow. That is why, from time to time throughout this book, I have included my own experiences with hunger.

It wasn't until after the end of my marriage that I came to understand firsthand what it meant to be a suddenly single mother with two small children, promises of child support that didn't arrive, no regular income, and no health insurance.

I will never forget how alone I felt the morning my landlord called to say that my children and I would be evicted if the $425 I owed in back rent wasn't paid immediately. I had $200 in the bank, a stack of unpaid bills on the kitchen table and no food in the house. I tiptoed into the bedroom and looked at my children still asleep in their beds. For a while, I just stood there helplessly, wondering how I could possibly rescue them.

As welfare reform and food stamp cuts continue to take their toll, more and more single mothers will look helplessly at their children. In the year 2000, nearly one in three households headed by single women were food insecure. In fact, the poverty rate of families supported by single mothers was almost four times higher than that of married couples with children. In the aftermath of divorce, even formerly middle-class mothers often found themselves pushed into poverty. Single women with children also represented three-fourths of all homeless families. That is why their stories appear here so much more often than the stories of single men or married couples with children. It is the children in these families who will suffer most.

Some of these children are not only in danger of losing the food they need, they are in danger of losing their homes and their mothers as well. That is because mothers who are overwhelmed often give up their children rather than see them go hungry or live on the street. They may tell themselves and their frantic children that it is only for a little while, but that little while often becomes a lifetime in the damage it causes. As David Liederman, executive director of the Child Welfare League of America, said, "Parents will survive as long as they can and when they can't do it anymore their kids will come into the foster care system."

The robust economy we kept hearing about until the slowdown of 2001 was putting more people to work, but a lot of them still weren't earning nearly enough to pay the rent and the medical expenses and have enough left over to buy food. With the current economic downturn and the full force of incremental food stamp cuts, hunger will increase even more.

In 2001, 63 percent of all poor children had at least one employed parent, but that parent was earning poverty-level wages, which the Census Bureau defined as $17,650 for a family of four. Each year, generally in the fall, the U.S. Census Bureau issues a report that provides statistics on how many people are poor and how poverty is distributed by age, race, region and family. The poverty thresholds were originally developed by Mollie Orshansky of the Social Security Administration and are adjusted each year for inflation.

But as Ted Koppel pointed out in a special report on hunger in America's working families, aired on November 25, 1998, no matter how abundantly stocked the shelves of our supermarkets are, a lot of these families earning poverty-level wages can't afford to buy the food.

Amartya Sen, a Nobel Prize winner in economics, once said, "Even famines, like those in India, can occur where the food supply is high if people can't buy the food because they don't have enough money. . . . The gross national product overlooks the fact that many people are terribly poor."

America's famine is a famine of plenty—a silent famine of children that is growing more urgent each day, and almost no one can safely assume that they or their children are immune. There is no vaccine for this epidemic and there is no guarantee that losing a job, a spouse, a health insurance plan or simply having a poorly placed investment in the stock market might not set us and our children on the same downward spiral. The only thing we can know for sure is that if we fall, there will be no federal safety net in place to catch us.

The sad truth is that there never really was. Like the legend of the emperor's new clothes, the safety net was only a myth, a smokescreen that we all applauded because we were too blind or too frightened or too indifferent to see the naked truth. The concept was given prominence by members of the Reagan administration in order to justify major cuts in social and nutrition programs back in 1981. At the time, the administration argued that a safety net would protect vulnerable people from the otherwise harmful federal cutbacks. But later, budget director David Stockman said, "It (the list of safety net programs) was a happenstance list, just a spur-of-the-moment thing that the (White House) press office wanted to put out." In a similar vein, former White House domestic policy advisor Martin Anderson added, "Providing a safety net for those who cannot or are not expected to work was not really a social policy objective. The term safety net was political shorthand that only made sense for a limited period of time."

Whether the illusion of a safety net was perpetrated by an impulse of the moment or an unconscious twist of public policy, the impact on real safety was devastating. Again and again, the programs designed to help lift families out of poverty have failed to do so and the "safety net" has failed to catch them. Again and again, American families have been let down and left vulnerable by the very programs that were supposed to protect them.

Yet, as badly off as the chronically poor are when it comes to an urgent need for food, the newly poor are often even worse off. That is because many families who were once middle class still have assets that make them ineligible for help. They don't have enough cash to buy food, but because they still own a house or a fairly new car they are turned away from our food stamp offices.

That is why so many middle-class families are now appearing on overcrowded soup lines and in emergency food pantries. It is also why some of the desperate mothers I met on my journey have become thieves, a new breed of American thieves, food thieves, petty thieves with grand purposes, thieves who rob food shelves, not cash registers, in order to feed their hungry children.

As these families recalled what they had experienced and what they had done, I occasionally witnessed firsthand the transformation of people who had once embraced life to people who had grown numb and apathetic or angry and bitter.

I also saw how hunger can sometimes destroy the great richness of children's lives and replace it with physical suffering, mental decline, apathy, illness and despair. More often, however, I saw the almost unstoppable American quality of courage and hope. I saw it not just in the children and families who had experienced hunger, but in the generous, spirited people who realized that there was hunger and poverty in America and did their best to help.

Again and again, as I made contacts in preparation for writing this book, I reached people who told me they felt blessed in serving the hungry. They spoke of having a sense of mission or a calling. Although I knew I was somehow driven to write about hunger, that concept had not yet occurred to me. Since then, I have realized that my own connection began earlier and ran far deeper than I had originally understood.

When I was six years old, my parents took me on a car trip across the country. On the way, we drove through the Mississippi Delta. For the first time in my life, I saw tar-paper shacks and children in rags begging for food. I cried and asked why no one was helping them. "Try to forget about it, honey," my father said. "It's too big for us. We're just little people. There's nothing we can do." But I couldn't let go. Finally, to comfort me, my parents stopped at Woolworth's and bought me a small black doll. I took it everywhere I went. For years I fed it, dressed it, took care of it and pretended I was helping.

Now, once again, at the start of this new millennium, I am standing at a crossroad in my own life, but this time I know that my father was wrong. I know that whether we are "little" people or famous celebrities, what each of us does or fails to do can make the difference between life and death.

Back in 1974, after my first hunger article was published, many organizations had rushed to aid Martha Roca. I visited and brought food a few days after the article appeared. When my daughter Rebecca and I arrived at her house, we found that she was receiving hot lunches. Somehow she was convinced that they were coming from us.

"Thank you. Thank you, darling dears," she kept saying as she led us into the kitchen. She opened her refrigerator and showed us that she was saving every empty carton and container, the way richer women sometimes save the velvet-covered boxes that their most treasured jewels have come in.

After I left, I made several calls about having an evening meal delivered; it seemed promising. Then, rather suddenly, I became busy with traveling and writing articles about hunger in other cities and I stopped bringing her food. I did not know that everyone involved would assume, as I had, that someone else was taking care of her.

Some months later, on a cold, dry Saturday morning, I returned with my small daughter, carrying our usual bags of groceries. As we walked toward Martha Roca's house, we talked about how much we had missed her and how much happiness she had given us. Rebecca told me she could already imagine Mrs. Roca opening the door a crack then laughing with pleasure and saying, "Hello, darling dears, come in, come in." I knocked on the battered old door, supporting one bag on my knee. There was no answer. I knocked louder, waited then tried again.

"She has to be home, she never goes anywhere," my daughter said with concern already filling her eyes.

Finally we went to the next house and rang the bell. A heavyset woman peeked out of the window from behind her curtain, recognized us then opened the door. Her eyes grew softer. "I'm sorry," she said. "I know you're the ones who always brought the food but this time you're too late. They carried her out of there last week."

She must have seen the horror on Rebecca's face because after that she spoke only to me. "If I'd known she was hungry, I would have brought her something, I really would." Her voice trailed off. "I never heard a sound from her. She never asked me for any help. She just starved to death right there in her bed."

I tried to comfort my weeping daughter by telling her that Martha Roca was very old and that she had already lived for eighty-four years. "Think how much sadder it would be," I said, "if she was only a little girl—a beautiful little girl like you with her whole life ahead of her."

Today, my daughter is a grown woman, but the impact of that early experience is still with her. She now works with homeless women and children, doing her best to make sure they get the food and emotional support they need.

Stalin once said, "A single death is a tragedy and a million deaths are a statistic." In that same way, when we hear that 36 million people are hungry and that somewhere between 12.1 million and 14.5 million of them are children, it is hard for us to absorb the numbers or to really feel them. Numbers are for the mind and stories are for the heart. Numbers and even facts shift and change from year to year, city to city and study to study. Sometimes they numb us and turn our hearts to stone, but direct experiences and true stories lift the stones away. They unite us through time and show us the way back to the common ground. They draw power from the images they evoke. In each story there lies a fragment of our own story and a piece of the larger story, the human story that all of us share. That is why, instead of simply presenting numbers and facts, I journeyed from the East Coast to the West Coast, meeting people, listening to their individual stories and learning from them. Some were inspiring, some were heartbreaking and some were shocking, but they all contained a sharp knife of insight and a deep flame of truth. They all gave me the courage to continue and the strength to listen, even to horrifying things, without turning away. They gave me the eyes to see the enduring patterns of love and hope. While each story was as unique and as complex as a fingerprint, it also symbolized our common human hand and the plight of huge numbers of voiceless people.

The stories in *Growing Up Empty* are longer and more detailed than they were in *Starving in the Shadow of Plenty*. That is because the stories of hungry children were often inseparable from the stories of their parents. I could not understand the problems of the children without also knowing the struggles of their parents. Sometimes, understandably, parents wanted to protect their children from talking about hunger directly and chose instead to speak for them. That was not my first choice but it was one that I respected. Whenever possible, I have tried to let mothers, fathers and children speak for themselves so that they could reveal their individual personalities, the unique circumstances of their lives, and finally be heard and understood. I believe that they have been kept silent for too long. I believe it is time we learned more about the hungry than where they live, how old they are and what they ate or did not eat for dinner. I believe it is time we listened to these families' dreams and fears and yearnings, time we got to know who they really are and time we realized that they are a lot like us and our children and our children's children. Because the fact is that they are our neighbors, our parents, our brothers, our sisters, our sons and our daughters.

Our politicians have danced around the problem of hunger for too long. They have denied that it exists and, at the same time, they have handed it over to the more charitable and hoped that it would disappear. But the truth is that hunger in America is far too vast to be contained by charity alone. It was too vast even before the recession, the layoffs and the cutbacks and now it will be far worse. As we move into the twenty-first century, if something dramatic is not done, more and more of America's families will become hungry and voiceless. Their children will needlessly starve unless those of us with voices raise them in unison once and for all. It is no longer enough to honor Robert Kennedy's or Martin Luther King's dream one day a year.

One of the places that I traveled to was Marks, Mississippi. It is also where King stopped on March 25, 1968, and actually cried over the conditions of hunger and poverty he saw there. I found that very little has changed in Marks in the last thirty years. Even today, narrow shacks and shanties line the streets and barefoot children still wander aimlessly without enough food to eat.

While I was there, I met a single mother who is the descendant of slaves. She had her first child at the age of twelve. Today, she is twenty-three and lives with four children on food stamps and fifty-eight dollars a month in child support. But she dreams of leaving Marks and going back to school to become a nurse someday so that she can give something back to the community that set her people free.

In a north Philadelphia ghetto, I met a woman permanently crippled by an abusive husband who broke her spine while her starving children watched in horror. Now she teaches them about the goodness of God from the chair in the living room that she cannot leave.

Both of these women were born into families that have been poor for generations. But poverty and hunger are no longer confined to the traditionally poor or to the traditional stereotypes of the hungry. To my astonishment, I found that hunger exists among enlisted personnel in every branch of the United States military. I learned that not only do our soldiers stand on our front lines, they and their wives and their children also stand on our food stamp lines and our free bread lines. I also found hunger, devastating, desperate hunger, among the immigrants who grow and harvest the food we eat and the refugees who came here after starving in war-torn countries because they believed that in America they would find a safe haven.

Nor is the middle class immune to hunger. In a prosperous suburb I met a doctor's wife who had been deserted without warning and left without support when her husband fell in love with his young assistant. Driven to desperation, she stole Acme Supermarket scrip from her synagogue in order to feed her hungry children.

In San Diego, California, I met a homeless mother who grew up in a middle-class home. A former athlete and dancer, she lived in the St. Vincent's shelter with her sons while attending college full-time so that someday she could earn enough to buy a home for herself and her children.

Although these women have never met each other and their stories are very different, they are bound together by the common misery of poverty and hunger, by their fierce love for their children and by a nobility and bravery that never failed to inspire me.

As I write these words, I know there are *over 36 million* more Americans who are suffering from hunger and food insecurity. They are scattered throughout thousands of towns and villages and cities. Most have stories that we will never hear and many will be even hungrier as we sit down to dinner tonight in the richest nation in the world.

What troubles me most deeply is that at least 12.1 million of them are children, children under the age of twelve, children whose days should be filled with playtime and schoolwork and hope. Instead, many of these children are struggling every day in the most unimaginably basic ways for the shelter and food that other American kids take for granted.

Wherever I went, without exception, I found them. Until, after a while, I realized with a certain quiet horror that I did not have to choose specific locations. It did not matter what town or city or village I stopped at, the hungry children, even the starving children would be there, often hidden, perhaps deliberately, from the casual traveler's view or even from their own busy neighbor's view but not from the view of those who are willing to seek and to see.

I know now that right here in my own state of Pennsylvania, I could have found the entire range of families that I have written about from the always poor to the newly poor, from the working poor to the single mother, from the immigrant and refugee to the military family and homeless family. But the same could be said of Massachusetts, Washington, New York, California or any other state in the Union.

What I have tried to do in these pages is to provide a cross section of families in rural, urban and suburban parts of the country, families suffering from chronic hunger, divorce-related hunger and hunger linked to domestic abuse. I have also found employment-related hunger and hunger among the old and among the young. That is because, like any other spreading epidemic, hunger has made its way into every category, every community, every educational background, every race and every religious persuasion.

As I traveled, it became painfully clear to me that whoever the hungry were, wherever they lived, whether they had known hunger from generation to generation or were experiencing it for the first time, the sense of terror that they felt was universal and almost unimaginable.

For that reason, the focus here is not so much on the differences between the newly poor and the always poor, the rural poor, the urban poor, the enlisted poor and the suburban poor as it is on the similarities. This is the story of what happens to families who, for whatever reason, do not have enough money to buy the food they need and have to rely on inadequate public policy or insufficient private help.

Most of all, my emphasis is on the common experiences that hunger inflicts on children and on the needless physical and emotional losses that hunger creates in them.

Like all statistics, the statistics that appear in this book are subject to change, to argument and to interpretation. Because of that, I would like to stress that the primary reason they appear here is not to establish the final definitive word but to let the reader know that the families I spoke to represent many, many millions more and that their misery is great.

Our passion should be to end hunger, not to argue over the shifting statistics of a particular area or group. My purpose is to find the children, not to number them. It is to serve as a road map for those who are invisible and as a microphone for those whose silent cries for help have gone unheard throughout the generations.

When people are not seen or heard, it is easy to let them slip from our consciousness. It is easy to throw them scraps from prosperity's table at Thanksgiving and Christmas and convince ourselves that we have done our part. It is easy to forget that growing children need three good meals a day, not two good meals a year. It is also easy for Americans to believe that the middle class and the rich have individual personalities and dreams but that the poor are all alike and somehow less important or less admirable.

I have seen firsthand that the housekeeper is often more generous than her mistress and I have come to realize how poor the response of the wealthy sometimes is. I have also witnessed how rich many of our hungry neighbors actually are, rich in spirit, rich in love, rich in the quality of the dreams they hold for their children, rich in their willingness to share whatever they have and rich in their fiercely protective instincts. I've grown to respect them deeply for those instincts.

I know I will never be able to capture all of the pain, spirit or beauty that I have been fortunate enough to witness, but I also know that I must convey whatever I can.

If I have departed from traditional journalistic form in the process by becoming emotional, by presenting more narrative detail than is customary or by becoming too close to the people I've written about, so be it. I have reached a time in my own life when there is nothing I have to prove but a great deal I have to do. If I have risked sentimentality, it is because I find nothing more worthy of deep sentiment and deep anger than the needless starving of America's children throughout the generations.

My strongest drive is to convey the fact that as federal aid is slashed, suffering and hunger increases among us and that as federal aid increases, hunger proportionately decreases. It is to show that, urgent and admirable as they are, all the grassroots efforts and all the food rescue efforts of the last quarter century still haven't defeated hunger in America because they alone can't make up for the shortfall caused by cuts in government programs.

That does not mean that we should stop our individual or group efforts. I know now, from personal experience, that even on the smallest scale, every family's food stamps and each of our independent acts of giving can mean the difference between life and death. The answers will come from our collective action as a nation, from our politicians' responses and from the individual things that every one of us does. It means not forgetting, as I forgot to bring food to Martha Roca, and it means not allowing our political leaders to forget. It means spreading the word by telling those who don't already know. It means not turning away from the people who need us and the work we were meant to do.

My fourteen-year-old son, Adam, recently came to me and said, "No offense, Mom, but I think that you've wasted a lot of your life." He had been upstairs in my study looking through a file and had come across a bunch of my old letters and clippings.

There was a yellowed review from the *Washington Post* that described *Starving in the Shadow of Plenty* as "a professional victory for American journalism."

"How could you have stopped?" he asked with dismay and what I thought was contempt in his eyes. "How could you have turned away from something that you were meant to do? Why did you waste all those years writing other books?"

I didn't know how to answer my son. I felt suddenly ashamed of what I hadn't done, rather than proud of what I had achieved while I was still so young. I hesitated.

"Your sisters were small. Their father had just left," I finally said.

Adam, sensing my discomfort, put his arms around me. "I'm sorry, Mom," he whispered.

"So am I," I answered. "But I can't change that now. All I can do is start with today and make a commitment to do my best with the time that is left."

Chapter 1

Hunger and
the Middle Class

"In the end, it is the children who bear the greatest costs including
the lifetime of lost learning and lost potential for advancement
associated with even a short stay in an impoverished family."

Rescuing the American Dream,
THE CHILDREN'S DEFENSE FUND

Divorce and the Downward Spiral

Ruth blushed deeply when she opened the front door of her gabled Victorian home. She was embarrassed because she knew that no one expected to find hunger here among the beautiful estates, expansive green lawns, expensive shops, BMWs, swimming pools and thoroughbred horses. Her upscale suburb is a blend of old and new money. Affluence manifests itself in the architecture, the attitudes, even the supermarkets.

"I found myself in this situation literally overnight," she said, her thin arms waving like sea plants as she led me through a central hall, past a winding, carpeted staircase into the once formal dining room that now serves as her makeshift office.

She was a pretty woman even now after four years of hardship, thin but still sensuous, a thirty-eight-year-old college graduate with thick brown hair and a deep commitment to Judaism.

"About an hour before a big family bar mitzvah, my husband, who's a physician, told me he was in love with his office assistant. It was a total shock. I was standing in the bathroom putting on my makeup. My eighty-four-year-old father was sitting downstairs on the living room sofa all dressed up in his suit and my kids were running around the bedroom chasing the hamster. Out of nowhere, my husband opened the bathroom door without knocking and told me, like it was a weather report, that he was having an affair with a twenty-two-year-old kid. My legs got weak. I started shaking. I couldn't even turn around to look at him but I saw his reflection in the mirror.

"'Alan, I can't deal with this now,' I finally said. 'How could you tell me a thing like this when we're on our way out the door? How can I stand there with you and all these relatives and make polite conversation and act like nothing is wrong?'

"'Yes, of course. I understand. I'm sorry,' he said, quietly. He lowered his head in deference to me. My husband was always a master of the bedside manner. 'You go. We'll talk when you come home.'

"So, I took the kids and my father and I went, which was probably the worst mistake of my life, besides marrying him in the first place, but I needed time to think. I wanted to appear calm and in control."

Ruth suddenly stopped talking and motioned me toward a chair with green upholstery.

"I'm sorry," she said, pressing my hand into her palm. "I didn't even think to offer you a chair. I just started talking my head off. This subject always gets me going. I should never have let him out of my sight," she continued once I was sitting, "but I didn't know then what I know today. When I got home, two hundred dollars was on the table. He had cleaned out his papers, packed his bag and left." She shook her head, her body bent forward a little and her shoulders fell. "Not even a note. That was in August. On that day, that one summer day, our whole world changed. Can you imagine?"

I put down my notebook and thought of telling her that my own husband left, in much the same way, two years after he graduated from medical school. I thought about saying that I understood, not just the economic crisis and the fear of hunger, but the other feeling of loss. Ruth seemed like she was about to say something. I laid the bundle of my own feelings and memories aside and picked up my notebook again.

"You look upset. I'm sorry if I upset you. You want a glass of water?" she asked. "We've got plenty of water."

"Yes. Thanks," I said as I glanced around the room. There were court briefs, letters and legal documents piled on the table and stacked on the chairs. When Ruth came back with the water and saw me looking around, she sniffed and grabbed a Kleenex from a box that sat in the middle of the dining room table.

"You think this is a lot of paperwork," she said as she handed me the glass. "This is just the beginning. This is nothing." Her eyes moistened. "I have crates and crates of legal papers upstairs. It's been a long fight. I'm in a situation that I never expected to be in. All I ever wanted to have was a happy, complete family because that's the thing I had missed the most in my own childhood.

"I know now that I'm like a lot of women, millions of women who've been left alone without support, but I didn't know that then. I had no idea what to do when he walked out, absolutely no idea. He has a private practice in the city. It cost $350,000 to finance. I had cosigned the loan, so when he disappeared I shared his debts but not his assets. He had emptied our joint account, so I had no money at all for about a week. When we ran out of food, I began borrowing money from my father, but he didn't have much because we had already borrowed most of my father's retirement money when we bought this house.

"I started by calling lawyers right out of the Yellow Pages but they all wanted retainers of fifteen hundred to three thousand dollars just to get started. I didn't have it, of course. So, tell me what does a woman do when, all of a sudden, something like this happens that she never expected to happen?"

I was silently taking notes, still searching for something reassuring to say. My own husband had promised to send child support, then stopped after a few months. I had finally asked a cousin who was an attorney to help but I never received monthly payments again. There was no point in telling her that.

"What would you do?" she asked, studying my face, moving her eyes over every inch. "I mean, there is no suddenly-single manual. Every attorney I called said, 'Go to the bank. Don't you have access to joint funds? Did he cancel them?' When I told them he had taken everything, the lawyers said they were sorry but they couldn't help me. My father got impatient. He told me to stop crying and forget about him. He knew I'd been badly hurt, but to this day, I don't think he understood what I was up against economically." Ruth grimaced. "You need a few thousand dollars to start the legal process, just to start. When I tried to explain that to him he threw his hands up and said, 'Then be your own lawyer.' But how could I represent myself and protect myself? How much time does a mother of three children with no legal training have to go to all the libraries and do all the legal research and figure out a strategy to match his?

"I cried till my eyes were swollen shut then something inside me snapped and I began searching through every box and every drawer and every file in the house. I didn't even know what I was searching for. There was really nothing specific. It was like I needed to do something with my pain and my anger. It was almost as if I was searching for an explanation of what had gone wrong with my marriage. Of course, I didn't find that, but while I was searching, I did find an office account in a file in the back room that my husband had forgotten about. There was still five thousand dollars in it. I used to manage his medical practice so I was listed as a cosigner on that account. I knew his social security number." Ruth moved her chair closer. She looked at me with huge, ocean-colored eyes. "What I did probably wasn't legal," she said softly, "but I was desperate. So I wrote a check and I took the five thousand dollars.

"That's how I finally got a lawyer. After that, his attorney kept sending things to my attorney. For every letter my lawyer got he wrote a letter that was the mirror image. A lot of it was meaningless, but if something crosses a lawyer's desk, naturally he has to look at it, and every single minute that he looks at it is billable. Within a few months, the entire five thousand dollars was gone and so was the lawyer. In the end, I went to Jewish Family Services. They gave me an attorney pro bono but he was a kid just out of law school. When I mentioned my husband's lawyer, this kid started quaking in his shoes.

"If Alan had worked for a company and received a regular paycheck, it would have been easier because the courts are set up for that and they could have attached his wages. But, as a physician, he was self-employed, and we were still married so they couldn't attach his wages and they couldn't establish what his income was. My kids were hungry. I was hungry. My father was hungry. We were living mostly on potatoes because, at that point, I knew a place that sold five pounds for a dollar.

"Alan always came to the court appearances looking like a million bucks, wearing an expensive suit and talking softly and calmly. He'd smile and bow to the judge. He'd make eye contact and nod like it was the two of them against his crazy wife. Of course, I was all frazzled and on the verge of hysteria."

Ruth paused just long enough to take another sip of water. She was clearly past the embarrassment and so intent on talking or thinking out loud that sometimes it seemed as if she barely knew I was there.

"Somehow, through it all, I got a support order. The judge said that if he went four weeks without paying, they would schedule an enforcement hearing, but the enforcement hearing would take another four weeks, and if at any time during those eight weeks he paid one week's support, the whole count would start over. So that's exactly what my husband did, very intentionally, very methodically. He outsmarted the system. Every seven weeks to the day, he sent one check.

"When I told the court what was going on, they said they'd look into it. But tell me, what's a woman with three kids and no independent resources supposed to do for money and food while the court establishes a pattern of review that takes a year and a half?" Ruth shifted her feet on the stained green rug. "Every seven weeks, he sent one week's support. He's still doing it and we're still drifting here without a life raft.

"Before this happened, we were an average, middle-class family, Americans working our way up. Actually, we were better off than middle class. But overnight, my kids and I were thrown into poverty. No, I take that back. We weren't thrown, we were hurled into it.

Everything just shattered around us the way it did for the Jews at the start of World War Two. It was our own private hell, our night of the broken glass. I tried to develop a new career, but how do you go back to school and get degrees without money or food? I was all alone in the middle of a major life crisis and it wasn't like I could work full-time anyhow. My kids have a lot of special needs. I have twins who are eight. They're doing well now but they were born prematurely. All three kids still needed a lot of attention.

"Luckily, I have a nursing degree. I finally ended up getting part-time work as a nurse, but I was low man on the totem pole, of course, partly because I had taken so many years off to be with my kids and also because my job was only part-time. I had no security, no benefits and no sick leave. The truth was, I didn't even earn enough to lift us out of poverty but, at least, I could finally buy food so I was pretending to the kids that our troubles were over. I was trying to hold them together by making them think our life was finally normal again.

"Then in the fall of '97, I lost my job. He was still cutting us off for seven weeks at a time. So, now we had no food, no money for the mortgage, the telephone, the electricity or the water and here we were still living in this neighborhood, in the middle of all this afflu-ence. Now, my kids were hungry again. Actually, this time, they were starving. I thought about selling the house but I couldn't because it was in his name. I knew that my kids and my father needed food immediately, so did I. I couldn't qualify for food stamps because I was still married and the house was an asset. I didn't know if the school had a free breakfast or lunch program and I didn't know about food pantries. I'd never even heard of them and I was too embarrassed to ask if anyone had free food to give me. I felt so lost. I thought I was the only one who had ever gone through anything like this. I'd wake up in the middle of the night with my heart knocking and my covers soaked with sweat. My life was rapidly going downward and I saw no way up."

Ruth sniffled. "I just felt more and more out of control. Who would have expected to go hungry when you're married to a professional? Women just don't know that they have to go into their marriages covering their rear ends."

She buried her face in her hands and rubbed her forehead.

"I started selling everything I could find that was worth anything, even the kids' toys that still looked new or had their packaging.

"Then I got the foreclosure notice for my house. My husband had declared bankruptcy. Suddenly, there were posters on our front door. Three weeks before the sheriff's sale, our water was shut off, then our lights. The kids brought me all the pennies and nickels and dimes that were left in their piggy banks. They told me to use it for the mortgage." Ruth sniffled again then whispered, "They're such great kids. They actually thought it would pay off the debt." She rubbed her eyes with the back of her hand. "I forget what I was going to say. I'm sorry. Oh, yes, food, food. For me, it all goes together, so it's hard to talk about not having enough to eat without talking about not having enough to keep the house or lights or water going."

"It does go together," I said, thinking about the huge amount of stress she must still be under. "Life doesn't fall apart in separate little pieces."

"Well, the irony of all this is that I run one of the programs for my synagogue. It's volunteer work that I offered to do because I could no longer pay the dues or tuition for my children's Hebrew lessons and I felt like I just couldn't keep taking from the synagogue without giving something back.

"So while all this is going on, I was asked to take control of all of the scrip from all the Acme Supermarkets as part of my job. When they asked me to do it, I got very excited because I knew it would provide us with access to food. I tried to act casual like I could take it or leave it. It's a fund-raiser for our synagogue. We sell the scrip to our congregation for full price but we get it from Acme for a discount. So between you and me, I began to take, I mean to borrow, some of the scrip that belonged to the synagogue."

Ruth cleared her throat. She laughed a hollow, rusty laugh and then coughed. "Nobody noticed," she said as she watched me and waited for a response. "At least nobody said anything. Sometimes, I half thought that they knew and that they gave me control of the scrip on purpose so I could feed my kids.

"Anyhow, at the point where I started using the scrip, we'd been eating peanut butter and bread day after day. I still had one jar of peanut butter left but I didn't even have the money to buy my kids bread for the sandwiches. What would you do?" she asked again, looking at me without expecting an answer. Her right shoulder flinched forward then back, and for a moment I saw the tiny muscles under her eyes twitch. "I'm a mother," she said. "These are my children, my babies we're talking about. Am I really going to make them eat peanut butter for weeks on end when I have access to all this food scrip?

Before I could speak, Ruth said, "No, I'm not doing that, I had to do something, I had to, there was no choice. But, to be frank with you, it was very hard to take the scrip out of the drawer and put it into my wallet, very hard, especially the first time. After that, it got a little easier and that's how I fed my kids.

"Of course, I kept falling more and more in debt. I planned to give it back as soon as my husband sent money but he never sent money regularly, so it turned out that I couldn't." She pulled her hair back tightly behind her head for a minute then let it fall loose on her shoulders again. "I guess some people would say I was stealing the food. I guess they might prosecute me and put me in jail. I really don't know, and to tell you the truth, I don't like to think about it because it scares me so much."

For a moment, I tried to envision a news article about a doctor's wife driven to steal food for her three children because her husband refused to pay support more than once every eight weeks. It seemed to say more about our laws than about Ruth's instincts.

"Around this time I had learned the system, I had gotten street smart," Ruth said, interrupting my thoughts. "So I was also going to the food pantry where they give out free food. That allowed me to reduce the amount of scrip I needed but none of that food was fresh.

"Talking about fresh food might sound trivial under such desperate circumstances, but up until this time I had never ever used canned vegetables in my life or even jarred gefilte fish, so none of us were used to it. I mean, it was like we knew it existed but we had never even tasted it." Her voice trembled softly. "I realize, of course, that you have to be flexible when you're without money. You have to change those kinds of values and I tried. I decided to make it like a game for the kids. So I'd say, 'Guess what?' And they'd sit there on the floor, all shiny-eyed and excited and say, 'What, Mommy?' in those sweet, trusting little voices of theirs. I wanted to cry and rush over to them and pick them up in my arms and say, 'I'm so scared. Oh, God, I'm so scared of what's going to happen to us.' But I'd wait until my voice worked again and I'd say, 'We're going to try all these new kinds of really cool foods that we've never tasted before.' I was like, 'Wow, look, they come in cans and packages where you just add water.' They would laugh, high little giggle laughs, and clap their hands and jump up and down and I would laugh too, but underneath I felt just terrible about it because I knew they couldn't eat in a healthy way and neither could I.

"I'm supposed to have a low-fat diet because I have high cholesterol but that's not what was available. When you're poor you take whatever you can get, not just with food, but with everything in life.

"If you're at the food pantry and you see some Soft Scrub or cleaning fluid or laundry detergent, your impulse is to take it as fast as you can get your hands on it without seeming too greedy. You don't question what brand it is because that stuff is hard to get at a food pantry. It's like wartime scarcity, like living through a war where everything is rationed.

"Don't get me wrong. I'm not complaining that they don't give you enough. The people at the Jewish food pantry have been wonderful to me. I've never been put on the spot or felt like I had to offer an explanation of why I kept coming back so often or why I've been in this situation for so long. They are very good about trying to meet everybody's needs without asking embarrassing questions as long as the supplies last.

"But I've noticed in the last couple of months that there was less food in the pantry than I have seen there in the last two and a half years that I've been going. There's almost never any toilet paper or paper goods. So, if someone has donated four rolls of toilet paper, you want to grab the whole package, but you know it wouldn't be right so you open it up and just take one. That way there is enough to go around, well, not really, but at least you've done your part. It's not like there is a policy about it but it's just common sense, fair play, sharing the limited resources.

"The pantry I go to is in a synagogue in the city, not my usual one, which would be more embarrassing, if you know what I mean."

I nodded. I did know what she meant. She meant that at her own synagogue she could still pass for someone who managed without charity or free food. The congregation might know she was separated and up against some hard times but they didn't know how desperate her life had really become and she didn't want them to.

Ruth ran her hands over her stomach and pulled it in.

"When I was young, I used to be chubby, and after the kids were born I was still always a little overweight, so for a while I tried to convince myself that this was my lucky break, less money, less food, less temptation. It was my chance to become magically thin and gorgeous. Whenever I got really hungry, I tried to imagine myself in a red mini-dress, sleek as the girl he left me for. That way I could avoid eating and save more of the food for my kids. For years I'd been trying to lose those last five pounds and the diets never worked. But suddenly, I had dropped eight, then ten, then twelve pounds. I started to look thin and drawn, actually skinny; all bones wrapped up in cloth. I looked a lot like my mother before she died. I was pale. My energy was lower and I knew it was no longer becoming."

Suddenly, Ruth stopped talking. She stared off into space, not even blinking. "Ruth," I said, putting my hand on her arm. "Are you OK?"

"Yes," she answered, still staring. "I was just thinking about my mother. Before she died she said someday a man would come and take her place in my heart. He would always take care of me." She sighed deeply. "Her generation still believed in princes. She'd turn over in her grave if she knew what was happening and how I was getting food for the children."

"Do the boys realize that you're getting food at the pantry?" I asked.

Her eyes fixed on a square of light in the center of the table; she touched it with her index finger and nodded.

"I think they figured it out when they were off from school for a teachers meeting or something. Yes. They had a friend over. The pantry is not like a supermarket, you know. It's just one little room with these donated odds and ends and it's only open from eleven to one on Wednesdays. I had almost no food left in the house and I knew we couldn't wait another week. It wasn't that I was ashamed exactly. It was more that there was so much else going on in their lives and they were so worried about losing the house and being out on the street that I just didn't want to add to it. They're still worried about that. We've had a temporary reprieve because my husband didn't want to lose the money he'd invested but it's still entirely up to him. So I kind of presented it as if we were going to the pantry to help out but they kept hanging around. So after we talked a little bit and I saw it was getting close to one o'clock, I finally said, very nonchalantly, 'And this is for us.'"

"Do they ever ask why they can't go to the supermarket or choose more expensive things to eat?" I asked, thinking of the way many children, including my own, always liked to find their favorite foods and pile them into the cart regardless of price.

"No. They never do. I guess I'm lucky that way. They were sick for so much of their childhoods that they aren't used to going shopping like other kids. They just weren't exposed to it when they were younger. They are not like the kids you see having a temper tantrum over the candy bar they can't have."

Ruth shuddered. It was a small involuntary tremor but enough to let me know that something deeply troubling had just crossed her mind. When it stopped she said,

"My kids have been very damaged by hunger and by being poor. At first I was shocked when I realized how much they had suffered because I thought I had done such a good job in shielding them. I still think they are not as scared about being hungry as they are about the sheriff's sale and about not having a place to live. Of course, the two go together but they haven't quite figured that part out yet. For the most part, they just eat whatever I give them and they don't really understand that what I'm giving them is all I can get."

"You mean they trust you to provide for them?" I said. "They just assume that somehow you'll be able to do it because you are their mother and you always have?"

"Yes," she responded. "And that makes me feel even worse because they believe I can do something that I might not be able to do.

"My father is different," Ruth added. "He comes from a different culture. He won't eat whatever I give him. For him, food is not just food. The kind of food he eats is as important to him as shelter. It's as important to him as life itself. He is an orthodox Jew. Kosher food is not an issue for me or for the kids, but for him it's extremely fundamental. I absolutely have to provide kosher meals for my father or he won't eat at all. Even during World War Two, when he was in North Africa and Italy, he'd go for days without any food rather than eat the beans that had pork in them. That's how committed he is. Now, in Judaism, when it comes to life and survival, the Bible says you don't have to keep kosher but he doesn't see it that way. I think he'd rather starve to death. Ordinarily, keeping kosher is twice as expensive. If it weren't for Jewish Family Service, I'd never be able to do it."

Ruth paused and reconsidered.

"Well, maybe I would somehow. Actually, I'm pretty resourceful. We never really know until we're tested. Each day is a miracle. When my mother died, I was only six, so it's not like crisis and tragedy were unknown to me. Her death was the first earthquake in my life. This was the second. But, one thing I have to say is that growing up without a mother, I developed good survival skills. What about the women who are less resourceful than I am? What the hell do they do? It's not like I'm putting someone else's intelligence down, but what happens to a woman and her kids if she doesn't have these skills?"

Every year hundreds of thousands of middle-class women like Ruth find themselves unexpectedly separated or divorced and waiting for support checks that don't arrive or are barely enough to live on. Without marketable skills, they and their children are often plunged into poverty and hunger.

Statistically, single mothers without the support of a husband, even single mothers who have been used to luxury, are likely to be poorer than any other group. Single working women who head families are also twice as likely to be poor as single men because they are unprepared to enter the workforce. The work they do is often menial. In her book *No Shame in My Game*, Katherine Newman wrote, "They bend their backs to change the linens on the beds we occupy in hospitals, they work over vats of grease to make the French fries we eat, bag the groceries we take home from the supermarket, clean the floors and the toilets in the hospitals, then go home to raise their children on wages so low that they sink below the poverty line even when they work full time."

In *Falling from Grace*, Newman points out once again that when women who have always been secure and comfortable are suddenly unable to control their economic lives or the lives of their children, they often feel profoundly lost. They are used to expensive suburban houses, fine restaurants, beautiful clothing, private schools, even lavish bar mitzvahs and weddings. So when poverty hits, it often strikes them harder and deeper, at least from a psychological perspective. They usually enter their new world emotionally unprepared and so ashamed that often they try to keep their situation a secret from their friends, their extended families and their parents.

Even when they find jobs, they can almost never earn enough to remain close to the lifestyle that they and their children were used to, especially if child support payments don't come. Millions of divorced or separated women, like Ruth, find securing support or alimony payments difficult or impossible. In 1995, the Census Bureau reported that 11.5 million single parents had custody of their children but only 6.4 million of them had formal agreements for child support. Of those who had agreements, only half, or 3.2 million, received partial payments or any payments at all.

When no-fault divorce was implemented in the '70s, it emphasized property settlements over alimony. That emphasis still holds today. It splits the property but often neglects the vast differences in occupational training and advanced education between women who stayed home raising children and men who built highly marketable and lucrative careers, careers that resulted in the huge difference between what they and their wives can earn. This difference usually allows men to remain in the middle class after a divorce while women, even after property settlements, often plummet into the lower class and sometimes fall into extreme poverty and hunger. This is especially true if they are unskilled or if they are young professionals who have invested heavily in their husband's education and have little or no joint property or savings.

They are also suddenly alone, trying to cope not only with the extreme hardship of poverty and hunger but also the emotional pain of a failed marriage and the financial irresponsibility of their husbands. When the husbands who vowed to love and protect them are gone, the families enter poverty with a double sense of loss.

As Ruth later confirmed, every delayed or missed payment and every legal manipulation is another painful sign that she and her children are no longer loved, valued, or safe.

It is terrifying for these families to live without the support and love they counted on and terrifying to feel like social outcasts in the only culture they have ever known. Suburban children from middle-class homes often feel particularly alone in their sudden poverty but, in fact, they are not.

In 1999, 1.9 million poor children under the age of six were living in the suburbs. That almost matched the 2.1 million poor children living in the cities. In fact, between the late 1970s and the early 1990s, the rate of poverty for the young poor children living in the suburbs grew by nearly 60 percent. That number is expected to increase another 30 percent by 2010.

These families are often still living unnoticed next to their middle-class or upper-middle-class neighbors. The majority are white. They also make an extra effort to hide their poverty and as a result, despite their growing numbers and growing need, they remain invisible. Many suburbs don't even seek state and federal funds to help them.

"For my kids and for me, there is this huge pride factor," Ruth explained. "I mean, you know how cruel kids can be. Maybe I'm oversensitive but I'm still afraid that if I sent them for free breakfast or free lunch, the other kids at school would pick up on the fact that my kids weren't paying and it would be humiliating for them. So, I get free tuna fish from the pantry and luckily they like it. I can almost always give them a tuna fish sandwich to take to school. By the way," she added, glancing at her watch, "they'll be home any minute. I don't mind if you meet them but I'd rather you didn't talk to them about food and hunger. I think it would embarrass them.

"Occasionally, here and there, an aunt or uncle will give me twenty dollars and say, 'Do something that makes your life a little easier.' Then, I'll give each kid a dollar seventy-five to buy lunch in school and make it seem like a treat. You know, just to give them the feeling that they can do it, that they are still like the other kids. I mean, these kids had their hearts cut out when their father left. All the 'I love you's' mean nothing now. So one of my big goals is not to add more sadness to their lives. I could probably feed them exclusively from the pantry and save myself some grief but I think the kind of food they would have to eat would make them too aware. For example, they'd have to give up fresh milk altogether and drink powder. They don't like powdered milk. They don't like to go without cheese or fruit or what my father considers a few essential items like kosher chicken for Sabbath dinner on Friday night. But to provide them with that, I still have to take Acme scrip from the program that my synagogue runs."

Ruth cupped her hands tightly around her cheeks and the tears came into her eyes again.

"Another thing that I do is collect a lot of peanut butter crackers and little bags of potato chips." She sniffed. "Someone, I have no idea who, donates them to the pantry all the time in huge quantities. So I keep them here in a basket on the kitchen counter and I say to my kids, 'If you're hungry you can take as much as you want.' I know the food is crap in terms of nutritional value but it gives them a feeling, like, you know, like there's food in the house. Maybe it's not what they would choose. Maybe they'd rather have Fruit Roll-Ups and Rice Krispies Treats and all that other sort of stuff, but I like to think it's sort of appealing to them, because they can take it themselves right out of the basket. I like to think that it creates a feeling of abundance."

Ruth stared at me with the light of new understanding in her eyes and said, "You know something that I realized just now talking to you? It's not only about providing enough food to keep my kids from going hungry, it's also about providing a certain sense of dignity, the dignity that they lost when their father walked out and we became poor."

The bell rang. Ruth opened the front door and suddenly three bone-thin boys, all with shaggy blond hair and sea-blue eyes, stumbled in. Their shoulders were hunched by the weight of their backpacks. The oldest took a neatly folded piece of paper out of his pocket and handed it to his mother. He had meticulously written the words "potato chips" exactly ten times on each line. The entire page was full. Ruth nodded.

"He does this sometimes. It started a couple of months ago," she said apologetically. "The doctor told me it was an obsessive-compulsive disorder but I've noticed it's always about food." She put the paper down on the table and glanced at me then back at them. "Say hello to my friend from the book club, then go ahead and get your potato chips. You know where they are. How about you guys?" she added, turning to the smaller boys. "Are you hungry too?" They nodded in perfect unison.

"We're always hungry," the older boy said, looking directly at me. "That's because my dad doesn't love us anymore. I hate my dad. He doesn't care what happens to us. Every day, we go to school hungry and all we get is tuna fish."

"You don't have to be hungry now," Ruth said, interrupting. "Go ahead, take the whole basket of chips upstairs. Eat as much as you want. I'll call you when I'm finished talking."

"He doesn't mean it. He's just going through an angry stage," Ruth said as soon as the boys had climbed the stairs. I wanted to talk further with the boys but Ruth had made it clear that she preferred I didn't.

"What about dinner?" one of the twins asked with a sad twang in his voice. "Won't it spoil our appetites?"

"Don't worry about it," Ruth said casually. "If you're full, you're full. We'll go straight to homework and you'll just have a bigger dinner tomorrow night.

"Usually, we have dinner together every night, but today we're all out. There's just one can of tuna fish and I need it for their lunches tomorrow. I'll have to go to the synagogue in the morning and borrow some scrip."

I could see that there was more tension with the children than she wanted to talk about. Ruth stood up, sighed deeply, then sat down at the table again.

"I've been so distracted that I didn't get to the pantry before it closed on Wednesday. My husband has been suing for custody. He's trying to say that I'm unfit and there is a trial date set," she said finally. "The judge could sense the tension between us and the way the kids were caught in the middle so he ordered family counseling. Do you know how hard it is to sit in a room with a counselor and not be allowed to say your husband hasn't sent money in four weeks, your water was shut off and you have no food in the house for your kids? But you're not allowed to do that because, believe it or not, you can't walk into counseling and talk about support. There's another problem. As long as my husband is technically operating within the law, even if he's only providing one paycheck every eight weeks, he can make it look like I can't provide a safe place for the kids to live and enough food for them to eat because I'm incompetent. That's exactly what he's hoping for. The court sees the whole thing in weeks of payment and somehow, for them, once every eight weeks cuts it. Once you have a support order that the court has agreed on, the rest is your responsibility, even if he's manipulating it, even if he's with-holding seven out of every eight weeks.

"So I'm trying to keep quiet in family counseling and choose my battles. I do that when it comes to food too. I'd rather have the elec-tricity turned off than have my kids go hungry. I can always light a candle like we do on the Sabbath and pretend that living without electricity is just another game. I've made food for them a priority over other things no matter what I have to do to get it."

Then Ruth laughed. It was the short, rusty laugh that I had heard before but this time it sounded a little harsher.

"Food has made me a thief," she whispered, dropping her fore-head into her palms. "God forgive me. I've made feeding my chil-dren such a priority that I steal from my own synagogue."

Chapter 2

Hunger and
the Always Poor

"I want to tell every well-fed and optimistic American that it is intolerable that so many millions should be maimed in body and in spirit when it is not necessary that they should be. My standard of comparison is not how much worse things used to be, it is how much better they could be if only we were stirred."

MICHAEL HARRINGTON
The Other America

Generation after Generation
of Urban and Rural Poverty

I knew that Marks, Mississippi, was the last place Martin Luther King visited before he was shot to death in Memphis, Tennessee. It was also the last place that he cried over the rural hunger and poverty he saw in America.

So, when I found myself in Memphis for a Food Chain conference, I decided to rent a car, drive to Marks and see how much things had improved. I figured I was getting close when my cell phone stopped working. I looked for a pay phone. There weren't any. There wasn't a movie theater or hospital either, so I headed down the main road looking for the Quitman County Development Organization, an African-American resource center that had agreed to help me.

The center was started by Robert Jackson, the son of a dirt-poor sharecropper who left Marks as a young man then returned after attending the University of Southern Mississippi. In 1977, Jackson joined forces with the Reverend Carl Brown, who had also grown up in Quitman County but had spent twenty-five years in California. At first they operated out of Carl Brown's church, where they served breakfast to some of the hungry kids. But by 1980, they had raised enough money to renovate an old building and create a separate center. When the white city fathers refused to rezone the building, Jackson and Brown dug in their heels and had the entire African-American community boycott the local white businesses. After a month, the founding fathers finally relented. Today, there is a plaque on the Quitman County Development Center that reads "We walked for 29 days and the wall of opposition fell.'"

There is also a mural on the wall that shows black slaves picking cotton. Under it someone has written, "Lest we forget whence we came."

In Marks, Mississippi, it is not very likely that they will forget. Even though almost a century and a half has passed since Abraham Lincoln signed the Emancipation Proclamation, the dream of most black residents is the same as it always was. It is still to escape from Marks to freedom, opportunity and equality. Although slavery was outlawed seven generations ago, many of the African-American residents continue to live in shacks with leaking roofs and no indoor plumbing while the white people continue to inhabit huge plantation-style homes with gated private driveways. Most of the black children still go to underfunded public schools and most of the white ones still attend the town's private academy.

Even recently, when blacks tried to set up a school and day-care center in an abandoned schoolhouse in the white part of town, there was an uproar. Although they came with money, their white neighbors refused to sell them the land. Being unable to buy land if you are black has always been one of the biggest obstacles in Marks. It is a town that does not want to change.

As I drove through the dusty roads that hot Saturday afternoon in May of 1999, I carried Martin Luther King's words on the seat beside me.

I was in Marks, Mississippi, the other day [King wrote more than 30 years earlier]. *I tell you, I saw hundreds of little black boys and black girls walking the streets with no shoes to wear. . . . And I saw their mothers and fathers and I said, "How do you live?" And they said, "Well, we go around to the neighbors and ask them for a little something. When the berry season comes, we pick berries. When the rabbit season comes, we hunt and catch a few rabbits. And that's about it."*

Now, as I peered through the dead, dry heat, I saw for myself that time in Marks, Mississippi, had all but stopped. I passed the town's only "supermarket," which looked more like a corner store, then drove down Cotton Road and saw the shacks and children in the streets, still hungry and still barefoot. But I knew that they were different children. I knew that they were a whole new generation of children facing the same old problems. The children that Martin Luther King had seen were now the parents or the grandparents of the children I was looking at, but most of them were still living in these shacks and, like their parents before them, they were still out of work and often out of food.

The problem is not limited to Marks, Mississippi, or to the Delta. Many rural families face daunting economic situations. Earnings in rural areas are usually far lower than in urban communities and the gulf seems to be widening each year. Stereotyped images of happy, healthy, freckle-faced kids living on farms, milking cows, growing food and raising their own chickens are largely gone. They've been replaced by suburbs that are spreading as rural areas recede. The Mississippi Delta, along with two Appalachian mining counties in Kentucky, three Sioux Indian reservations in South Dakota and two Texas counties along the Mexican border contain the very worst concentrations of child poverty in the nation, and other rural areas are also struggling. But even knowing that at the cerebral level didn't really prepare me for the abject bleakness and all-consuming deprivation of Marks, Mississippi.

Except for a few mangy dogs and ragged kids who save their best thrift-store clothes for Sunday, the streets of Marks were deserted. Even the Quitman County Development Center was empty. Although I had called ahead, it had been difficult to line up anyone for an interview because so few people in Marks had telephones. In an effort to be helpful, codirector Bernard Tuitman went into the coin-operated laundromat and approached the only person in the place. He asked her if she'd be willing to talk to a writer about hunger and poverty.

Talese, a slender, delicate twenty-three-year-old, reluctantly agreed to talk but only until her clothes had dried. We went upstairs to an empty office that the codirector had given us permission to use. Talese crossed her arms in an awkward moment of silence then gazed across the long conference table and waited for my first question. Feeling a little out of place, I pulled the tab off of a can of diet ginger ale and asked, rather awkwardly, what it had been like to grow up in Marks.

Talese's eyes filled with something that looked like a blend of hostility and amusement. "It'd be a hell of a lot easier if I was a rich white girl like you," she said. "What you doin' here anyhow? What you know about hunger? The white folks live across the river in them big, fancy houses. They never come here to talk to us."

Her words hung in the air. I took a sip of my ginger ale and swallowed. Something made my eyes burn. She noticed and stared at me.

"I think it's the bubbles," I said, dabbing them with my index finger.

"I'm just tryin' to tell you the truth," she responded.

"Yes," I said. "I understand."

She smiled. Her eyes were still wary and challenging but her anger seemed to be subsiding.

"No. You just think you do. Ain't no way you could understand but it ain't your fault. You come from someplace else.

"My mom and grandmom picked cotton all day. They picked till they couldn't stand up. They weren't allowed to wear their hair long and they weren't allowed to wear makeup or pretty clothes because the white ladies didn't want no white men lookin' at them. They weren't even allowed to talk to white people. When I was little, I followed them out into the fields every day and I picked cotton too, but I want my kids to have a better life than I've had. I want them to go to college and get out of Marks.

"There are only two jobs for black folks here today, standin' in water from morning to night skinnin' catfish, or cleanin' the rooms over at the gamblin' casino fifty-four miles away, and even those jobs are taken. The casino's a hundred and four miles of drivin', round trip, each day. I did it for two and a half years, so I know. There were thirty rooms to clean. I left early and came home late. I never got to see my kids but the money was good so I did it till my car broke down and I lost my job.

"Now, we get four hundred dollars a month in food stamps for five of us, that's about twenty dollars a week each.

"I also get fifty-eight dollars a month in child support for one of my kids." Talese leaned across the table and glanced out the window. "We stay with my brother. That way we can use the fifty-eight dollars to get clothes and the other things my kids really need for school. Of course, like a lot of other families around here, we ain't got no plumbin' or electricity."

A fly that had been circling landed on the table. "Bein' hungry and poor is real hard on the kids," she said as she swatted it with her hand. I felt the slap as if it was meant for me.

As the Children's Defense Fund study *Falling by the Wayside: Children in Rural America* points out, in 1990, one in ten rural children lived in extreme poverty with family incomes below one-half of the federal poverty threshold. "Many of these families did not receive federal assistance and when they did, it was often well below what was offered in metropolitan areas."

Lack of public transportation, lack of public assistance offices, lack of telephones and lack of outreach all contributed to the difficulties.

Some rural people had to travel more than fifty miles, often without a car of their own, just to apply for benefits. One respondent said, "This is a rural area. There are no buses. Many persons have to pay someone to drive a hundred miles round trip only to be refused to be seen if they are fifteen minutes late."

Talese put it this way. "I could get welfare but I don't want it. I made myself a promise that me and my kids would never be on welfare. They make us feel so ashamed. All they'd give me is one hundred sixty-eight dollars for four kids anyhow, and they are so nasty to my children and me that it just ain't worth it. Besides, I want to work. I want to work so much that for a while I took my kids and moved to Virginia because I heard there were jobs there. I did housekeepin' for white folks and we all stayed in one hotel room which we was sharin' with another family. We did that for three months. We only came back because my mother got sick. She has cancer so I came home to take care of her.

"We try to eat healthy, stuff like pinto beans, collard greens, potatoes, okra and watermelon but we run out all the time. Those stamps ain't nearly enough for the five of us. And we have to share the food with my brother and his girlfriend. Don't misunderstand. I ain't complainin'. They kind enough to give us a roof over our heads, so we give them food. It's only right that we take care of each other. That's how families are around here.

"But to get the food stamps is a hassle. I have to turn in report forms every week sayin' I've been out looking for a job. Now, everyone knows there ain't no jobs in Marks, but they require it so I do it. Sometimes they come to the house to check. If they don't find no food, they cut people off. They think it means you're sellin' your stamps. We're always scared they will come to our house and find no food. We don't sell our stamps. We just eat our food. When we get near the end, I say, 'Don't eat that. Leave it on the shelf so they can see it if they come.' But the kids can't help themselves. They're just kids, you know, and they're hungry kids."

Talese shrugged.

"A lot of people in Marks have given up. They don't even try to get stamps. I see their kids marchin' down the dirt roads once, maybe twice a day, pickin' berries and lookin' for trash.

"But I'm different, I'm feedin' my kids and I'm gettin' out. It's not that I don't like it here, I do, I love Marks, Mississippi. I was born here, it's home to me, I got family here. But there's just no way to stay and survive. We got three thousand people and one little market with high prices. We got no jobs and nothin' for the kids to do. There ain't even prostitution here because no one has any money to pay for it. I want my kids to have everythin' that those white kids across the river have because I love them. I had my first when I was twelve. I'm twenty-three now and my kids are eleven, ten, seven and four. Havin' babies is about the only thing a girl can do around here to feel like she's good for something."

As I listened to Talese and thought about what she said, it became clear that young women like her have very little in their lives to make them feel valued. Even their most basic everyday needs for food and shelter frequently go unmet. Whatever sense of importance or power they have seems to come directly from creating and rearing their babies. Childbearing gives them a reason not to give up and die, but it does more than that. It gives them a reason to hope. Each time they give birth, they feel essential again, at least for a while.

"I was eleven and on the honor role when I got pregnant with the first one. My boyfriend was sixteen. We hardly knew what we was doin' and we never heard of birth control. My aunt gave me turpentine to abort it. She tried to force me but I wouldn't drink it. I don't believe in abortion. Kids are too precious. My kids mean the world to me but I also have a dream of my own and I ain't gonna stop till I see my dream. Someday I'm gonna graduate from high school and go to Coahoma Community College and then I'm gonna become a nurse so I can help the elders.

"My grandmommy died in my arms when she was fifty-six. Just before she died, she said she wanted me to be an RN. Now, it's my dream because it was her dream for me. We was real close. I comforted her and she comforted me. I made her happy and I believe if I could make her happy, I can make other people happy. I don't care if they are black or white. The white folks made us slaves but they also set us free. You never know who you might need in life so it's good to help whoever you can, then, when you're down and out, the person you helped just might help you.

"You got any kids?" she asked quizzically, tilting her head and resting a ragged sleeve on the table.

"Yes," I said. "I have three."

"Then you know what I'm talkin' about. If you're a mother, you don't want your kids beggin' for food and eatin' nothin' but the rabbits they catch in the fields.

"If you're a mother, you ain't no different from me."

Unlike the untraveled back roads of the Mississippi Delta, Philadelphia is part of the familiar America. It is a city of 1.6 million people, a city celebrated for containing the most historic square mile in the country, the place where the United States was conceived and ratified. Every day, tourists arrive from all over the world. Guides take the visitors through Independence Hall and by the Liberty Bell, past Georgian and Federal buildings, expensive shops and renovated town houses. For single professionals and growing families, Philadelphia is an upscale urban environment. It is dominated by the Avenue of the Arts, skyscrapers, museums and a rapidly expanding waterfront.

But a mile or two north of Center City, hidden from the casual view of tourists, there is another Philadelphia, a bombed-out, boarded-up part of town where falling-down row homes with graffiti-covered walls house thousands and thousands of the city's always poor. This is where gangs congregate on street corners and where women and children often live in fear, not just of hunger and poverty but also of violence born of that poverty, violence even from members of their own families. This is where I first met Bertha and her two young daughters.

I parked in front of a run-down row house and noticed that years ago someone had painted the now-peeling porch gray. That was when the windows, which were long since covered with boards, still let the sunlight in.

I never would have found the house or Bertha if not for Rita Ungaro-Schiavone, a petite tireless woman who started Aid for Friends back in 1974. Rita had been an acquaintance ever since my first hunger article was published. The nonprofit, almost all-volunteer organization she founded still helps feed and support Philadelphia's isolated and homebound. Now, as she opened the door to Bertha's house, Rita explained, "We keep a spare key because the kids are in school and there's no way that Bertha can get to the door."

"Bertha, honey, we're here," Rita called as she turned the lock. The long narrow room was so dark that I squinted trying to take it in. At first, I could barely make out a birdcage but I could hear a parakeet chattering and see the outline of its stand next to a microwave and an old TV. Straight ahead there was a candle burning in a jar beneath a poster-sized portrait of Jesus Christ. As my eyes adjusted to the darkness, farther off to the right I could see a broken brown couch still covered with what looked like its original plastic. Directly in front of me was a worn brown easy chair that had once matched the couch. It had been converted to a makeshift hospital bed by placing a board on top of a couple of wooden crates to extend its length. That's where Bertha was sitting. In fact that's where she had been sitting for most of the last eight years, ever since she was paralyzed from the waist down by her husband.

"I brought your lunch and I brought Loretta," Rita said in her hoarse, cheerful voice as she led me over to Bertha. There was something about Bertha that I was instantly drawn to. I wasn't sure if it was her warmth, her strange blend of frailty and power or her capacity to forgive. I didn't know why but, unusual as this setting was, I felt as if I had just entered a holy place.

I walked closer and saw that Bertha's face was round. Her cheekbones were high and her skin was a soft brown with freckles scattered randomly across her nose and cheeks. When she smiled, the first thing I noticed was that several of her teeth were missing, but I was quickly drawn to her large almond-shaped eyes. They were deep and as dark as burned wood. For a moment, I stared at her, mesmerized.

"I see the love shinin' out your eyes," she said.

There was something about her voice that made me think of the sea, more specifically of the tide moving forward on a calm day.

Rita reached for the light and broke the spell. Suddenly, I saw roaches, dozens of roaches scurrying everywhere. I had never realized they came in so many sizes.

"Sit down, honey. Don't be afraid. They ain't gonna hurt you," Bertha said with a trace of amusement in her voice as she gestured me with her eyes toward the couch with the plastic cover.

"I've lived with roaches all my life," she said after most of them had disappeared and I had reluctantly settled down on the sofa and turned on my tape recorder. "I've lived with hunger too," Bertha added, then she paused and closed her eyes for a minute. "When I was a kid, every night when we said our prayers, you know what we prayed for? Well, I'll tell you. We prayed for food. Most days our stomachs ached like rubber bands was tied around them. Sometimes it got better. Sometimes it got worse, but it never went away for long.

"My mother was a beautiful woman but she was an alcoholic. When she was sober, I could feel the beauty of her, the quiet of her, but she wasn't sober much.

"We was hungry because she had no food to give us. The whole family, at least a lot of them, was on alcohol. We moved around all the time. Someone was always pushin' us out because we couldn't pay the rent. Mamma used to throw chairs at the rent man but he didn't go away for long. We always ended up in houses that didn't have any lights. I never knew it was because we couldn't pay the electricity. When Mamma was drunk, things got real bad. She used to hit us with a belt in the tub when the wash powder was over us. Me and my sister, Joy, and my brothers Corneal and Seymour and

Jerome was cryin' all the time. Either it was the hunger or it was the beatin's. We felt like we was always hurtin', always hungry, always thirsty.

"Once when things got really bad, Mamma tried to jump out the window. I remember, I grabbed her leg and wrapped my whole body around it to hold her back. 'I love you, Mamma,' I kept sayin'. 'I love you.' I don't know how old I was but I know that I was very young because it was before I got raped and that was when I was seven."

I stared at Bertha, without speaking. At that point I think the roaches could have crawled on my legs and I wouldn't have felt them, or if I did, I'd have felt ashamed that I'd noticed.

"Mamma had went to the speakeasy looking for money to buy food. Seymour and Jerome went with her to wait outside and keep her safe. Me and my little sister was at home alone countin' the cars going by to pass the time. That's when a man came lookin' for Mamma. He kicked in the door. I was hollerin' that Mamma wasn't there but he wouldn't listen to me. This man was big. He was so tall that I remember lookin' up at him like a giant, then suddenly he was draggin' me through the halls, the dark halls by my legs and I was screamin'. I remember the details and I remember the smells. I remembered it as I was growin' up and I remember it today." She shivered. "I can still smell his scent and feel his sweat on me and I be screamin', 'Help me,' and I be runnin'. I had no clothes on because he had already tore them off. I started runnin' but he caught me and pinned me down. I begged him to get off me, I begged him not to kill me. I thought he had a knife because it felt like I was being torn apart, like somethin' was stabbin' me from the inside out. I thought I was dyin' because I couldn't breathe and I couldn't see anymore. But he wouldn't stop. I was gettin' weak, very weak. I opened my eyes, it was gettin' dark, a dim light still came through one of the curtains from outside. That's how I knew that it was gettin' dark. I closed my eyes again and prayed for God to make him stop. By the time everythin' was over, it was completely dark.

"Finally, he carried me back to where my sister was waitin'. He carried me because I wasn't able to walk and he said, 'If you tell anyone, I'm gonna kill you.'"

When Bertha stopped speaking, we were all completely still. A jagged trickle of tears slid silently down her cheek. I stood up, walked over and dried them with a tissue.

"When they brought me back from the hospital, my mamma moved us up to Twenty-Ninth and Dauphin," she said very quietly as her damp palm pressed into mine and her fingers clamped shut. "Most of the houses on that block were boarded up, but I still remember a lady that lived on the corner. Her skin was smooth like chocolate milk. I remember her because she was the one that used to give us food. She would sneak food over when my mamma was away and give it to us, mostly old bread. I don't know how she knew when Mamma was at the speakeasies and we was home alone or how she knew when Mamma took us with her and dragged us through the snow without no proper shoes. But I think she knew about the frostbite because one time she brought me socks.

"When I was in the fourth grade, I met my husband George. We had went to the same school. I knew him but I didn't like him. I didn't like his character because he used to put mirrors on the steps and look up girls' dresses. When I went up the steps, I said, 'What you doin', George?' and he said, 'Shut up, Pocahontas.' He called me Pocahontas because my hair was braided up the top of my head just the same as it is now.

"I didn't talk to him after that for many years. I was very quiet. I was quiet because I had a lot of fear in me, a lot of flashback. I didn't talk to him again till I was sixteen. I was livin' with my grandmother. The girls around the block used to say they wanted to take me to meet this boy called George and I said, 'No. I don't need to meet nobody.' They said, 'But you're sixteen, goin' on seventeen and you never had a boyfriend.'

"I said, 'I'm fine. I just want friends and you're my friends and that's all I want.'

"But I was destined to live it again. They say that when you come from abuse, you marry abuse, and that has a lot of reality in it. The same can be said of hunger. I knew it as a child, I know it as an adult and my children also know it. The sufferin' was renewed each year the same way the leaves on the branches of the trees comes back each spring.

"But I didn't know that then. At that time, I still had it in my mind that I was goin' to make it. I thought I was goin' to learn how to speak English properly. I was goin' to go to college. I was goin' to get me a job and be somebody someday. But I was also goin' to serve the Lord because I felt the drawing. I wanted God in my life because he would show me the path. He would give me greater insight, more direction.

"So, when I met George again, I didn't know whether God wanted me to have a mate or not. I thought maybe God had sent me George because he knew those were the loneliest days of my life, especially when I used to see people on Christmas day with their families and friends and boyfriends. You know in college how people go out on dates and stuff, and I was always alone. I never knew what it felt like to be lonely until I started seein' couples. I thought it was normal to be alone. I thought I was supposed to be a nun. But other people thought there was somethin' wrong with me. They'd say, 'Bertha, you got to have a boyfriend.' And I'd say, 'Not now,' and then they brought George to me. George looked like he was from the ghetto just like I did. You know, way down to earth. He made everybody laugh, even me, he gave me somethin' to laugh about. He was the only one that brought out the laughter in me and that's where I made my mistake. Through the laughter, I began to trust again."

Bertha paused, looked over at the poster of Jesus then back at me.

"But it wasn't just laughter, he did more than that. He showed me some concern. I had a room in a house in Mount Airy and the landlord wasn't puttin' on the heat. I had three blankets and I was still cold. I was goin' to community college and I was goin' to a hospital to work as a nurse's aide. Then I caught pneumonia.

"George came and brought me soup. He was also doin' the shoppin' for me and payin' for the food, and you know what I did? I said to him to please leave me alone because I was scared of it because I'd been hurt by a man. I was all confused in my mind. I wanted to have a friend but I was too scared to trust a man. A lot of people don't believe in havin' a friend without him touchin' you."

Bertha looked at me, then she added, almost apologetically, "He was being so kind. I was hungry and I was sick and he was bringin' me soup. He was addin' food to the laughter and in my life I had always been hungry for both."

Bertha's hand was still clasped in mine and I could feel her begin to tremble as she spoke.

"Part of me needed him but a part of me still remembered the things that happened when I was seven, so I was afraid, and because of my fears I was rigid. Have you ever heard of rigid? How you say it? Rigid? Frigid? I don't know how you say it but that is what I was. When he would touch me, it would unnerve me. At first, I would be fine and then I didn't be fine. I was unbalanced. I was ashamed. I was even coverin' up in the swimming pool. I'd keep a towel or blanket over me.

"I had these memories of bein' raped and I wondered if George understood. I asked God why I had to have so much problems within myself that I couldn't be normal.

"On my wedding night, I was in the bathroom cryin'. Eventually, I came out but he had the lights on and I wanted the lights off because I didn't want to be seen. This was my husband, this was my wedding night. I knew I was a basket case but I was afraid, I was married and I was afraid.

"George handled me slow and gentle and we talked and then he loved me. We kissed each other, rubbed each other, fondled a little and slowly I forgot everythin'. I forgot the hurt. I forgot the hunger. I forgot the year I was seven. I enjoyed myself, I relaxed, I had some pleasure in it. It was easy for me to learn because I was attracted to George and I loved him.

"When I married him, he was just startin' boot camp. He had to go back to the base the next day so we just had that one night together in Atlantic City, then he was gone again. From time to time, he'd come home durin' the trainin', first from Aberdeen, Maryland, then from Fort Dix, New Jersey. In those days, he was always kind.

"The abuse didn't start until he came back from Korea almost two years later. He said that, when he was in Korea, he had tasted the clubs and the bars. He said every weekend he was dancin' and par-tyin', then he said he still wanted to do that, so I said, 'George, I can make a party for you right here.' He said, 'I'm talking about a differ-ent kind of party, Bertha.' So I said, 'George, I dance for the Lord.' Then he looked at me and said, 'It's me or God, Bertha. One of us has to go.'

"After that he told me he was workin' two jobs and that's why he never came home no more, but there was no money. When I got a job as a teacher's aide, he took my money and said he owed it to his friend. I said, 'But, George, we need food in the refrigerator. We need food for our children.' He said, 'Don't tell me what to do. I'm the man of the house.'

"He was withdrawin' more and more then hollerin' and screamin'. He was gettin' after the kids too. He'd say, 'I'm their father. I'll hit them if I want to.'

"So just like before, the past had come back to me. I had tried to avoid it but it was all there again, the beatin' and the hunger. I tried everythin' I knew to get food for the kids. We was refused welfare because George was able-bodied. The Salvation Army gave me some vouchers. It was forty-five dollars, I could take the vouchers to Acme, but I could only get them one time and we was so hungry that some nights I prayed I would wake up dead." Bertha shrugged. "I know that don't make any sense but you understands what I mean."

Our conversation was interrupted when the door creaked open, and standing in the arc of sunlight I saw Sophia, a tall, slender, strik-ingly beautiful eleven-year-old.

"Come over here, Sophia, and say hello to Miss Loretta."

Sophia smiled shyly and nodded.

"Tell her what it was like when we was livin' with your father."

Sophia's smile vanished. She was silent and seemed frightened.

"Miss Loretta is our friend, Sophia," Bertha said sternly. "She be sent here to us by God to make a book that will help people. Go on, do like I say. Tell her."

"That's OK," I said. "Only if Sophia wants to talk about it."

Sophia studied me for a moment then sat down on the couch beside me.

"I like your red hair," she said, softly. "That's a pretty color. I'd like to draw a picture of you in your house. Do you live in a house that stands by itself?"

"Go on," Bertha repeated. "Tell her."

There was another short pause and then a sigh. "It was bad," Sophia whispered. "It was real bad. We was always hungry. If we was lucky, we'd have a little bread or oatmeal. Mom was working, but when she came home on payday, he always took the money away from her to buy whatever he wanted. We never had nothing in the refrigerator. I don't know what he did to that money. I don't know if he ate it or what but whenever we said we was hungry, he said, 'You should have eaten before.' I guess that's what he did. He must have ate before he came home. And sometimes he'd start hitting us with his shoe for being hungry. We'd look in the cabinets but they was always empty, too, just like the refrigerator. Finally, one time my mom went to the Salvation Army to get us food. We was excited but it didn't last long. Every day I was hungry and tired. Sometimes I got pain and tightness in my belly like I was bleeding inside."

Sophia sniffled and I watched as a single tear traced a path down around the side of her nostril. She seemed to want to tell me more.

"If I did eat, I'd get diarrhea," she said. "I'd be getting headaches every day and I was dizzy all the time. I couldn't stay awake in school. One day, I felt so weak I couldn't even walk. They dragged me to the school nurse. She took one look at me and said, 'Take this child to the hospital.'

"After that, I'd get free breakfast and lunch in school. Sometimes he'd bring home a little food at night and give it to us but only as much as he thought we needed. He thought Mom bought us too much food and spent too much money so he took the money away from her to pay the rent, but then we got all these calls that the rent wasn't paid.

"Sometimes, the people at Acme would see me and my sister, Fianna, there and give us food, mostly leftovers. They knew about us and they felt sorry for us because they understood that we was starving."

Sophia stopped talking and looked at her mother. Suddenly, her mouth curled down at the corners and her eyelids closed halfway. "Are you gonna tell her what he did to you, Momma?" she asked. "Now that we be talking about everything, are you gonna tell her or am I?" She drummed her foot nervously on the floor as she waited for an answer.

"I'll do it," Bertha said, after hesitating for about a minute.

I noticed that her voice had taken on a different tone. It had become very calm again but her eyes looked glazed. It was almost as if she had memorized someone else's story or a part in a play that she had grown used to reciting.

"One night," she began, "when George come home, I was in the kitchen. The manager at Acme had just given some food to Sophia because he felt sorry for her. It was soup bones and old vegetables that they was gettin' ready to throw away. Sophia was thin, very thin at that time. She ran home with the food, all excited, and gave it to me. I said, 'Praise the Lord, Sophia. The Lord has provided for us,' and I started cookin' it to make a soup. While I was cookin' and lis- tenin' to my gospel music, George came into the kitchen. He was walkin' back and forth, back and forth, and I said, 'What's wrong with you today, George? Why are you pacin' like that?' He didn't say nothin'. I was stirrin' the pot and he just kept pacin' the floor back and forth, back and forth. The kids ran into the kitchen. He yelled at them to go to the front room and to stay there. But they smelled the food and they was hungry. He yelled again, 'Get out and don't come back in here.' Then he turned the music off.

"I said, 'George, please don't be screamin' at the children and don't turn that music off. I love that music and I'm tryin' to cook the food here for dinner so the kids can have somethin' nice and hot to eat for a change.'

"He sprung around on the back of his shoes, then his eyes got real small. He was talkin' very fast and I knew he was using some kind of drugs that made him act crazy. Then he said, 'I didn't tell you to buy no food. What you think, you wear the pants in this family now? You hidin' money from me? That's it! I'm leavin' you, Bertha. I'm going back out into the world and party.'

"I was calm. I said, 'George, that's your choice. I can't force God's will on no man.' I had found out the month before that he was smokin' pot and takin' other drugs even though he never did it in our house because he didn't want to disrespect me and the girls. Sometimes the effects stayed with him a long while. This time, George didn't answer me; he just kept watchin' me stir the soup. The kids wanted to come back into the kitchen but they opened the door slowly, only a crack because they could hear him yellin' and they was scared. That's when he took the chair and pushed it under the door-knob.

"'What you doin', George?' I asked. 'Why are you lockin' your kids out their own kitchen? You been usin' them drugs again?'

"He still didn't say nothin', he just kept starin' at me, then before I knew it those kids had bust back into the kitchen again. They pushed the chair right out of the way. George hollered at them and this time he threw them out and put the chair back up to the door. He tried to secure it real tight. Then he grabbed my hair and dragged me across the floor. After he let my hair go, he grabbed onto my hips and lifted me straight up."

"I saw him," Sophie blurted out, talking very quickly. "I saw him do it. I be hiding behind the refrigerator and I saw him. He had her up in the air like a stick, straight up. He be holding her next to that brown table. Her body was stiff and straight up like a board."

"I was beggin' him to put me down," Bertha broke in. "I was screamin', 'Stop it, George. Stop it. Put me down!'

"'You want to go down?' he yelled, laughin' real crazy. 'Is that what you want? Did you say "Put me down"?'

"The next thing I remember I was hittin' the table. He lifted me way up and slammed me down again. My spine crashed into the edge of the table. I still remember the pain of the impact. That pain went straight through my body and it took me out of here. I remember that, but after that . . . I don't remember nothin'.'"

"Mamma was on the kitchen floor," Sophia gasped. "She was shaking real bad. She had her eyes closed and she was moaning and all I knew to do was put my head on her chest and ask God to make her stop shaking but it didn't work. She wouldn't stop. My daddy took one look at her and he ran straight out the door. I think he was scared of what he done because he didn't come back for two days."

Once again, I was silent, stunned silent. It wasn't grief or sympathy, it was awe that seized me. What could an outsider, a stranger like me, possibly say to this woman and her child? What affected me even more deeply than the horror was their spirit, their capacity to go on loving and forgiving despite all the suffering and the pain. Bertha was also silent for a moment, then a sound broke loose in her throat but she clasped her hand over her mouth.

"When I came to myself, I couldn't see," she said quietly. "And I couldn't move from my neck down. The lady who lived upstairs heard my screams, and after George ran out she ran in but nobody called the cops and nobody called the ambulance." There was another long pause, then Bertha said, "I still believe that Jesus loves me. I believe that because he spared my life. It is a miracle that I am alive and it is proof of his love. I don't know how long I was unconscious but I remember the lady upstairs sayin', 'I've been tryin' to bring you awake for a long time. I've been tryin' to bring you out of it.' Then she got her husband, Junior, who was very big and who was not really her husband, to pick me up and carry me to my room.

"A year later, I asked her, 'Why didn't you call the cops?' And she said, 'Because I knew George since he was a little child, because he used to sit on the steps of the church in a deep dream. I knew somethin' was wrong with him then and I know somethin' is wrong with him now. I'm sorry he broke your spine, Bertha, but I know he couldn't help himself and I knew he would come back soon to take care of you. I'm just like a mother over him and I didn't want to see him go to jail.'"

As soon as Bertha finished speaking, the parakeet began to chirp. Sophia walked over and opened the door of the cage. The bird jumped onto the rim of the door then flew to Bertha and landed on her shoulder as if it too had heard the story.

"I'm OK now. Don't worry about me," Bertha said to the bird as she held out her hand so it could perch on her finger. Then turning to me, she added, "I just hope there ain't no one else in the ghetto goin' through what we been through."

I nodded, knowing that researchers in several parts of the country had recently focused on the link between poverty, hunger and domestic abuse. A random sample from one low-income urban neighborhood in Chicago found that poor families receiving welfare experienced three times the amount of physical violence as other groups. In fact, they found that over 60 percent of women living in poverty had been severely assaulted by a male partner and over a third had been threatened with death.

Several other major research efforts conducted by the University of Massachusetts, Northwestern University and the Better Homes Fund found remarkably consistent and similar patterns of domestic violence in families receiving welfare. All of the studies also found high levels of physical and mental health problems among abused women. The University of Massachusetts study found that 31.7 percent of those who had been abused now had a physical disability, a physical handicap or other serious physical, mental or emotional problems. Like Bertha, a high percentage had also been the victims of childhood domestic violence and sexual abuse. They concluded that these high rates of violent victimization across women's life spans have important implications for antipoverty policy, Welfare to Work legislation and understanding how to help poor women in a general way.

The studies also confirmed that women living in abusive relationships often seek employment, probably in an effort to achieve self-reliance and independence from their partners, but they frequently do not succeed because the violence that they are experiencing at home often makes it impossible for them to perform at work. Some haven't developed the resiliency to retain jobs while dealing with abuse, others are prevented by the physical disabilities they've suffered, still others are stopped by the abusive partner who is afraid of losing control of "his woman" if she works.

A 1990 Ford Foundation study found that 50 percent of all homeless women and children were fleeing abuse. They reported that a woman is battered every thirteen seconds but, in the absence of money, these women often face a terrible choice between homelessness and continued abuse. To make the situation more desperate, shelter providers in Virginia found that more than two thousand women who ran away from abusive relationships and sought shelter in that state in 1995 were denied entrance because of a lack of space.

For all of these reasons, women living with poverty and hunger are more likely than women in the middle class to feel that separation or divorce is impossible. Poor rural women are even less likely to leave than poor urban women. That is because while all abusive men tend to isolate their partners, women in rural areas also face geographical isolation. They often live miles from the nearest neighbor, friend or family member. Inadequate transportation and a lack of nearby shelters frequently combine with a lack of money, making escape feel nearly impossible. Even if a rural woman does manage to seek help and bring charges against her abusive partner, in small towns where everyone knows everyone else, police officers and judges may be less likely to acknowledge the seriousness of the assault.

Studies by Child Protective Services have also found that between 30 percent and 60 percent of men who batter their partners also abuse their children. Of course, even when the children themselves are not the direct victims of physical violence, they are affected by what they see. Many, like Sophia, have been beaten themselves and have also watched helplessly as their mothers were beaten. They have seen the fighting, the bruises, the destroyed property and the broken bones.

Although there is no single profile of the woman who is battered or the man who does the battering, it is clear that the additional stress of poverty increases domestic violence.

While 33 percent of American women experience abuse, the number rises to between 50 percent and 60 percent for those living with poverty and hunger.

"I used to save some of my food from school and try to sneak it upstairs to Momma," Sophia suddenly blurted out. "But, if my dad caught me, he would take his belt off and beat me with it or grab me and pull me down the stairs. Momma couldn't even wash her hands or go to the bathroom and he left her all alone in that room, that plain old room, the room we wasn't allowed to go into."

"I was up there screamin', 'Where's my kids? I want my kids. I'm not gonna die here. George, I want my kids. Sophia! Fianna! George! Somebody help me! But nobody came, nobody watched over me except the Lord and I don't remember how I ate or how I stayed alive.

"That was in 1984. I was in bed for two years before the Lord graduated me to this chair. It was right after George got killed in a motorcycle crash and the Lord set us free."

The parakeet chirped again then arched its wings and flew over to Sophia. She held up her finger like a parenthesis and waited for it to land before she spoke. "I was glad when Daddy died," she said as her gentle face twisted up in pain. "I was glad because he said he would kill me if I told anybody what happened. Now, I knew that I would finally be able to go to church and tell people and get food for Momma and bring her downstairs and take care of her."

"It was very hard for me when George died," Bertha whispered. "I was glad in a way and yet I was sorry. I sent the kids to the funeral. I wanted them to understand him and not hate him. I wanted them to know that certain things are inevitable and that in everyone there is some good. When he come back from the war, he was a totally changed person. Part of me still loves the George I married and I still dream of him that way, the George who taught me laughter . . . the George who brought me soup."

For a moment, Bertha's eyes filled up with tears but she quickly collected herself.

"Today, Rita brings me soup and my children brings me laughter so I'm not worryin' about my condition or how little we have. The doctors tell me we waited too long. They can only do what they can do, which means they give me pills to keep down the pain, but I don't have time to think about what I'm gonna face tomorrow. Tomorrow will tell for itself."

"In some ways I'm like the mom in the house now," Sophia said proudly. "I take care of Momma and I feed her but I loves to do it. It's a blessing to do it. I loves it because she took care of me. Now it's my turn to take care of her. She can't go to the bathroom or brush her teeth or comb her hair or cook the food but even now, in so many other ways, she still takes care of us. She makes sure that we have our education and we have clothes and that we go to the youth services at the church. She works on our homework with us. Sometimes, after we do our work, we have popcorn. We listen to tapes, we relate together and because of Momma, I'm on the honor roll at school. I want to be a doctor and my little sister, she wants to be a judge. I love our life the way it is now and I appreciate it more because I never forget all those years when I tried to help Momma and he wouldn't let me."

I watched Bertha's hands open in her lap then close again.

"These children are a gift and a jewel but I am also devastated that they have to do all this for me. I want them to have a childhood. I don't want them to live in bondage. I want them to have pleasure, to roller skate, to polish their nails and go to the movies. My girls help me with everythin'. They brush my teeth. They bends my legs to keep me from becomin' stiff. They wash the clothes. They keep the surface of things clean and they fix the food that Rita brings.

"After George died, at first our food came from the church. But the church was helpin' the homeless and they didn't have enough. Then welfare gave us money and food stamps but we ran out all the time. One day, I was lyin' here and I was prayin' for help and the Lord just led me to the Yellow Pages, where I saw Aid for Friends. I called them myself. They came and did an evaluation and then they began bringin' food.

"Aid for Friends always brings us as much as they can but they don't always have the support that they need either. My longing is to see that they get those supporters because Aid for Friends was long overdue. Just as there are hungry people all over the world, we have a lot of people right here in Philly that be in need. Me and my kids was in great need and we thank God for Aid for Friends and for Rita. They brings the dinners ready to eat. The kids just has to warm it up. They also brings us bags with breakfast cereal, juice and oatmeal. They gave me a microwave, a toaster and a refrigerator. At Christmas, they brought us gifts. I can't even begin to express all they've given us. With their help we have survived. Because of them, me and my children triumphed over tragedy. Because of them trash became treasure and we learned to rebuild our lives."

"Don't you ever get angry, Bertha?" I asked, wondering how she stayed so even and so strong despite her helplessness.

"No. Why would I get angry," Bertha answered with her face a perfect heart, "when I'm still right here livin' and there's always hope?"

"But you live in that chair," Sophia chimed in with a touch of bitterness in her voice, "You can't even walk. You can't come to my graduation."

"That's normal for me," Bertha responded, looking at Sophia, then at me. "Miss Loretta," she said, "I believe there's always a reason for the things that happens to us. I see myself as a tiny speck of dust and yet at the same time I also know that I am somebody, that I have a purpose. Me and my kids, we shine brighter than the ones born with a silver platter. With George gone, we have closure, a new life has begun. We have food, we have a home and, glory be to God, my kids . . . they have a future."

Chapter 3

Hunger and
the Military

"To kill with sword and with hunger and with death and with the beasts of the earth."

REVELATION, 6:8

From Front Lines to Food Lines

"The first time Carol called, it was the end of August. She asked me to stop by but didn't say she and her baby were hungry. When I got to her house, I found the eighteen-month-old trying to eat from the garbage pail in the kitchen. Carol was too weak to get out of bed. Her husband had been in the field for ten days and they'd been completely out of food for three."

Lisa Joels, the founder of HELP (Helping Enlisted Lives Prosper), was talking to me as we drove toward the base commissary at Quantico, a Marine training center in Dumfrees, Virginia.

"Carol called again at the end of September," Lisa added. "She asked how to get a free Thanksgiving turkey. I said, 'Hey, I'll be happy to tell you but Thanksgiving is two months away. Do you have any food in the house right now?' There was a long pause before Carol said, 'No.' It's really very hard for a lot of military families to admit that they have nothing to eat at the end of each month so they hint around at it and wait for me to ask."

Lisa pulled into the base commissary parking lot and turned off the engine.

"These kids bought so heavily into the idea that the military would take care of them that now they think it's their fault and they feel ashamed. They think that they must be doing something wrong. They aren't, though. They just run out of food and food stamps every month like all the other poor families in America."

Military pay varies. Lisa explained, "It varies by rank, marital status, and length of service. At the bottom of the scale in 2000, a newly enlisted, single Marine earned $887.70 a month before taxes, with a housing allowance of about $215 a month. If he was married, his salary stayed the same but his housing allowance went up to roughly $385 a month. It's just not enough."

We began walking down the aisles of the commissary and now, as Lisa spoke, she piled bread, cheese, drumsticks, potatoes, spaghetti, bananas, peanut butter and jelly into a cart.

"This stuff should last them until the next food stamps arrive," she said as she stood back and looked at the food in the cart. "I think I've got it down to a science."

"How can you afford to buy people food?" I asked, once we were back in the car and driving toward Carol's house.

Lisa shrugged. "My husband's an E-7 with eighteen years behind him. There are two of us working and we only have one kid. We're also very careful but I think I'm blessed. The more I give, the more it seems to come back to me, contributions, office equipment, furniture, you name it. I started this organization after I went to Philadelphia and listened to Colin Powell speak at the President's Summit on Volunteerism. He said, 'Go out and help a neighbor. The hardest thing you'll ever do is hold a stranger's hand.' It was at a vulnerable time in my own life and his words really got to me.

"My son has cancer and he had just gone into remission. I felt so grateful that I wanted to give something back. I'd heard that a lot of enlisted families were having a hard time but I'd never explored it. This time was different, I felt energized and determined. As soon as I got back home, I began driving around the base and knocking on the doors of all the new families. First, I introduced myself, then I asked them how they were doing and if they needed anything. It didn't take long. When I got about four houses into it, I found a girl living in a totally empty house. She didn't tell me anything was wrong, she just seemed really glad that someone had stopped by to welcome her. She invited me in. As soon as I got inside, I said, 'Hey. Where's your furniture?' She said, 'We don't have any.' I said, 'Where's your car?' She said, 'We don't have one.' I said, 'Where do you sleep?' She pointed to a sleeping bag crumpled up in the middle of the floor. Then I asked if she and the baby had enough food to eat. First, she nodded yes, then her eyes filled up with tears. I was dumbfounded. I came home and I said to my husband, 'My God, Barron. You're not going to believe this but, honest to God, I just found these people right down the road from us who have absolutely nothing. She's sixteen years old with a four-month-old baby. Her eighteen-year-old husband was too proud to say, 'I have no bed. I have no food. I have nothing.'"

Lisa shook her head sadly then said, "Since starting HELP in 1997, I've found more than fifteen hundred families at this base alone in situations that were just as bad or worse."

My own husband had served in the military. He'd been taken straight from a neurosurgical residency and placed aboard a submarine as the medical officer during the Vietnam War. When I called him that night and told him what I'd learned from Lisa Joels, he couldn't believe it either.

The next morning, we parked the car in a relatively run-down area of the base reserved exclusively for enlisted families and walked up a brown dirt path where modest, 1950s style attached brick houses stood in small clusters. Lisa knocked on the door of one of them. A young, sharp-featured boy of about twenty-one dressed in tall black boots and military fatigues opened the door partway. He peeked around the edge then stepped outside and quickly closed the door behind him. He had obviously been waiting for us and didn't want us to come in. The first thing I saw were his eyes. Although they were an unusual shade of pale blue, it wasn't the color that struck me most. It was the impenetrable flatness, the hardness and the distrust.

"Thanks," he said, reaching for a bag of the groceries. He was clearly uncomfortable when Lisa opened the door and whisked past him carrying the packages. I glanced inside then took a breath before walking in behind her. Despite what I had been told, I still wasn't expecting to see this level of chaos and poverty in a military home. There was nothing in the living room besides what looked like about a week's trash that the baby had spilled and was crawling around in. Lisa stepped around the trash and walked directly into the kitchen, then opened the refrigerator. Except for some red liquid that had congealed on the shelves and one slice of unwrapped bread, it was completely empty.

"Carol stresses out," Alex said apologetically as he saw us taking in the scene. "She's been having a really hard time coping lately and I haven't been around to help. I've been working ninety-six-hour shifts. I'm away four days at a time training lieutenants in the field. I've been doing it for three years now. I'm away from home so much that I can't even get a second job to help make ends meet like a lot of the other guys do. I really want to take better care of my family," Alex added, as he saw me watching the baby. She was trying to eat one of the empty McDonald's wrappers that was on the floor. I bent down and picked her up, then opened the loaf of bread Lisa brought and asked if it was all right to let her have a slice.

"Yeah. Sure," he said as the baby grabbed it.

She crammed it into her mouth, devoured it and began crying for more. Alex handed her another, ate one himself, then suggested that we'd probably be more comfortable sitting outside on the stoop.

"I'm sorry the place is such a mess," he said, apologizing again. "Carol lost a baby a few weeks ago, and she hasn't been herself since."

"She did?" Lisa said, spinning around. "What was the problem?"

"I don't know," Alex answered. "I wasn't here.

"But I'll tell you one thing I do know," he added, once we were all outside on the stoop. "From the time I was fourteen, I raised two sisters alone and ran a hundred-acre farm in Kentucky. I worked eight to twelve hours a day on that farm and I went to school in between. Then I took another job on the weekends that paid four dollars and fifty cents an hour. It was hard, very hard, but it was a lot easier than this is." He lit a cigarette and looked at me. "I knew marriage wasn't going to be easy, but I love my wife and I wanted to marry her. The way the Marine Corps made it sound, they were going to help take care of us, they made me think we'd have everything we needed." He squeezed his eyes shut for a minute as if they burned then opened them again. "They've done exactly the opposite. They've torn this marriage apart. They never said you'll get no food allowance for your family. They never said you'll need food stamps and WIC and you still won't have enough. They never said we're going to take you away from your wife and kids nine months out of twelve. They never said the Marine Corps is no place for a family, period . . . but they knew it, they knew it all the time."

In the old Marine Corps, there was a rule that an enlisted man could not be married without his commanding officer's permission. He had to be an E-4 and have two years of service before he was even eligible to bring his wife and family with him. In those days everyone said, "If the military wanted you to have a wife they would have issued you one in your duffel bag."

The young men objected because it went against their hope of being able to get married and take care of their families the way they thought a real man would. That was the main reason many of them joined the corps in the first place.

Even today, most people think that if a family is in the military they get free medical care, free dental care, and free housing. They assume it because, directly or indirectly, they have been led to believe it. Although they have usually not been lied to, they have not been told the whole truth either. Most do not realize that there is no food allowance for wives or children. The housing is free only if it is available. If the family wants a dental plan, they have to pay for it because it is only free for the soldier, and even the soldier has copays for fillings and extractions. Nor is the term "free medical care" entirely accurate. Some things are covered, others are not. If a family is stressed by lack of money and food, for example, and needs non-emergency mental health care in order to cope, they too have a copay. If they are too poor to afford food and clothing and if it costs twenty dollars every time they go in to talk about it, it stands to reason that they are not going to have very many visits.

Theoretically, the commissary saves families lots of money

because it lowers the prices of the items that are being sold by about 30 percent, but in fact, here too the truth is more complex. Since the commissary never has specials, only standard markdowns, it is often actually more expensive than clipping coupons and buying specials at the regular supermarkets. While the Post Exchange has wonderful prices on the clothing it discounts, it carries mostly expensive brands, even for children. So, in the end, it is sometimes considerably more expensive to shop there than at Wal-Mart, Kmart or other less expensive stores.

Under federally established poverty guidelines, the first three military ranks, E-1 through E-3, are eligible for food stamps unless they have assets worth more than four thousand dollars, in which case they are disqualified. But, even with food stamps, a lot of military families have the same problems as Alex and Carol. Toward the end of the month, all the food they purchased with their food stamps has been eaten. Their paychecks have been spent and their refrigerators are empty. There might be a bottle of catsup or mustard and maybe some WIC milk, but many families will be completely out of food. Others will be eating ramen noodles three times a day because they can get ten packs for a dollar at the base commissary and because their next payday is often still a week or more away.

Junior enlisted families also usually end up losing their telephones. That's often because they've made so many desperate long-distance calls home for help and money that they can't pay the phone bill. Pacific Bell and many other phone companies require a payment of three times the highest bill just to get a disconnected phone turned back on. So, once they lose their phones, that's it. Most of these families will never be able to get them back again, at least not during that tour of duty.

As a result, these young men and women often find themselves more deeply isolated than they have ever been. They are often hundreds, even thousands of miles from home without the support systems or the life skills necessary to deal with hunger, poverty, separations and other difficult conditions.

"The only group that's ever helped us since we came here is yours," Alex said, turning to Lisa. "Navy Relief only drove us deeper into debt. Do you know what I have to do? I have to make a monthly contribution to my platoon for parties and trips that I never take because I'm always in the field. It comes out of my paycheck. The contribution isn't exactly mandatory, but I've been told in so many words that if I don't make it, there are plenty of shit details they can put me on." Alex's mouth twisted slightly and his nostrils flared, then he spit over the edge of the wrought-iron rail onto the brown grass. "Most people here are like me. They joined the Marine Corps to get away from something. They wanted structure because they never had it at home, they thought they were tough enough to handle it because they'd already gone through a hard life, but they were wrong. Nothing prepares you for this. I was angry when I came here. I still have a scar between my eyes where my mother punched me with a fistful of rings when I was five. My mother always beat me and my grandmother stabbed me in the hand." Alex laughed a hard, bitter laugh then tossed his head. "My family put the "D" in dysfunctional. I think I was searching for my father when I came here, a lot of us probably are. Have you seen those recruiting ads?" Alex asked as a bitter smile crept across his face. "The ones that show a father with his arm around his son and the father is saying, 'He's not just my son, he's my hero.' Well that's the military playing on our need for approval. They act like our families will suddenly love us now and respect us."

"Yes, I've seen the ads," I said, surprised by his openness and his understanding of why young men like him are especially vulnerable.

"But my father was different," Alex added as his expression softened. "He was gentle and I was very close to him. He died a week before my sixth birthday and I can still remember standing at my bedroom window looking up at the sky and the stars and thinking that my father was up there floating around somewhere. I was praying—just praying—to St. Mary that he would come back home to me." His eyes clouded over then filled up. He looked away so I wouldn't see. "I've cried two times in my life, just two," he said, regaining control. "One was for my father, the other was for my grandfather. After my father died, my grandfather was the only one who was there for me. He had been in the Marines too, the old corps. That's one of the reasons I joined, I came here looking for a better life. I was hoping I could change things, turn my luck around, but I ended up with more rules, more punishments and more poverty than ever and I still had no sense that I was valued.

"I was after a dream. One of my teachers in school used to call it the American dream but that dream turned into a nightmare. Now, I feel like I'm in a goddamn prison with every other weekend off." Alex waved to another Marine who was walking up the path, then he stepped on his cigarette and ground it into the earth until every strand of tobacco was buried, until the thin white paper had turned brown and disappeared in the dirt.

"When I finally get home for my big weekend off, I still can't relax because I have to worry about feeding my baby daughter and feeding my wife. For myself, it doesn't matter," he added, raising his shoulders and puffing up his chest a little. "I can last four days without food if I have water. I've lived with so little for so long that I've got my body trained, but my wife and my baby need to eat. I know my kid is growing up without enough food and I don't know what the hell it's going to do to her. I'm scared to death she'll be stunted or retarded or something."

"How often do you run out?" I asked.

"At the end of every month for sure," Alex answered, pensively, "but to be honest with you, sometimes it's a lot more often than that. Even when we do have food, we usually don't have enough."

"Hey, Carol. How ya doin'?" Lisa called as a young woman walked up the path. She was rail thin and sallow. Her jeans and T-shirt hung loosely on her frail body. As soon as Alex saw her his face lit up.

"Hi, baby," he said gently. "How'd it go?"

Carol shook her head as if to say no. "I've been trying to get a job," she explained to me after we'd been introduced. "But we don't have a vehicle and most of the jobs around here require that. Actually, we do have one, but it's been missing second gear ever since we bought it, and we can't afford to fix it. We can't even get down to the food stamp office to recertify for the stamps."

"That's how it usually goes," Lisa whispered, pulling me aside while Alex handed Carol the baby. "One problem compounds another for these young enlisted families. They're still paying three hundred four dollars a month for a car that's been sitting there broken for over a year."

"It's a 1994 with seventy-six thousand miles," Alex said, over-hearing Lisa. "We owe about thirty-five hundred dollars on it, and if we don't keep up the payments, we'll lose both the car and our credit." Carol walked into the house and came out with a piece of the cheese. "Thanks for the food, Lisa," she said as she handed it to the baby.

"Boy, she's really hungry," Lisa observed. "When's the last time that baby ate?"

Carol started to say something then she looked at Alex and stopped. They both seemed uncomfortable, as if they thought an admission of hunger might incriminate them or discredit them as parents. Maybe they were afraid, as Lisa mentioned later, that the baby might be taken from them by the authorities.

"My job is to be a big tough man," Alex said, breaking the silence. "But the only way I can feed my wife and kid is to send them back to her mother's house or call you." Then Alex spat on the ground again. "Maybe they think that's OK. Maybe they believe that a hungry soldier is an angry soldier and an angry soldier is a good killer and for them, maybe that's the bottom line. All I know is that I've been in the field three hundred of the last three hundred sixty-five days. I was hurt out there, hurt bad enough so I needed surgery. After the operation, I wasn't supposed to be out of bed for two full weeks. They gave me five days off and then sent me back. They were doing war games. The doctor told me not to lift more than ten pounds or stand more than thirty minutes. They knew that, but I was out there standing five hours at a time and lifting sixty or seventy pounds. I'm testing ballistic plates that are supposed to protect people from live rounds but sometimes they don't work. That's how me and two other guys got hurt.

"I've put in three years, and I've only got shit to show for it." Alex looked at my notepad. He smiled then stood back and looked a little surprised. "You really are taking me down word for word." He paced for a minute, as if he was thinking over the risks and possible consequences, then said, "Hell. I don't care what you write. I don't give a damn. Why should I? I'm getting out of here soon. My dream of a good life here is dead. I'm a short-timer now, so I don't have to follow the rules anymore.

"Besides," he said rhetorically, "how much worse can it get? As soon as I see someone trying to jerk me or my friends around, I speak up. They make excuses that I'm in the field all the time because of my expertise, but the truth is I'm out there because I stood up for another Marine."

The baby tugged at Alex's bootlaces then reached up his leg for the rest of him. Alex smiled a broad, beautiful smile that didn't match the anger flashing in his eyes just a moment before, then he picked her up and kissed her forehead.

"When I finished boot camp, I was the proudest soldier in the world. I loved the fact that I was a Marine. It was second only to my marriage and the birth of my daughter. They didn't tell us it would be like this. When we finally hit payday, the first thing we do is run to the commissary because we're so damn hungry all the time."

"The baby always has food," Carol interrupted, looking uneasy again. Then, as if she sensed that we might not believe her, she added, "We make sure we have enough for her even if it's only ramen noodles."

Of the five armed services, it's probably the Marines and their families who find hunger and poverty the hardest to talk about. That's because pride marks their self-worth in a very basic way. It is the smallest group of America's fighting forces and it has always been unique.

The Air Force has officers and airmen. The Navy has officers and sailors. The Army has officers and soldiers, but the Marines have only officers and Marines. At first, that may not sound like a significant distinction, but the Marines are the only group that has given its name to its enlisted personnel. Much more than the other services, the Marines have always been known for instilling pride and responsibility at the lowest levels of the organization. They have 8.8 enlisted men for every officer. The heart of the organization actually resides with the lowest level Marine—the peon, the man who is often called the grunt in the trenches. Forty-nine percent of Marines are E-3s or below. That's about twice as many as in the other three services. Marines recruit from the bottom half of American society. They lure in kids like Alex, kids who have hard lives, weak high school records and big dreams. They appeal to them by holding out what is often their last hope for honor and financial security. They advertise on radio and TV promising large bonuses without mentioning that the bonuses are only for certain critically needed specialties. At the time they enlist, many young Marines feel deeply alienated from mainstream American society and they are desperately hoping to become part of something larger than themselves.

During the 1970s, the Marines hit their historic bottom. They had suffered more losses during the Vietnam War than they had in World War II. Drug abuse was rampant, and racial relations between African-American and white recruits were poor. The Marines haven't drafted anyone since 1970, but, with the end of the general draft in 1973, many of the young men who had been enlisting in the Marines in order to avoid being drafted into the army suddenly stopped. For a while the bottom dropped lower and more than half of the Marine recruits were high school dropouts.

Over the last quarter century, recruiters, eager to make their quotas again, began to offer what seemed like an appealing alternative to the loneliness and alienation that had become so widespread among their troops. They began to actively seek young men who wanted to have wives and children. They made big promises,

promises of security and a good life for the entire family, a life that boys from poor families could not imagine being able to offer their brides any other way. Unfortunately, they were just promises, but they were promises that the boys believed and as a result, today 53 percent of the fighting forces are married.

"Alex is what I call a broken Marine," Lisa said as we drove back to her house. "It's really a shame the way they build these guys and their families up and then break them down. It really upsets me. The recruiters ratchet up their hopes, then, when they get here, it's nothing like they thought it would be. The Marines have abused Alex just like his mother did. He still doesn't have the skills to handle all the emotional baggage so he's acting out. He was looking for a second chance and they failed him. They failed him and that's why he's leaving, that's why they can't retain him.

"The command structure here resents the help I offer these enlisted families. They have never taken me seriously," Lisa said as she introduced me to her husband, Barron, then she laughed. "Maybe it's because I'm African American and my husband's a handsome white guy. Maybe it's because I'm not an officer's wife. Maybe it's just because I'm a woman. I don't know, but whenever I found a problem, I always took it to the top of command. They became defensive about that, they felt I was criticizing them. I tried to make them understand that I didn't come to Quantico with an agenda and that I'm not trying to cause trouble. But until those in command come out here and see for themselves, until they carry a bed or bring food to an empty house, they won't understand what's going on here."

"The lack of appreciation for all Lisa's work irritates me," Barron said. "Because she's done more on her small, grassroots level than anyone else around here to help these people."

"It's really very simple and very logical," Lisa added. "We have families on this base, usually officers' families who are throwing away perfectly good things, especially when they are being relocated. We also have families on this base who are without. As far as furniture goes, the solution was obvious. Barron and I got a truck and began picking up the stuff that people were getting rid of. Then every Saturday morning, we put it out on a lawn and gave it to whoever needed it. I've also started classes for the wives in money management, cooking, and life skills. Coming up with enough food for everyone is the toughest part. We still don't have a good system for that."

"My wife teaches outside the front gate," Barron said warmly, taking her hand in his, "because they won't give her a classroom. We still haven't gotten many of the top officers on this base to admit that there is a basic problem with the way these Marines are valued and compensated. Civilians haven't been given an opportunity to help make things different for enlisted families, because they don't know what's going on here."

Lisa nodded and leaned toward me. "For a long time, Barron and I literally carried the couches and the beds and the tables ourselves. We did it until our backs gave out. Now we have volunteers. We've given up every Saturday for three summers and received no money. Still, like I told you before, whenever we really need something, it just seems to turn up." Lisa's expression became pensive. "My mother died three years ago. She had eleven children and very little money, but she always had enough to help those who had even less. Now that she's passed, I think she's helping me from above. I really mean that because all of a sudden, we're getting through to people. Even the colonel's wife goes out collecting trash with me now. Colin Powell may have heard through the grapevine that he got me off the couch, but he has no idea what he's started."

HELP is a revolving door. It probably sees more families than any other service organization at Quantico. Its role is unique. But it's just one organization on just one Marine base. Poverty and hunger exist among all enlisted families, not just the Marines, and they have for many years. For the most part, the problem has been kept quiet but, once in a while, it has led to a tragedy that the press has picked up, like the death of Danny Holley.

Back in August of 1984, the Associated Press reported that the young son of an enlisted soldier in Marina, California, hanged himself after leaving a note for his mother that read, "Dear Mom. I love you and I hope you won't be mad at me but I think if there was one less mouth to feed, things would be better." He was thirteen years old.

Danny had collected cans for a penny apiece to help buy food for his sister and two brothers at Fort Ord in California while his father, Army Sergeant Johnnie Holley, was stationed in South Korea.

"The troubles of the Holley family were not much different from those of many other army families," said Cynthia High of the Army Emergency Relief Office when she was questioned about Danny's death.

The family had moved that June from West Germany to Fort Ord, one hundred miles south of San Francisco. The housing they were promised was unavailable. Money from their bank account was held up and their car hadn't arrived. The Army was trying to help them but there were many other families on base with financial troubles and a lack of food. Actually, the Holleys were better off than a lot of others. They had received an interest-free loan of thirteen hundred dollars and emergency food supplies, but they were still having trouble making ends meet and thirteen-year-old Danny took it very hard. It was a tough time in many ways. He didn't know anyone on the base, his dad was away and his family was frequently hungry. The family had been given a book of bus tickets that they'd use when they had to go to the doctor or somewhere else but the tickets had run out, and as Danny's mother put it, "We had nothing so we just stayed home."

Actually, Danny didn't stay home; he roamed the neighborhood collecting the cans. He took his self-appointed job seriously and sometimes collected as many as nine hundred cans, enough to bring home nine dollars. He gave his mother the money and told her that it was to buy food for his four-year-old sister, Erin, his eight-year-old brother, Johnnie, and for Christopher, who was only two. But despite his efforts, the children were often hungry.

"He was always very responsible," Danny's mother said as she sat in her kitchen crying shortly after his death. "He was so good-natured. He used to get up in the morning and make me a cup of tea and bring it to me in bed. He was a good boy. But whenever we were hungry and there was little or nothing to eat, he'd always say the same thing he wrote in the note. He'd always say things would be better if there were one less mouth to feed."

Of course, Mrs. Holley didn't think he meant it literally. It never occurred to her that he might actually take his own life.

Then, without further warning, one morning his brother found him hanging in the backyard. He was rushed to a hospital and pronounced dead an hour later. After Danny's father was flown home for the funeral, hundreds of people called the local *Monterey Peninsula Herald*, where the death had been written up, wanting to donate groceries. People, overcome with emotion, also called the relief center at the base and the local Salvation Army, but for Danny Holley it was too late.

In 1982 (about two years before Danny's suicide) military salaries fell nearly 14 percent behind civilian pay. Congress recently approved a 4.8 percent pay raise that began on January 1, 2000, with a second raise scheduled for July of 2001. But at the bottom of the military pay scale, where help is needed most, the January 2000 raise was only about forty dollars a month before state and federal taxes. It still left a military-civilian gap of more than 11 percent.

Advocates for the military families consistently point out that the acute problem comes when an enlisted man marries and has children. That is partly because there is no additional food allowance for the family of an enlisted man, and also because housing allowances are never enough to cover the costs of housing, food and all the other added expenses of families. In fact, they usually aren't even enough to cope with housing expenses alone. As a result, families who are living in areas with high rents often end up moving forty or fifty miles away from their duty stations to areas where housing is less expensive and more available. But even that has a downside, because it means that now they have to maintain both a car and costly insurance.

If they live in military housing, the government pays for their utilities, but if they live off base, the utilities are often a large additional expense. Unfortunately, many bases have very little housing and extremely long waiting lists.

Military installations usually do not keep track of how many of their troops receive public assistance in the form of food stamps, WIC or other subsidies, partly because they don't want to know. The idea itself is embarrassing to both the command structure and the enlisted families. The Pentagon claims that only 450 members of the armed forces are living below the poverty level of $13,332 for a family of three. But according to spokesman Bill Swisher, a recent survey of 165 soldiers at Walter Reed Army Hospital found that 41 percent were using some form of public assistance or private charity.

This number is especially surprising because enlisted men, known for their pride, tend as a group to resist any form of help or charity as long as they possibly can.

According to the Defense Commissary Agency, military families at Fort Belvoir, Fort Meade, Fort Meyer, Andrews Air Force Base, Quantico, and Patuxent River National Air Station used more than $800,000 worth of food stamps and WIC vouchers in 1999. And, according to Pentagon figures, more than 21 million WIC vouchers were redeemed at military commissaries in 2000.

As advocates for military families pointed out to me again and again, something is very wrong when the men who are willing to fight and die for us on the front lines must wait on long lines for free food, supplement that with food stamps and WIC and still not be able to feed their families adequately. As one advocate at Marine Community Service put it, "All the military pride in the world isn't going to pay the bills or put food on their tables. In fact, military pride just makes it harder for many armed service members to accept public assistance, even when they desperately need it. We have a lot of difficulty reaching those in need, because they don't want us to know they have a problem. It's not in their nature."

John and Donelle grew up in Charlotte, North Carolina. They've been together since she was twelve and he was thirteen. As far back as Donelle can remember, they were always best friends, but they weren't married until three days after boot camp had ended, by which time Donelle already had one baby and was about to deliver a second. John spent the first month alone at Quantico getting everything ready for his family's arrival. He was lucky to get a small World War II–style bungalow right on the base and some free furniture at Lisa Joels's Saturday-morning giveaway. He was excited and all set to pick up Donelle and the baby but he had run out of money and had no food at all to put in their new house. He explored the options, then finally went to Navy Relief and took a cash advance on his next paycheck.

John knew about food stamps and he knew about WIC. He was fully aware that he was eligible for both, but he didn't want them— not for his family. He was ashamed even to consider it. It flew in the face of every dream he'd ever had about being a man, a provider and a real husband. It flew in the face of the promises he'd made to Donelle.

John grew up in the projects and knew hunger as a kid, but his beautiful wife, Donelle, had always been economically comfortable. John always believed that if he came into the military, he could take good care of her and his family. In fact, that's why he chose to enlist. When he asked Donelle to marry him, he got down on his knees and promised her a good home and a good life. He said, "I swear to you, honey, I ain't never going to put you in a ghetto like the one I grew up in and I ain't never gonna let you be hungry. I'm gonna become a Marine, Donelle, and that means I'm going to take good care of you and the kids."

Donelle loved everything about John, especially his promises. It was true that she had grown up in a calm suburb of Charlotte and been economically comfortable, at least in John's terms, but she'd also had an abusive father and always wanted her children to have a good one. As she saw it, this was her chance to marry the boy she had always loved, to be economically secure and to raise her children right. Then when the children were old enough to go to school by themselves, she planned to start college and become a teen counselor for domestic violence. She hoped to help other kids who were having a tough time the way she had always hoped that someone would help her. Young as John and Donelle were when they first met, the love between them had never wavered. When they decided to marry, they both vowed that it would be forever. But all that was before John chose the Marines and before hunger and poverty ruled their lives.

John earns $1,017.80 a month, but this is taxable income, and it's never enough for their family of four. "I want to be a good provider. I don't want you to do without. I don't want you to go through this," John told Donelle the day he finally broke down and decided they would have to use the food stamps he'd kept hidden in a drawer for months. By that time the baby was starting to walk and needed shoes. They had no money for food, let alone shoes, and it was almost two weeks until payday. Painful as it was, it had come to a point where John had to admit to himself that they had no choice. Since there was no gas in the car and no money to buy gas, John walked to the commissary. He stood on line for fifteen minutes, feeling painfully humiliated as he held one loaf of bread, some baby food, and the stamps. Even then, he had promised himself he would use stamps only for essentials and nothing more. When the cashier finally rang up the bill, it was $3.55. She asked to see his green eligibility card. When he realized that he had forgotten to bring it, John walked home again, deeply ashamed and still without food.

By the time I visited Donelle, John had finally resigned himself to both the gift of extra food and the terrible loss of self-esteem and pride. They had been using food stamps for several months. But, as we sat in Donelle's immaculately clean bungalow, she explained that, even with the stamps, their problem had not been solved.

"The stamps only last us a couple of weeks, three if we're really careful. Right now, as usual, the food stamps is gone, and we're also out of cash. Until yesterday we had some cheese and some milk from WIC, which we also started to use, but now we ate that up too. I gave the food to the babies first, then to my husband, then I ate whatever was left. I try hard," she said, turning to face me. "I write out weekly menus. I include everything we will eat at each meal. I plan ahead to make the food last as long as possible. I take a cooking class from Lisa Joels, and another class that taught me how to budget the food, but it still don't work. It don't work because there ain't enough food to make it work. I'm depressed and John is discouraged. Taking those stamps really hurt his pride and it hurt our marriage. It made him feel like he had failed me. I think it changed him forever. Even if we had one of those plastic food debit cards that President Bush has been talkin' about, it wouldn't help because the shame is on the inside. Everyone who's ever taken food stamps from the government knows what I'm talkin' about. It's their attitude. They made us feel like failures for needin' them.

"After this station, John's going to be sent overseas for six months or a year. When that happens, I'll probably go home with the kids. At least then we'll be able to eat. My mother works for Easter Seals. She's married to a guy who's a truck driver. He earns a lot more than John and he treats me a lot better than my own father ever did. When I grew up, we weren't rich. We could never afford any of the fancy stuff but we weren't poor either. We always had enough food. Now we are poor, dirt poor, and it's just a lot of stress, much more than I ever imagined. Some days, it gets so bad that I think I'll crack up if I don't take the next boat back to Charlotte. I'm trying to be strong for John. I'm trying to hide it from him but, of course, he knows, and no matter how kind he is or how hard I try, things just ain't the same between us anymore."

Donelle stopped talking. She picked her crying baby up and held him for a while, then she told me about how hard it was to see her dreams die when she was still so young.

"When we was growing up in high school, John always brought me presents, mostly they were small, sentimental things like roses and Victoria's Secret perfumes. He also wrote me little love notes. Now, he don't do that anymore. I know, in my head, that it's because we have no money to buy anything that ain't essential, but I still can't help feeling in my heart that it's really because he don't care for me as much as he used to. It seems like the Marines changed him. They made him distant and defensive and angry. He used to talk to me. He used to like going places with me just to hang out. Now, he's less interested in me and the kids and he's serious all the time. Now, it's like whatever he says goes, like nothing is my decision. Sometimes, I think it's because they order him around all day, and then at night he takes out his frustration by doing the exact same thing to me and the kids. I think it's that and never having enough food or anything else we need.

"He just applied for a second job at Home Depot and Ikea. I really don't want him to have another job because I know that it will take away from his time with the children. It's bad enough that he'll soon be gone for six months or more; at least, I want the kids to know him while he's here. If he starts working nights and weekends, we'll never see him. I don't think we're strong enough for that."

She leaned across the table and looked out the window, her voice was barely a rustle. "Right now I feel lonely even when he's home. The only reason we're still together is because I love him so much and I think he loves me. When we was younger, the notes he wrote always made me so happy. Now he says he's too big for that. He says that was just high school stuff.

"This morning I was devastated because last night I had decided to make a really big effort. After the kids went to sleep, I had lit candles and had soft, romantic music playing. We had just used up the last of our food at dinner but I still had some Kool-Aid left. I put it in champagne glasses and dressed in my best nightgown then I got into bed next to him and I said, 'Honey, if you're tired, we don't have to make love, we can just hold each other.' He lay there for a while without moving a muscle and without touching me, then he said, 'What's on TV?' When I heard that I just froze. This morning I couldn't hold my feelings in no more and I said, 'Our love life has slipped to nothing, and whenever I want to talk you just want to sleep or watch TV.' Then I started to cry and I said, 'John, what happened to us?'

"I'm only eighteen but I already feel old and used up. There ain't no joy in our lives anymore. All we do is struggle. We struggle for money and we struggle for food. I used to think money didn't really matter but I was wrong. When you don't have it, it takes over everything else. It destroys your whole life. Before he left for work this morning, I was about to tell him I was leaving him, but I didn't. Instead I said, 'John, please pick me a flower today or write me a poem.' Then I began to cry and he looked at me and he said, 'Don't cry, Donelle, I'll bring you a flower because I love you more.' I said, 'No, John. I love you more.' Then, for a minute, we both started laughing because, when we was little, we always used to fight about who loved who more. Now I'm just waiting to see if he really comes home with a flower."

Difficult as life is for John and Donelle, many military families in more expensive parts of the country where base housing is not available are even worse off.

For six years, Pat Kellenbarger, the energetic, passionately outspoken director of Military Parish Visitors in San Diego, California, has been helping some of these families cope. The group, sponsored by the thirty-three Presbyterian churches of San Diego County, began forty years ago. It now provides food and other emergency assistance to enlisted military families twenty-four hours a day, seven days a week.

"San Diego is a beautiful place to live with wonderful weather," Pat told me. "But it is also one of the most expensive cities in the United States, and that affects people in the military just as much or maybe even more than it affects other struggling people. There are thirteen bases here in San Diego County, but there is very little base housing. The military housing that does exist is so scattered that it creates its own problems. Public transportation is extremely poor here unless you live right in the heart of the city, and even then it is very expensive. Car insurance is also very costly. Under the age of twenty-five, it costs a minimum of one hundred dollars a month, and after an accident, it goes up to two hundred dollars a month.

"In May of 2001, San Diego's base housing had a waiting list of more than five thousand families and area availability dropped to one-half of one percent vacancies. The cost of those apartments had also risen by seventeen percent since the previous September. As a result, the military families who were assigned to San Diego as their first duty station often ended up with literally no place to live.

"In all the years I've been here," Pat continued, with an angry tremor creeping into her voice, "there isn't a week that's gone by that I haven't found a military family sleeping on the floor or eating on the floor for a lack of chairs and tables and beds. It's not just that they have no place to live, these families have no money for their most basic needs, like a bed to sleep on, diapers for the baby or food to eat.

"We've had some small pay increases in the last three years. They were better than a sharp stick in the eye but not nearly enough to keep up with the rising cost of living. The number of calls for assistance have continued to rise each year. There are more people on our food lines than ever before and more people on our bread lines. There are more families doubling up and living together illegally. There are more fights and just a lot more stress. Some of the wives have tried to go to work but they can usually only get minimum-wage jobs. Child care costs one hundred ten dollars a week, so they end up working for the baby-sitter. They are away from their kids and they still don't have enough money to buy food. I had a chaplain here recently who was visiting from Japan. I invited him to come to my food ministry. I give out food one week and bread the next. This happened to be a bread week. I give out bread at five locations. There are often hundreds of people on my bread lines. When he showed up, I put him to work passing out the bread. He just kept shaking his head and saying, 'I can't believe this, I can't believe this, I can't believe this,' over and over again.

"One time, I walked into a house that was completely empty except for a pile of dirty clothes in the corner which the parents were sleeping on and drying themselves on. The baby was in an open Samsonite suitcase. There were McDonald's papers all over the floor, and when I asked the girl about them she said, 'My husband knew he was going to be in the field for three weeks. He also knew that I would be here by myself with very little money and no dishes or pots or pans. So he went down to McDonald's on Sunday when hamburgers were thirty-nine cents and bought twenty-one of them. I've been eating one hamburger every day for the last twenty days.'"

Pat ran her hand through her short gray hair and sighed deeply. "When I asked this girl where home was, she said, 'Detroit.' When I asked her how long she'd been waiting for her things to arrive, she didn't answer me directly. She just said, 'We've been here for four months.' So I said, 'Do you mean to say you came here eight months pregnant with nothing?' 'There was nothing to bring,' she answered. 'Your mother didn't even let you bring the bed you were sleeping on in Detroit?' I asked. She thought for a minute then said, 'My younger brothers and sisters needed that bed.'

"It never ends," Pat said softly, with more sadness than anger in her voice. "They have no food and they have no housing. Last night I was with a family that had a four-month-old baby. They had found a forty-dollar-a-night motel to stay in and they had been there for a week. They've been looking for an apartment, but of course they won't find one. They are from Wyoming. They seem young and vigorous so I said, 'Hey. I have an idea. Why don't you guys go out to the Marine Corps campground at Lake O'Neil? It's only twelve dollars a night, and you can check out cots and a tent. There are hot showers, a laundromat, and a telephone.' I said it as if I was coming up with the idea for the first time but they didn't go for it. They said camping was not what they expected when they enlisted in the Marines and that they would have to think about it. They told me that they had some furniture in a storage unit which could stay there for thirty days and that they were still hoping an apartment would open up by then. They realize that they will be deeply in debt from the motel bill but they still don't believe how bad the housing situation here really is. They're still in shock. I've seen it over and over again so many times that I think I'm jaded now. But for each new family, of course, it's the first time and it often takes a long time for the hope they arrived with to die. This particular family has some food from WIC that they keep in the little motel refrigerator. It's supposed to be for the baby but I know that all three of them are eating it. They're probably trying to live on it. He's right out of basic training. He just checked into his unit, put his name on the housing list, and went to work. I don't think he really understands that there is at least a four-month wait for housing. But there is; that's why I suggested camping. I was trying to put a light face on dark times, and maybe I shouldn't have, because the truth is that desperate times call for desperate measures. But how do you tell that to a couple of kids on their own for the first time in their lives? Once I had a family with six children who stayed at a campground for five months. I helped them get food."

Then Pat Kellenbarger smiled for the first time and her face relaxed.

"We do have a marvelous food ministry," she said. "It's not exactly manna from heaven but sometimes it seems like it. We get fresh fruits and vegetables, juices, bread and canned goods given to us as part of the Christian Food Co-op. Twenty-six agencies get food from this one truck. There's more than twenty tons of food on the truck. I get more of it than the others because I feed more people than anyone else in the co-op. The Senior Gleaners help collect and harvest the food and many other small agencies and church groups are part of it. It's not just for military families. They also feed the disenfranchised, the lost members of our society, the shut-ins, the low-income groups, the orphans in Mexico, the Indians on reservations and, of course, the enlisted military families. I'm currently feeding about four hundred military families every month. That's roughly twelve hundred people. I do it at Camp Pendleton, Chula Vista, El

Cajon, East County, and right here, just north of us in San Diego, where there are three military housing areas very close together.

"Hunger in the military has been kept even more of a secret than hunger in the rest of America. The old message that the military takes care of its own is so deeply ingrained in the American belief system that it is extremely hard for people to absorb anything else. It's even hard for me to believe and I see it every day."

"It's hard for me too," I said. "I was talking to other groups about hunger and I kept seeing soldiers and their wives and children on food lines. I couldn't understand it."

Pat nodded. "I watch young military wives in the supermarket. I can pick them out every time because they are the ones who always walk straight through the produce department. They don't even stop because, even though San Diego is comparatively cheap for fruits and vegetables, they know they can't afford to buy them. By the time they buy the diapers, the macaroni, the tampons, the toothpaste, the boot polish and the starch for the uniforms, there's not much left. Fresh fruits and vegetables come after boot polish and starch because an enlisted man has to look sharp and act like nothing's wrong even if his family is going hungry."

"Like the Spartan boy," I said. "The wolf is eating away at his heart but he still has to smile."

"Yes," Pat said, "exactly. Enlisted military families are often dying inside but they still try to keep the show going. They have the same needs as other poverty-level families and then some. The women are away from their parents and friends and the husband is often absent for long periods of time. Unlike some bases in the interior, the bases in San Diego are 'sending bases.' That means that entire units at Camp Pendleton are picked up with men and equipment, in toto, and moved to places like Okinawa for six or seven months at a time. Suddenly, the mother and kids are at home by themselves, seven days a week, around the clock, with no husband and no support system.

"Many of these girls are shy and immature. They are afraid to make friends, afraid to reach out, afraid that they will be taken advantage of. They are young and they are not experienced, at least not as money managers. They go from maybe a ten-dollars-a-week allowance as high school kids to what they think is going to be a gigantic amount of money when they see it on paper. They think they're going to have all this money, but then it goes so quickly. I kid them about their payday pizzas. They live for payday so they can order in a pizza. I say, 'Why are you paying twenty dollars to have a pizza delivered to your house? For twenty dollars, you could make ten pizzas,' and I show them how."

Then Pat explained that her ministry goes to three sites each week. The military families bring their empty bags then stand on line and wait while she does a quick visual calculation of what's on the truck. "OK," she says, after she's assessed the situation, "each person on line gets twelve potatoes, six ears of corn, four cucumbers, five oranges, a bag of apples, three packs of ramen noodles, two bags of chocolate chip cookies, two bags of prepared salad, three bottles of juice, six loaves of bread and four onions." She has volunteers who then put the food into bags. In 1999, the Military Parish Visitors helped to feed ten thousand active-duty military families in San Diego alone. They have a staff of two and about eighty volunteers who are mostly retired people from the nearby churches.

Pat also advises the families to join the SHARE program, a co-op where they pay fourteen dollars a month and do two hours of service in exchange for about forty-five dollars worth of food, including six to eight pounds of fresh meat. "But families often can't take advantage of SHARE," she explained, "because to do so they have to pay the fourteen dollars by the fifth or sixth of the month. Many of them have their rent and other things due the first of the month, and by the fifth, they don't have fourteen dollars left."

As I listened to Pat, I realized that while the problems of hunger and poverty are always most severe in the high-cost areas like San Diego, Norfolk, Quantico, Washington, D.C., Seattle, and Honolulu, they are made even worse for the women and children, both economically and psychologically, when the men are sent off for six or seven months at a time. They are made psychologically worse because now the wives and children must navigate their paths through poverty and hunger alone in a strange city. They are made economically worse because when their husband is taken away from his family, there is a reduction in the family paycheck of about $210 a month. That reduction represents his COMRATS (commuted rations) or food money. It is the only food allowance that the family has.

As Pat explained it, "There is no food allowance for women or for children, but when daddy is home and eating with them, at least he gets about seven dollars a day for his food, which they all share. When he's sent away, they take the seven dollars a day out of his paycheck. They act as if the rest of the family requires no food. Most young families don't understand this until it happens because it wasn't clearly explained to the husband, and it was never explained to the wife at all. I get these frantic phone calls from wives every two weeks saying, 'Pat, my husband's paycheck is a hundred five dollars short.' Of course, the wife has to keep buying food for herself and the kids. The telephone bill doesn't change, and the kids still need shoes, but it takes thirty days for his one-hundred-dollar family separation allowance to pop in. The military is famous for sending men out on exercises for twenty-nine days and then bringing them back just before the thirtieth day. It's not a mistake," Pat adds. "It's done on purpose, because they have to be gone for thirty days to be eligible for the one-hundred-dollar family separation pay.

"Both food stamps and WIC are accepted instead of cash at the commissary. Most young military families would not make it without WIC supplemental food and formula. To get it, they have to be pregnant, nursing, or have kids under the age of five. Families can earn up to three thousand dollars a month and still qualify for WIC if they have enough kids. But like all government programs, the rules they have to follow are rigid, unforgiving and sometimes, at least from a mother's perspective, they are also senseless and cruel."

Marge Johnson is one of those mothers. I met her at NAV-

CARE, a modern, one-story military clinic for Navy families. The building, which is painted white with a single blue stripe around the perimeter, is located on Clairmont Mesa Boulevard in San Diego. Marge arrived pushing a baby in a stroller and looking tired; perhaps weary would describe it better. I was standing at the other end of the parking lot when I saw her walking toward me with a slow, heavy step and glazed-looking eyes as two blond-haired, blue-eyed hellions, Taylor, five, and Cody, seven, hung on each of her arms. They were there for school physicals. Timothy, her youngest, had just turned one. That, I was to learn, was one of Marge's problems. At the age of one, literally overnight, he had become too old to qualify for free WIC formula.

"I was breast-feeding Timothy exactly the way I breast-fed both of my older boys," Marge explained as we took our seats in the crowded waiting room. She pushed her shoulder-length red hair back from her face with her hand and sniffed. "The older boys are seventeen months apart. Back in Kentucky, I nursed both of them at the same time, one on one breast, one on the other. That's common in Kentucky, and they thrived. This baby is developing slower than my others, and I keep thinking it's because I didn't have enough to eat when I was pregnant. At least when I was nursing it made me feel I was finally doin' right by him. Then, about six months ago, I got depressed. My anxiety got so bad, I began having panic attacks every time we ran out of food. Finally, the doctor put me on Zoloft which, wouldn't you know, went right to my milk, so I had to stop nursing. It just tore me up inside to stop nursing this baby. I think that nursing has always been therapeutic for me. It was a release when my milk let down, but the stress about always being hungry and having the kids be hungry had reached a point where I could just feel my chest tightening up. Toward the end of the month, I couldn't drive and I couldn't think. Even Cody, that freckle-faced little hillbilly, could tell. He would just say, 'Mommy, are you feeling scared again?' Then he'd come up next to me and little as he is, he'd just hold on to me and the baby and Taylor real tight, like a big group hug, until the panic passed. It's been real bad lately, even with the Zoloft and the group hugs. This is the first time I've been out of the house in a month."

Then Marge gasped as if there was not enough air in the room. She grabbed my hand. Her fingers were cold but her palms were sweating. Suddenly, little Cody noticed. Without a word, he came over, took her hand out of mine and put his arms around her. After a few minutes in the comfort of his small arms, she seemed to relax again.

"WIC gave me supplemental formula and it meant the world to me," she said when she could speak again. "But, like I told you," she added, still breathing rapidly, "they cut me off when the baby turned one. They said I needed a doctor's note in order to keep getting the formula. So I came here to the clinic. I just can't understand why they don't let me decide what my baby needs. A mother often knows that even better than a doctor does and I know that next to breast milk, formula works best for my baby. When they cut him off the formula last week, he got sick. He got cramps and a rash, so I came to the clinic and I begged, I actually pleaded with them to let my child have the free formula. 'I'll give you two months to wean him,' the doctor finally said, but I could hear in her voice that she didn't understand. She was real cold. She told me to just start mixing the Enfamil with milk. When she gave me the prescription for two months, I was so upset that I almost put a one in front of the two." Marge wiped her eyes with her index finger. "To tell you the truth," she whispered after the children had gone into the examining room, "the only reason I didn't do it was because I was afraid I'd get caught and go to jail for trying to steal the milk. Then I got afraid they'd send my husband overseas and all three of my kids would be alone."

She raised her chin and said sadly, "Oh, God, I wish we were back in Kentucky. We weren't rich there either but we were never without. We grew and we planted. We're not allowed to do that here. The lawns have to be clipped. We're not even allowed to have a veg- etable garden. I was used to preparing good, nutritious meals for a family of ten on very little money. It's not that I don't know how to do it." Marge's soft eyes hardened and her voice dropped a little. "I know exactly how, I just don't have enough money to work with.

"Everyone thinks when you're in the military you're set for life," Marge added bitterly after we'd left the clinic and had begun to drive toward her house. Her voice was almost a wail now. "They mislead you on purpose and that's the real sin that they commit. They play on your weakness and on the injuries you've already suffered. They tell you half-truths to draw you in. They make you think you'll have enough money and your dreams will come true, then once they've got you here, you're stuck. You're like a prisoner.

"Take today. All I've got in my wallet is the rwo dollars my aunt sent us to buy ice cream for the kids, and if she hadn't sent it, I wouldn't have anything.

"That's my husband, Andy," Marge said as she opened the door of a small, neat ranch house in an area reserved for enlisted families. Andy took the baby from Marge and turned away without smiling or saying hello. "He enlisted at seventeen when he was still single," Marge explained. "Now he's been in for eight years. He's an E-5 and he has nine or ten medals. He also has one ribbon and nine bars but he's still just an enlisted man, not an officer. He gets $492.70 on the first of the month, and $533.26 on the fifteenth. That's a total of $1,025.96 a month, which is less than $13,000 a year. And, for a family of five with three kids, that's just not enough.

"Once a month, we get the generic supplemental food," Marge told me when we were settled down again in her living room. "It's distributed to enlisted families and other poor people by the USDA for domestic food assistance. There's rice, macaroni, ham, peanut butter, canned pork, and canned chicken. I get it at the Sierra Mesa Recreational Center on the fourth Wednesday of every month. We get two portions of everything because we have three kids. I feed my family supper every night for a week on those commodities, but I feel very strongly that it shouldn't have to be this way. I've become outspoken about it lately, but my husband is still afraid that he'll lose rank or get court-martialed. He won't talk to you. He won't say a word. Look at him."

She pointed at her husband sitting and listening with his hands digging firmly into the side of the couch. He raised a clenched fist then released it and put one finger across his lips.

I had, of course, noticed that Marge's husband wasn't speaking. He had been sitting with us for quite a while without saying a single word but it hadn't occurred to me that it was because he was afraid.

"He acts like they've got recorders in the house, like they're God and they're listening from up above. That's how scared he is. They've stripped him of his spirit. They've stripped him of everything but his uniform, and he was so whole when he entered, so full of life."

"Is that true?" I asked, softly. "Are you afraid to talk to me?"

He nodded silently as I looked at his dying eyes and polished boots. He refused to say even the word yes out loud.

"See, he's terrified," Marge continued, with her voice rising. "He's scared to death. He believes that if they don't like something he says, his career's over. You know what I say? I say, 'So what! What's the worst thing that can happen? They can kick us out. They can give us a dishonorable discharge.' If they kicked us out, we'd move back to Kentucky. At least there we had food to grow and food to eat. At least there we had chickens and eggs and gardens."

Marge stopped and thought for a moment. Her eyes looked troubled. "Well, maybe I'm romanticizing what it was like back home. Maybe it was trailer parks and rotted teeth and withered, old-looking people who are still young, but at least there was a garden out back and we had enough food to eat. At least you could always find a patch of dirt and grow something. I do crafting now, Kentucky crafting. I go to Coronado and set up a stand near the ocean. I sell my crafts to the tourists to try to make a little extra for groceries but it still isn't enough.

"Here I am, twenty-six years old with three kids and a husband who fights for the country that won't give formula to his baby. Twenty-six years old and I still have to ask my own poor family to send money so the kids can have ice cream. I was adopted at six weeks by my aunt and my uncle. My uncle was a coal miner. When they started closing down the mines, I worked with my aunt cleaning those beautiful houses in the southeastern part of Kentucky. My aunt is a wonderful woman. She deserves a beautiful house and when I saw her, bent in half with rags in both hands, cleaning for someone else, I dreamed that someday when we joined the Navy we'd have a house like that and I'd share it with her. Of course, I knew that was a fantasy but I never dreamed I'd have nowhere to sleep but the floor. I never dreamed I'd have none of my family nearby and no formula to feed my baby.

"One day, soon after I arrived on this base, my husband was sent away for six months. The kids and I were sleeping on the floor and, as usual at the end of the month, there was no food or money in the house." Marge stopped suddenly and looked at her husband then she turned her back to him. "I'm telling you these things whether he likes it or not but I want you to know that none of it is his fault. He's a wonderful man, doing the best he can for all of us. But on this one day, I got so desperate that I just took the kids and got into the car and started driving aimlessly. I had no idea where I was going or what I was looking for. It was a cold, foggy Monday morning. All I knew was that the kids were hungry and I was wondering how on God's earth I would feed them. I was just praying out loud that I'd find a way. Then out of nowhere, through the rain and fog, I saw this long line of women and children. There must have been a hundred women on that line. I stopped the car and I got out. I walked across the street and I said to a woman who was holding a baby in her arms, 'Excuse me, ma'am, but why are all you women standing here in this line in the pouring rain?' She looked at me and said, 'Didn't you hear? They're giving away free bread; hamburger buns, hot dog buns, and bakery bread.' So I joined the women and children on that line and I got a loaf of sourdough bread. They could only give me one loaf, I think it was day-old bread but it had gotten wet so I don't really know. Anyhow, I got back in the car and drove home through the rain, holding that bread in my lap. I knew it wouldn't be enough to fill all of us up so I thought I'd feed it to the children first. The baby was crying and I was starting to get that panicky feeling again, then suddenly I began hearing a voice in my head and seeing a face, but it wasn't a hallucination, it was a real voice and a real face. I knew because I'd seen it before on TV. It was the recruiter's voice and the recruiter's face. Only this time, instead of smiling, he was laughing, laughing at us and beckoning to us with his hands and saying, 'Come on, join the Navy and let the journey begin.'"

Chapter 4

Hunger and the Working Poor

"They are one paycheck away from what is left of welfare, one sick child away from getting fired, one missed rent payment short of eviction . . . they can easily be reduced to indigence."

KATHERINE S. NEWMAN
No Shame in My Game

Long Hours, Starvation Wages

I first visited Annapolis, the state capital of Maryland, back in 1997. It was the year before Second Harvest reported that one in ten Americans had requested emergency food and the year before my own return to the field of hunger. Annapolis is the sailing capital of the world and a top tourist destination. I was there for a reunion of my husband's Navy submarine crew. The group of former officers stayed in the fashionable Lowes Annapolis Hotel on West Street and explored the area by foot.

We walked through twisting, narrow streets, lined with old brick and cobblestones. As we walked and chatted and laughed, we were greeted by several young naval cadets in crisp, white uniforms who studied at the prestigious U.S. Naval Academy. We admired the state capitol, the historic homes and the shiny new replicas of Revolutionary War–period buildings. I was especially charmed by the city dock, where hordes of tourists gazed at countless sailboats and enjoyed gourmet food and wine in charming, waterfront cafés. Everything seemed upscale, affluent and upbeat.

But in August of 2000, after seeing San Diego, with its gaslight district, its tourists, its affluence, its strong military presence and its hungry enlisted men, something made me think about Annapolis again. I began to wonder if hunger and poverty existed there too, alongside all the old charm and contemporary opulence.

My curiosity led to a quick Internet search, which turned up an organization called Food Link, an independent food salvage and distribution center that collects food from restaurants and supermarkets and distributes it to the hungry the same way that Food Chain does.

They immediately put me in touch with the Light House, a homeless shelter located on West Street. It was just a block and a half from the Lowes Annapolis Hotel where I had spent that reunion weekend.

When I reached Toni Graff, the executive director, she told me that in affluent areas like Annapolis, it's always easier for the boundaries between the working poor and the homeless to merge. She explained that in high-rent districts there is likely to be homelessness among the working poor because they are often just one or two paychecks away from eviction.

I learned that the Light House had been there for eleven years. In fact, on my previous visit, I had walked right past the hundred-year-old, two-story redbrick Federal building with its red tin roof and storefront design without realizing that it was a homeless shelter and an emergency food pantry. Even many of the local residents don't know that the Light House shelters or otherwise serves about twelve thousand of the area's men, women and children each year, a shockingly high percentage of the city's thirty-six thousand residents.

"We're not formal and we're not fancy," Toni Graff explained as she gave me a brief tour of the small, immaculate living area where rows of cots stood side by side. A TV and a couple of couches were all that separated the men's and women's quarters.

"We're just a small neighborhood shelter and crisis center that was started in 1989 at the St. Anne Church when an interim pastor saw four homeless people sleeping in the parish hall. But instead of turning them away like so many others would have, he decided to start a shelter. We don't have a lot of bureaucratic rules and we don't have a lot of money but we've expanded greatly since we started. Today, seventeen local churches are involved. Our community is based on need so it's made up of whoever comes to our door. Besides giving people cots to sleep on and something to eat, we have two guest apartments on the second floor for families so they can have a little more privacy."

Toni took me upstairs, showed me the apartments with their own kitchens and living rooms, then introduced me to Sonya Foreman, the managing director.

"We also own two houses," Sonya said with obvious pride. "Families with long-term shelter needs can live in them for up to two years. We've recently developed a modest financial-assistance program to help prevent evictions or other emergencies, like turning off the utilities. Oh, yes, and another extremely important thing we have is a very active food pantry. It provides a three-day supply of emergency food to local residents and gives out bag lunches to anyone who's hungry during the workweek."

Then Sonya's face turned serious. "But it's not enough. We've seen more need in the last two years than ever before." She drummed her fingers against the desk then pushed her dark curls away from her face. "We're packed. We're constantly full. We have a full-time staff of nine and a lot of amazing volunteers but we can't keep up.

"William Donald Shaffer, the former mayor of Baltimore and the former governor of Maryland, helps out here regularly," she added. "He's comptroller for the state of Maryland now so he comes here with a bunch of other volunteers he's recruited from the comptroller's office. They all pitch in and cook dinner for our homeless guests once a month.

"Like I said, we have a lot of wonderful people helping and we're grateful for their efforts, but the truth is that even the whole bunch of us working together are just Band-Aids for a problem that's far larger than we can heal. We have no idea how many adults or how many children are still out there without food or shelter in this lovely little town. Keep in mind that by definition, the homeless are hard to document because they don't live anywhere. Their lives are unstable and they keep moving from place to place. Often, the census takers can't even find them. It's actually amazing that they've managed to document more than ten thousand homeless children in the state of Maryland alone. The average age of those children is only six.

There are probably a lot more, but think about it, ten thousand little kids with no bed of their own to lay their head on. To me, that's a shocking fact.

"I hate to have to say this but just last month, in May, we turned away one hundred sixteen adults. Some were mothers with three or four kids so the actual number of people we turned away was much larger than one hundred sixteen. We don't even know how many times larger."

Sonya swallowed once, then swallowed again and bit down on her lower lip.

"By turning them away, I don't mean that we rejected them because they didn't qualify. I mean we turned them away because we didn't have room for them. We simply didn't have any more beds."

"Where do they go when they can't stay here?" I asked, remembering how cold the wind felt when it blew off the water in the evening and knowing that there were no other shelters nearby.

No one answered.

I looked at Toni and saw that there were deep frown lines running across her forehead and what I thought was sadness in her eyes. She hesitated for another moment then said, "We apologize to them and then we refer them back to the Department of Social Services. What else can we do? Technically, they will be taken care of by social services, but of course in reality we know that they will face a very difficult situation.

"Housing here in Annapolis is so expensive that it's often unaffordable for the working poor. You can't even touch a small one-bedroom apartment here for less than seven hundred a month. Don't get me wrong," Toni added. "I'm not saying homelessness is always just a cost-of-housing problem. Some of our guests, even those who work full-time, have more complex problems. Some have experienced abuse as kids or they are unbalanced or have drug issues, and others are just kids themselves without the skills to manage. But there is a belief in our culture that if you work you will not be poor or hungry, and the truth is that many of the people who work, even the people who work full-time, are very poor and often very hungry. They never get above the poverty line. They are not even paid enough money after taxes to cover their basic living expenses."

"Toni's right," Sonya said, softly. "A lot of people we see here simply can't make ends meet no matter how hard they work or how well they manage. That's why I have a real issue with the Welfare to Work reform. I think it does more harm than good. The people are poorer now than ever because as soon as they get a minimum-wage job, they are cut off from food stamps. It's not only demotivating, it's destructive. The government and everyone else knows that they still don't have enough money for food, rent and all the rest of it but they turn the other way and pretend that the salary will meet their needs. Most have no medical benefits, so they have to choose between medicine, food and housing. It's also obvious to anyone who thinks about it that people who are spending fifty percent or more of their income on housing are in extreme danger of losing their homes; all it takes is one emergency and that's how it often goes. If they can't pay the rent, they get evicted and, of course, they don't have the money for a security deposit to get a new rental so, if we have the space, they end up here.

"It's a straightforward issue but there are still a lot of folks who don't understand it. They say, if they can't earn enough to get by, tell them to go back to school and get their GEDs so they can get higher-paying jobs. But let's be realistic, we're talking about survival here. When your kids are hungry and your family is homeless, getting a degree is pretty low on the hierarchy of meeting your family's immediate and urgent needs.

"Actually, I'm not even sure how much difference a GED would make because we're seeing more and more people at our shelter who are already well educated. I mean they have high school or sometimes even college degrees. For the first time we're also seeing families here where the mother or father has more than one job or where both parents are working full-time and they're still living on the edge. If they have no money in the bank and are already in debt, as soon as they have that emergency, their whole world falls apart."

Sonya closed her eyes for a minute and shook her head. "I'm telling you," she said when she opened them again, "the working poor are adding a desperate new dimension to the homeless population."

Amy and her children were waiting for me in the small front lobby of the Light House Homeless Shelter the next morning. Two frail twin boys about three years old were sitting on the narrow wooden benches that lined each side of the wall. They were both working intently with colorless markers that magically made bright colors appear in their coloring books. Amy was so absorbed with the kids and the coloring that she barely seemed to know I had arrived. Even after I said hello and introduced myself, she looked up just long enough for me to notice that her face was pretty and delicate, then she looked back at one of the coloring books. She acted as if she had no idea why I was speaking to her. Although we had arranged the meeting the day before, I found myself wondering if there had been some misunderstanding. Then, unexpectedly, one of the twins smiled, held up his coloring book and offered me his marker. I sat down on the bench next to him and began to rub the page. He laughed and squealed with delight as the flower on the white paper suddenly turned green and pink and purple.

"Wow," I said, rather delighted myself. "That's really cool."

Amy smiled and rushed over to see. The ice was broken. Later, I realized that what had appeared to be coldness or indifference or lack of recognition on her part was simply embarrassment. It was hard for her to meet my gaze and hard for her to tell me how her life had unraveled.

Once we were settled in an upstairs office and she sent the kids off to play in another part of the shelter, Amy seemed to relax. She said she might as well start at the beginning, then explained that she had been taken in by her grandparents at the age of three weeks and had lived with them until her grandmother passed away eighteen years later. They had always been poor and her grandfather had always walked back and forth to work at the shipyard—that is, whenever there was work.

"We had no car and we had almost no money but our house was a refuge for everyone in need, just like a church is," she said, surprising me with the girlish innocence of her expression. "That was my grandmother's influence. She was so kind and so protective that, until I was five, she wouldn't even let me walk to the outhouse alone. But she was also realistic and practical. As soon as I was old enough to stand up on a chair at the sink, she taught me to wash dishes. She also showed me how to milk the cows, how to farm the garden, how to cook whatever we had and how to take food and make it stretch so we would feel the hunger less. By the time I was nine and my grandmother got sick, I knew how to take care of her and the house. I even knew how to pay the bills. We always had a lot of bills but no way to pay them. We were hungry then. Even with all her food stretching, there was never enough. Basically, we lived on the garden and the milk from the cows. My stomach got to the point where it was so small that if I ate more than a little, I got sick. What we got from the store was just a tiny bit of meat once a month, the cheapest kind we could get, you know, like soup bones, that sort of thing. I was hungry but it seemed normal to me because that was the way my life had always been."

Amy leaned forward and her soft, light-brown hair fell over her face like a screen. I tried to see her eyes between the strands but she squeezed them shut.

"When my grandma died," she whispered, "all the love in my life died too. It was as if the lights went out. I was with her when she had a massive heart attack and I was trying so hard to save her that they had to pry me off of her and drag me out of the room. I was studying nursing at the time so I thought I knew how to keep her breathing. After she died I went to the school and quit. I thought that if I couldn't save my own grandmother, I couldn't save anyone else. I felt that I had failed her. I decided I didn't believe in nursing anymore or in anything else really. I packed my stuff in a plastic bag and left the state with a cousin who had a car. We drove to Florida without jobs or plans. After that, my life took a downward spiral. I got pregnant and had a baby. Two weeks later, the father took off. I had no money, no food, no house and no transportation. I was living on the street. I'd nurse the baby religiously every four hours but there were days when I wouldn't eat at all because there was nothing to eat.

"I met a guy who felt sorry for us. He said he'd take me and the baby to his house. He had no money either and almost no food himself, but at least he had a place and he took us in. I shut my eyes every night while we did it and prayed he'd let us stay a little longer. I didn't even know his last name.

"I knew I needed help but I didn't know how to get it. I was ashamed to call my grandfather, I had no friends in Florida and I didn't know where the food stamp office was or how long I had to live at this guy's address before I could qualify. By the time I found out where the office was, I was desperate. I didn't even have enough money for a bus so I walked there with the baby. It was a long walk in a part of town where people slept on benches until the cops woke them up and made them move on. I walked for miles and miles. It took about two hours on foot before I finally found it. I waited on line another two hours, then when my turn finally came, the lady who worked there took one look at my papers and said I didn't have the things I needed to prove where I lived. I hadn't eaten anything since the day before and I was so hungry I was dizzy. I had the weak, shaky feeling that always comes with starving.

"As I walked back, one thought kept going through my head, it echoed as if I was in a tunnel with no exit. It was a thought that really frightened me at first because my grandparents had always taught me not to steal. But the more I thought about it the calmer I got. I actually felt some relief, and even though I still hadn't eaten, the hunger became less painful.

"When I was a kid and we had no money and nothing left in the garden, we could pretty much count on the neighbors to pitch in. They could usually give us something because they had a bigger field for growing. But now I had no neighbors and I had no grandmother and I had no growing field and I knew I had to count on myself. I also knew my baby had to count on me. While I was walking, I made up my mind that I wouldn't let my baby starve. No matter what it took, I would get my son what he needed; I would do it even if it meant giving up my life. When you're down that low you don't even think about it, you just do whatever you have to do to survive. Like they say, survival first. Survival with honor second."

"I walked into a supermarket," Amy said as her eyes glazed over. "It was a small one, sort of like one of those little corner stores with sawdust and narrow aisles that sell a little bit of everything. I was pushing the stroller with the baby in it and I was perfectly calm, calm as a shadow. I just began taking stuff. In those days they didn't have cameras in the supermarkets or those little beepy things, but almost before I knew it, the calm feeling vanished and something else took over. I sensed that I didn't have much time. I began stuffing food into the sides of the stroller and into the diaper bag and into my pocket-book. I was being very open about it like I didn't even care if they saw me. I know this sounds kind of crazy, but in that moment I felt as if, for the first time in a long time, I was finally thinking clearly. The woman in the food stamp office had said I couldn't have stamps until I came back the next day with more proof. But I knew that I didn't have any more proof and, even if I did, my baby couldn't wait, and why should he wait when there was all this food in the stores that no one was eating. Did she think I'd be standing there begging for food stamps if I had the money to buy food?"

As I listened to Amy I thought about how ironic it was that she and so many other American mothers felt pushed to steal the food they needed by the very organizations that were supposed to help them get it, the food stamp and welfare offices. "I wasn't exactly stealing on automatic pilot," she said, "because I had worked the whole thing out in my mind. First, I took the essentials like milk and diapers for the baby. Then I took some baby treats and a teething toy. After that I began taking other things I thought we needed, like canned goods for me and clothes for the baby and a couple of little rattles. When I couldn't take any more, I started to walk out. I thought I was being watched and I was right. The store manager followed me. He tapped me on the shoulder and said, 'Excuse me, lady, but you can't be doing that.'

"As soon as he said it, I began to shake. It was as if I had been having a dream or a nightmare and he'd just woken me up. Suddenly, I was scared to death and embarrassed and ashamed that I'd gotten caught. I told him I was sorry. I said I didn't want to go to jail and I didn't want to lose my baby and then I just started crying and sobbing. So do you know what that poor guy did? He took off his glasses and wiped his own eyes, then he put his glasses on again and he tried to comfort me. He patted me on the back and told me everything was going to be OK. He even said he would do whatever he could to help. He was really kind. He just said I couldn't do that and not to do it anymore. Then he told me to keep the necessities like the diapers and the milk and that he would personally pay for them. He said that he understood but he asked me to put the stuff back that I didn't really need, because I had totaled up about a hundred dollars worth of things.

"That night after we got home the baby drank part of a bottle of Mr. Bubble. It was the only thing I kept that I hadn't really needed, the one little luxury that I held on to. I thought he'd enjoy the bubbles because of the way they sparkle and get all silvery before they pop. I felt like they were magical and we needed some magic in our lives. Anyhow, I had to take him to the hospital to get his stomach pumped and I blamed myself. I thought it was my punishment from God for stealing and for being selfish.

"After that I decided that I would never steal ever again. I'd beg but I wouldn't steal. I'd go around anywhere and ask people for food. I didn't care what they thought of me. I'd run right up to them on the street and say, 'Please. Do you have a quarter or a dollar because my son is hungry and he needs to eat?' I met a kind lady that way, a generous lady who gave me five dollars and told me to try the social services again. I took her advice and went back. They still said I didn't qualify, but this time it was a different lady. She was a little nicer and she gave me a list of soup kitchens and food pantries and churches where I could get free food. I went to every single one because each of them had their own rules. Most of them would only give you a three-day supply of food once a month. So I made a list of my own, kind of like a calendar, that reminded me of when I could go to each pantry, and I went from one to another. Some of them would give me food once a week but a lot of them said that there was a longer waiting period. So I would go down the list and I'd alternate. I'd go to one this week to get food and another the next week. In the end, I'd hit them all and um . . . that's how we stayed alive.

"I was still very thin and, even though I was hungry, I looked good the way that models look good. Someone offered me a job working at a bar in a men's club, lap dancing and doing stuff that I wasn't proud of. I took the job and I got pregnant again, this time with the twins. I was desperate. I didn't know what to do. Finally I swallowed my fear and I swallowed my pride and I called my grandfather. I told him the whole story. I left nothing out, and when I was finished, do you know what he said?"

I shook my head.

"He said, 'Come on home, Amy. I still have a garden out back and I can plant enough food to feed you and your babies. I'll take care of all of you.'

"I think that was the day I began believing in God again. I moved back home. I had the twins and I started going to church. I was just so glad to be alive and have my babies and feel safe again. I met a deacon at the church who began helping me. He was different from any man I'd ever known. He was religious and kind and steady in his ways.

I always watched his hands when he prayed and, after a while, I dreamt about touching them. Then, one time, I dreamt that his hands touched me too, very gently. Eventually, I told him I had these feelings for him. His face turned red and he broke into a smile, then he looked at me longer than anybody else ever had. He told me that it was a lucky thing because he had feelings for me too and they were getting so strong that it was hard for him to be around me without letting them show. We got married that September.

"He earned five dollars and fifty cents an hour working for a hospital doing janitorial work. As deacon, he got no salary. That was his spiritual work. He did it for God and he did it for himself. He had two children from his first marriage who lived with him and I had three. We were living in a slumlord house but we couldn't afford to move anywhere else with such a big family. We couldn't make ends meet as it was. He got a second job cleaning a police station from 11:00 A.M. to 4:00 P.M. , then he cleaned the hospital from 11:00 P.M. to 7:00 A.M. Even then, we were barely making it. We still couldn't afford to pay the rent and buy enough food. The kids were hungry all the time. Finally, I went back to social services again for the third time. This time I had all the papers I needed to prove that we were really poor and that the five kids were really hungry. But the woman I talked to still acted like we must be doing something wrong. She warned me about food stamp fraud and she said my husband's salary seemed too low for all the hours he was working. She said they could put me in jail if the figures I was giving them had been altered in any way. By the time they eventually began giving us food stamps, I was scared to death that they might decide to put us in jail for something that we were doing wrong. Of course, the food stamps still weren't enough, so I started supplementing them with emergency food supplies from the pantries and churches again. I had the list just like before and I hit them all. Between my husband's two jobs, the food stamps and going to all the different places that gave out free food, my kids could finally get enough to eat.

"Looking back, it seems to me now that ever since I've had kids we've been struggling for food and shelter. What that's done to me and to my children, I can't even begin to say. I can't possibly calculate all the ways that it's hurt us, emotionally, physically and in terms of self-esteem, especially stealing food.

"A short time after we finally got the food stamps, the house we lived in was condemned for lead paint and snakes in the basement. We had to leave but, of course, we still didn't have enough money to rent anything else that was better. We couldn't come up with the first month's rent, the last month's rent and a security deposit. We just didn't have it, and I didn't have the heart to bring seven of us, a grown man and five kids, home to my grandfather's three-room cabin. So, there we were, out on the street with no place to go. I was homeless again, but this time I was homeless with five kids, a stable marriage and a husband working two jobs.

"We came to the Light House that April. We were very lucky because one of the two houses they own had just become available. They put us in their special transition program designed for families like ours. We stayed two years and paid three hundred fifty dollars a month for rent and maintenance. It was exactly the break we needed. A house like that would normally have cost us about a thousand dollars a month. It felt like the difference between life and death. It meant we could finally survive on the money my husband earned working the two jobs.

"He eventually got a better position. He's a supervisor of fuel technicians now and he earns ten dollars and fifty cents an hour. But he still only has hours, not a full-time salary, and we still have no health benefits. At this point we have a special deal that the Light House helped us get. It's sort of like we rent to buy. We pay nine hundred fifty-six dollars a month, but in the end we will own our house. It's a lot of money for us, even now with his pay raise, so we are back to really struggling again just like before. I come back here for free food. I also go to other pantries when I need to, but I'm a lot smarter now and I'm not desperate anymore. I have experienced kindness and that has made all the difference. I can trust again. My heart has softened because now I know that there are people who will help me and people who care for me.

"I've even gone back to school. I no longer blame myself for my grandmother's death, so I don't have to punish myself. I want to be a nurse again and I want to make the best life I can for my family."

Amy laced her fingers together and sat up straighter.

"But there's something else that's happened to me," she said softly. "I'm not angry anymore. Whenever I see people who need shelter or food the way I did, my heart just goes out to them, it melts. I don't care if I've just met them and will never see them again. I will share whatever I have. My house is a refuge for my family. But it's also a refuge for others who are hungry or homeless just the way my grandmother's house always was. Kindness has rescued me."

People like Amy, who have always been poor and trampled on, may never have come to expect kindness, and some may live an entire lifetime without it. But the way people are treated affects what they give back and even the way they dream. Federal programs, or any programs to help the hungry and poor, need to do more than prevent starvation and provide temporary shelter. They need to enhance people's sense of their own possibility, their sense of hope.

I have often been struck by the despair that permeates the poor communities I've visited, from the ghettos of North Philadelphia to the dusty back roads of the Mississippi Delta. If people have never been valued, they usually do not value themselves, and when they don't value themselves, they don't value their homes, their jobs or their communities. The well-being and pride of any neighborhood starts with the inner spirit of the people who live there. Hungry, broken-down adults and children must be rebuilt one person at a time from the inside out. Our federal aid programs do just the opposite. It's not just the budget cuts that are causing the hardship, it's the attitude of the people who administer the remaining resources.

Amy wasn't the first person to tell me how hard and dehumanizing it was to get food stamps. Over the years, I had heard and seen it again and again. But as I listened to the things she told me, once again it struck me as particularly sad that at the start of a new millennium the programs designed to help the hungry were still the ones creating the impediments. Robert Kennedy's team had seen the problem in the late sixties. I had seen it in the mid-seventies and the Harvard Physicians Task Force on Hunger had seen it in the eighties. They had pointed out that while the particular impediments took different forms in different parts of the country, in state after state the government required people to follow procedures that were laden with unnecessary paperwork and created nearly impossible obstacles for applicants. They also found that it was not an accident.

The government said that it was being done in the name of efficiency, but the task force called it "a form of expenditure control that kept eligible people from receiving program assistance." The justification for the behavior was the prevention of fraud and abuse but, as it turned out, "over 95 percent of the families receiving food stamps were, in fact, eligible for them."

The task force also found a food stamp office in Buncombe County, North Carolina, that was actually lined with conspicuous red-and-white signs that read, "Warning. We prosecute food stamp recipients." The signs were highly noticeable and intimidating, and although they went on to explain that the recipients were prosecuted for intentionally making false statements or withholding information, a frightening and adversarial atmosphere had clearly been established. This kind of atmosphere was not limited to North Carolina. It was found in virtually every state the task force examined.

One man was cut off food stamps because he had earned twenty-two dollars cleaning a lot. He had reported the income but because he didn't have a receipt to document it, the whole family lost their food stamps and their food for the entire month.

Whatever the rationale, for many years this kind of treatment by federal food assistance programs has had a profoundly negative effect on America's hungry children and their parents.

• • •

Today, Cathy Lewis is the managing director of a privately run homeless shelter. But once, she too was a homeless resident turned away and humiliated by her local department of social services and her food stamp office. That memory and her continued sense of economic vulnerability makes all the difference.

"I'm not going to kid you," she told me as she led me into her first-floor office. "This is a tough job full of stress. There's always another problem waiting around the corner, but to me it's worth every single migraine. It's worth it because, instead of knocking people down, we get them back on their feet, people like me." She wiped the sweat from her forehead and smiled. "Speaking of stress, I just started on a new prescription for migraines today. So, in a way, this is a good day for an interview, I mean you're getting a chance to talk to me when I'm all relaxed from my happy pills."

She took a gulp of air, smiled again, then grew serious.

"I have a fancy title now and I earn a little over twenty-four thousand dollars a year, but that's for me and my two kids. So after taxes come out, we're still pretty poor, or to use the professional term, still 'at risk.' Do you want to know how easy it is for a family at risk to cross that bridge into hunger and homelessness?"

She rolled her dark eyes and swayed a little. I nodded and sat down. "Well, I'll tell you," she said. "The wrong job, the wrong luck, the wrong guy, it's really surprisingly easy. You just kind of S-L-I-D-E into it. It's the downward spiral they all talk about. I never would have thought it could happen to me or my kids, but then, I guess none of us do."

Her eyes hunted for mine and something I saw in her face or heard in her words brought me back, once again, to the day my landlord threatened my children and me with eviction. It was a long time ago, more than twenty years, and we were never actually homeless, but that didn't keep my eyes from stinging as the margins between Cathy's life and my own suddenly blurred. I shivered in the August heat, surprised by how quickly she had moved right to the heart of things.

"I enlisted in the Army while I was still in high school. I met my first husband and my second husband there and spent ten years on active duty," Cathy said, leaning forward and letting her chin rest inside her palm. She sat there for a minute forming her thoughts, then said, "I left because I'd injured my back and because my youngest son, my three-year-old, had been diagnosed with childhood leukemia. I wanted to be where I could get him the best treatment. My husband was still enlisted. We had always done all right in the service because there were two of us and we both had salaries.

"When I left the military they gave me a lump sum of about eighteen thousand dollars. At the time it seemed like a lot of money, a huge amount. We rented a nice apartment and bought some furniture and, pretty soon, the money started to go. It was all the things working-class people get into, the car payments, the furniture payments, the rent, the tuition. My children were in a Christian private school and I had enrolled at Anne Arundel Community College. I was still thinking I'd train for something specific first then go out and get a really good job. We were doing fine with that plan until my husband got sent off to Germany and the marriage ended. I guess it was for all the usual reasons, distance, loneliness and a lack of trust. Then came the economic troubles.

"We no longer had his income and there was no child support because he wasn't my children's father. From January to the following February, there was a slow decline, a trickle-down effect as the eighteen thousand dollars whittled down. Then the trickle became a flood. Soon after that, I felt as if the dam had broken.

"I was looking for a job every day but I couldn't find one. I'd been out of the traditional job market for a long time and people kept telling me I wasn't qualified for the positions I applied for. It really upset me and in my head I was saying, 'What do you mean I'm not qualified? What do you mean I can't answer your phones and copy your documents? Why can't I file your mail?' For ten years I ran patrols. I lay in ditches. I shot targets. I had dozens of people working under me. I was just an E-4 but I was in a leadership position. I had major responsibilities. OK, so maybe I hadn't done these kinds of jobs before but I knew I could learn if someone would just give me a chance.

"All that winter I searched but no one hired me and the panic inside kept growing. It roared in my stomach all day and pounded in my heart at night. With every dollar I had to spend and nothing coming in, the pounding got louder. I was trying to quiet it by holding out on the bills. If I had a big gas or electric bill, I'd pay just enough so they wouldn't turn off the heat or the lights. I was trying to make the money last and the food stamps stretch. But no matter what I did, there wasn't enough of either, so we ate beans, dried beans, the cheapest dried beans we could get. I bought them in bulk to save money. When we got sick from the beans and all the gas, we'd have eggs or rice with a little bacon, just enough to add flavor. I'd get the thinnest sandwich meat you could buy. It was like ninety-nine cents a pack, just so my kids could have the taste of meat on their bread.

"We were all under enormous strain. The children's grades dropped. They were hungry all the time but they were bloated. They swore that if they ate another bean they would die. They said they would rather starve, but soon they got hungry again and begged for something to eat."

As I listened to Cathy, I visualized the huge underclass of families like hers, families who worked hard or wanted to but couldn't find jobs, families with "just barely enough," families who got hit by an unexpected crisis and were struck down. Then, I thought about all their imperiled children, children who didn't know each other but who were bound together by poverty, hunger and destitution, children like Cathy's living mostly on beans, rice or bread, children who could not possibly function like other kids who sat in the same classrooms, often only a desk or two away, but went home to a different world.

As the Center on Hunger, Poverty and Nutrition Policy has pointed out, even moderate undernutrition can have lasting effects on the cognitive development of children. Inadequate nutrition is a major cause of impaired mental development and is associated with increased educational failure among poor children. While this is recognized more and more by child development experts, it is still not well known to the general public.

Compelling new research shows a clear threat to the intellectual development of children who do not get adequate nutrition. "That is because, when children are chronically undernourished, their bodies conserve the limited food energy available, first reserved for maintenance of critical organ function, second for growth and last for social activity and cognitive development.

"Even nutritional deprivation of a relatively short-term nature influences children's capacity to learn. Deficiencies in specific nutrients, such as iron, have an immediate effect on the ability to concentrate. Children who come to school hungry are known to have shorter attention spans. They are unable to perform tasks as well as their peers."

That is why when Meyers, Sampson, et al., examined the effect of the School Breakfast Program on low-income elementary school children in Lawrence, Massachusetts, they found that impoverished children who participated in the School Breakfast Program had significantly higher standardized achievement test scores than impoverished children who did not participate.

The School Breakfast Program is authorized to provide federal funds to schools, but most school districts are not required to offer it and, even when it is offered, many mothers do not know that it exists.

"Going to school without a decent breakfast was real hard on the kids," Cathy said, spreading her fingers across her forehead and rubbing her temples with her thumb and pinky. "Their grades dropped, they became depressed, they also felt different and ashamed. Little things like not being able to afford a hamburger at a fast-food place and having to eat those damn beans really got to them. Let me tell you, this wasn't like eating soul food for fun. I tried to vary our diet. Once I got a neck bone and they scraped the fat off it and ate pure fat. That's how hungry they were.

"And like I told you, all during this time I was interviewing every day or I was out prowling the streets looking for interviews. Finally, I got an eighteen-hour-a-week, six-dollars-an-hour, part-time, no-benefits job." Cathy tilted her head and smiled a mock smile. "Then guess what happened? Go on. Guess."

I looked up at her over the top of my glasses. "They cut your food stamps," I ventured.

"You got it," she roared, hitting her desk with the flat of her hand. "They cut my food stamps down to eleven dollars because I had a job. Now that I was working, I was worse off than ever. Now we couldn't even afford the beans anymore. People at work began to wonder what was wrong with me. I had these huge shadows under my eyes all the time. If someone touched my hand, I was ready to cry my heart out. That little bit of warmth was all it took. One woman I confided in gave me some of her hours but it still wasn't enough.

"Each month I fell further and further behind in all our payments, including the rent. We began to get eviction notices. When the first one came and I saw what it was, I panicked. After that, I tried not to open them. I let them pile up. I hid them in a drawer so I wouldn't see them every time I walked past. I tried to ignore them as long as I could. Then, when I knew we were actually about to be evicted, I mean put out on the street, I put the furniture in storage and went to the Baltimore Department of Social Services. I walked up to the counter and burst into tears. I was so upset, I couldn't even speak. I couldn't get the words out. I had to walk away and sit down for a while to collect myself. Finally, with my voice still shaking and about to break again, I said we'd lost our apartment and had nowhere to go. The lady who worked there just looked at me. Her eyes were the color of cactus and, I swear to God, there were spikes in them. 'All the shelters are full,' she said very matter-of-factly. 'Do you have a car?' When I said yes, she opened her eyes a little wider and pulled out a spike. 'Then you and your kids can live in your car,' she said, sticking it straight into my heart.

"She gave me some emergency food stamps and sent me back to my car. I was frightened and I was outraged. I felt so naked and so pathetic that I wanted to say keep your damn stamps but I didn't. I took them because, if there was one thing I knew it was that I was going to feed my kids. If I had to sell my body to a stranger, if I had to steal, if I had to call my kids' father collect from a pay phone and say, 'I'm not doing well'—I was going to feed my kids. You reach a point when you get desperate enough or hungry enough that you will do anything to eat. Now, I'm not talking about selling my body for crack or alcohol. I'm talking about selling it for food for my kids. When people said, 'How'd you get homeless? Was it drugs, was it alcohol or did you have a breakdown?' I'd say, 'No, none of the above. Just hard times and a bad choice of men.' It was that simple. It really was. Anyhow, I knew we had to get to another town where they might have a shelter for us. Don't get me wrong," she said with a quick toss of her head. "Struggling, even hunger, was nothing new to me, but this was a whole different level, a whole new ball game.

"I mean, there we were in our car, me and these kids who I had promised to always protect and take care of, trying to find a safe neighborhood to sleep in where we wouldn't get chased away by the cops. Finally, we drove from Baltimore into Annapolis and parked near the waterfront in the tourist area. I figured we'd get showers and use the bathrooms there but it turned out that all those facilities were only for the people living on boats. People living in cars were outcasts. There were no facilities for them. We were using the food stamps to buy cold cuts and bread and eating sandwiches in the car. We slept in our clothes for three or four days. We were trying to become residents of the county so we could qualify for local benefits. I told my sons that if we couldn't get help soon they'd have to go and live with their father. They cried and said, 'Mommy, even if we're homeless, we want to stay with you.'

"That's when I went to the shelter and asked them for a place to stay. I had always been so proud and it was hard for me to admit I'd run out of ideas. Showing up at a shelter that Monday morning was a big deal for me but it was nothing to the staff. They saw people like me every day. They said they were sorry but they were full. They were kind about it but they were full. They told me to come back on Thursday. They said they'd see what they could do. Those were the longest days of my life.

"Looking back now, I don't know how we lived through it, sleeping in the car, washing up at gas stations and eating nothing but junk food. I never told my family what had happened till four or five years later. I was too ashamed. I guess I still had that Mary Tyler Moore 'I'm gonna make it' mentality."

Cathy took in a deep breath and let out a sigh. "I'm very careful with the choices I make now and the money I spend. I've been badly burned and so have my sons.

"My furniture was auctioned off because I couldn't pay the storage costs of one hundred five dollars a month. I lost everything I had, even the beautiful dining room set that I bought on installments and all the crystal I'd collected on three tours to Germany."

She put her elbows on her desk, then covered her ears and closed her eyes, as if to shut out the world.

"The fear of hunger and homelessness is still very real for me. I can still see myself living in that car. Right now, I'm living with another person, one of the sisters from my church, but before I found her, I was paying seven hundred dollars a month in rent and making eight dollars an hour. I began getting scared again. I began thinking we'd end up just like before. Luckily, this woman saw what was happening to me and opened up her home. She gave us two of her four bedrooms and I shared the rent. We are six people now with only one bathroom but we've managed just fine. We've never had a fight. We just go half on everything. This way my rent is only four hundred seventy-six dollars a month, but even paying only half the rent, it still gets tough. I worked two full-time jobs last year from February to May. I was here at the shelter from seven in the morning until three in the afternoon. Then from four to twelve I worked at the comptroller's office. I did it because my money was getting too low for comfort and I was getting terrified. I was beginning to feel that crazy train racing around in circles on the tracks inside my belly again. I tell you, I can smell the fear in my guts when it starts and I can see it like a ball rolling through the snow and gathering size. I always know when it's going to be a problem. So, right away, I will turn off my cable. I will turn down my heat. I will turn off my lights. I will stop talking on the phone. I will go back to eating beans. I will do whatever it takes."

Cathy shivered. "I haven't been on a vacation since 1991 because I'm too scared to spend the money. I'm also too proud to go to food pantries. I've been on both sides, so I know how demeaning it is to have someone look at me condescendingly and say, 'And what do you need today?' It makes me feel like I'm nothing. Right away I see 'big you' and 'little me.'" She held up her hands. "Look at this. Just remembering it makes my hands start shaking, but the fact that I've been there also makes me good at the job I do. I not only know what people are going through, to a lesser degree I'm still going through it myself.

"My oldest son is always hungry. He wants red meat and fresh vegetables and, of course, even now we can't afford them. It's very expensive to buy red meat and fresh vegetables so I go for the coupon sales and the canned goods. I went into Fresh Fields the other day, and when I saw the prices, I just turned around and walked out empty-handed. I watched that automatic door open, then I felt it close behind me. Even now, eating out for us is strictly fast food, like hamburgers at two for ninety-nine cents.

"I hold on to my money very tightly," Cathy said, rolling her fingers into a fist, then plunging them into the palm of her other hand. "It's self-defense. It's a primal reflex because I always want to make sure that we can eat and that my car and rent are paid.

"The men who know me now know how I feel. They know not to mess with my food or my money or my kids."

I watched as a tremor passed over Cathy's body. For a minute she looked like she wanted to cry, but instead she rolled her chair back on its wheels, then leaned toward me.

"I stash food," she whispered. She opened her eyes wider, waiting for a reaction. I must have looked puzzled or incredulous. "I'm not kidding you, Loretta," she repeated. "I stash food. Look. See, it's there right under my desk."

I stood up and looked and, sure enough, hidden under her desk was a black plastic crate. It was filled to the brim with hot chocolate mix, tea bags, chocolate chip cookies, oatmeal, canned goods and dried foods. I was about to say, "But you run the emergency food pantry. All you have to do is walk back there and take whatever you need." Then I realized that this had nothing to do with logic.

"You're afraid you'll be hungry again?" I said.

"Uh-huh," she answered, clutching the desk. "That's right, and my fear comes from the other place, the dark place under the trees at night, so if I've got nothing I know I can always eat this. I keep another stash in my car trunk. It's like I've been through a war and I've got post-traumatic stress syndrome. This is my bomb shelter.

"If my bank account drops below five hundred dollars, I panic. I freak out because five hundred dollars is what I know I need for gas and other stuff to get me and my sons back home to Texas. I'm not as proud as I used to be. This time I'd go home. I'm never living in my car again. I never want to be in that desperate place where I can't feed myself or my children. For their sake and my own sanity, I can't risk it, I'm too scared. I still have hopes and I still have dreams, big ones," Cathy said, her hand still clutching the edge of her desk. "My goal now is to get my degree and to earn more money. I want a salary of six figures before the decimal point and I want a house with four bedrooms and three baths."

"You do?" I said, surprised by the sudden turn in our conversation. I had assumed that her primary need was just to avoid poverty and hunger. Although it made perfect sense, it hadn't occurred to me that she actually wanted to become part of the middle class or the upper middle class.

"Yes, I do. You bet I do. And I don't want a town house either. I want a house with a yard. I've settled for too little for too long. Don't get me wrong, sharing a house with my church sister hasn't been traumatic, it's been wonderful, but I want my own house and I want to go on real vacations someday, not just read a travel book about the places other people go.

"Don't misunderstand," she said. "I'm not sorry about what happened to me because I've learned so much from it. If I had no test, I wouldn't have a testimony. If I had no mess, I wouldn't have a message. Each one of my great strengths is because I've been through a struggle. Before this happened, I didn't feel the way I do now about people who were suffering. Coming through hunger and homelessness has totally changed me. It threw me off my high horse and made me a better person. I want to help other poor people now just as much as I want to help myself. I am still poor in material things but I am no longer poor in spirit. That's because, here at this shelter, I'm doing the work that I feel called to do. I still get scared, sometimes I get very scared, but my biggest fear really isn't for myself anymore, it's for all the others out there without decent jobs or a place to turn. It's for the ones who've been cast out by the new Welfare to Work laws because I know what's going to happen to them. If they're lucky enough to get jobs, they'll join the working poor. A lot of them will be even poorer than they were on welfare. They'll lose their food stamps and many of them will also lose their homes. They'll have nowhere to go and groups like ours just can't house or feed them all."

The provisions of the new Welfare to Work legislation that Cathy referred to go on for hundreds of pages, but there are three major changes in public policy that are certain to drastically increase hunger and, indirectly, homelessness in America.

Until now, at least officially, the availability of food stamps was based on the need for food. But under the new welfare reform law, food stamps are limited to three months out of every three years for adults under fifty without children regardless of need. What that really means is that there is no longer a guarantee that people will not starve, even starve to death, in America. While the cuts do not include families with children, there is no way that existing food pantries and other emergency food providers can meet the suddenly increased needs of adults without having less for children.

The new law also takes food stamps away from immigrants who aren't citizens unless they qualify for specific exemptions. But fear, confusion, adversarial treatment and concern about deportation make many afraid even to ask. In fact, it sent thousands to emergency food pantries instead of food stamp offices even before the law took effect.

In addition, the law freezes the standard deduction. It also lowers the Thrifty Food Plan even further than the 1975 level that some of the Department of Agriculture's own workers called inadequate for more than short-term emergency use. That means that everyone including the children will now have even less.

As the impact of the cuts continues, the strain on emergency food providers will also continue and increase. They will be forced to turn people away without food because they will have no food left to give them.

The new welfare policy shifts the source of control from the federal government to the individual states and from federal entitlements to states' choices. Federal guidelines have vanished and Aid to Families with Dependent Children has been converted to a block grant called Temporary Assistance for Needy Families (TANF). It too gives discretion to the states without any guarantee that they will be responsive to the needs of hungry children.

The primary emphasis is on work, work as a promised answer, work as a panacea, work as a magic solution to welfare and to poverty. In theory, it's great. In reality, there are many strikes against the welfare recipient. First, relatively little emphasis is actually placed on training people for work that can lift them out of poverty. Second, competition for jobs is increasing. In fact, as huge corporations like Sara Lee, Lucent, CNN, Chrysler, DuPont and others downsize, currently employed blue-collar and professional middle-class workers are losing their jobs and scrambling for a limited number of new ones. Now, poorly trained welfare recipients are suddenly being asked to compete with these higher-skilled and better-educated groups.

Commonly held false beliefs about family size and the kind of people who receive welfare adds another strike and makes it even harder for them to succeed.

Actually, families who receive welfare do not have more children than other families. In fact, more than 70 percent of all AFDC families have two or fewer children and families receiving AFDC are about as likely to be white as black. In addition, more than two-thirds of the 14 million welfare recipients in 1995 were children.

People currently living on welfare, even welfare combined with food stamp benefits, are still living below the poverty levels in every state and below 75 percent of the poverty level in almost four-fifths of the states.

But as inadequate as welfare is, we are not moving most of these people from welfare to well-being. We are moving them from one form of poverty to another that may be even worse.

As the Children's Defense Fund study *Welfare to What?* points out, only a small fraction of former welfare recipients' new jobs actually pay above poverty wages and most of the new jobs pay far below the poverty line, which Census Bureau surveys defined as about $250 a week for a family of three in 1998.

The ability to escape from poverty through work is directly linked to the minimum wage. A national wage floor was first established in the United States during the 1930s Depression. At that time, with the exception of agriculture, business firms were forced to share more of their revenues with workers. For many years, the minimum wage rose in step with the top wages, but by 1997 the minimum wage had declined to the point where it no longer lifted its workers out of poverty. Seven states, including Alaska, California, Connecticut, Massachusetts, Oregon and Vermont had moved toward raising the minimum wage beyond the federally required level, but except for that small amount of progress, the maldistribution of money between the rich and the poor kept growing more and more extreme.

As William Greider pointed out in *One World, Ready or Not,* by 1997, 80 percent of America's wealth belonged to one-fifth of its people. The unspoken assumption was that this gross disparity was the natural, immutable order of things.

While many of the rich were raised in wealth, more than one in five American children was raised in poverty.

According to the Congressional Budget Office, income disparities were greater at the end of the twentieth century than at any time in the previous quarter century. Yet public awareness of the hunger and suffering caused by these disparities remained surprisingly low.

The United States was number one in the world in wealth and number twenty-six in the world in childhood mortality under the age of twelve.

A study done by the Children's Defense Fund found that an American child was two times more likely to be poor than a British child, three times more likely to be poor than a French child and at least six times more likely to be poor than a Belgian, Danish or Swiss child.

At the turn of the century, poverty in contemporary America not only hurt poor children, sometimes it killed them, if not directly through hunger then indirectly through diseases, parasites, inadequate health care and homelessness.

There is still a deeply held belief in the United States that poverty is a choice and that if people are willing to work, they will not be poor. But the reality is that half of America's poor children live with a parent who works. Millions of the families who work the longest hours at the least rewarding jobs never get above the poverty level or earn enough to adequately feed their hungry children.

Chapter 5

Hunger and
the Homeless

"Where youth grows pale, and spectre thin, and dies; where but to
think is to be full of sorrow and leaden-ey'd despairs."

JOHN KEATS,
Ode to a Nightingale

America's Wandering Families

Each night, when darkness falls, more than 100,000 American children have no home of their own to go back to. Some of them sleep in cars or abandoned buildings and eat whatever they can find. Some stay in overcrowded houses with friends or relatives. Others sleep in cheap run-down motels or overpriced residential hotels. The rest lay their heads down on the streets or in crowded, often dangerous shelters. Most move from place to place as they search for food and shelter. Every year their numbers increase.

These children and their parents signal the rise of a new, more desperate level of poverty and hunger in America. Twenty-five years ago, the homeless population was composed primarily of the mentally ill, the alcoholic or the drug addicted. Now that underclass has increased from single people who were lost long before homelessness ruled their lives, to families who are lost because it does. "Today homeless families account for between 38 percent and 77 percent of the homeless population, depending on the area. Two-thirds of the people in these families are children."

In the year 2000, unemployment was lower than it had been in thirty years but hunger, poverty and the number of children without homes was higher than it had been since the Depression of the 1930s.

Part of this was due to the increasing gap between the incomes of the working poor and the cost of living. More and more families who lived in wealthy cities like San Diego simply couldn't afford the rent and ended up on the street. Today, their children create an underclass of hungry street urchins who sometimes wander among the wealthy. Their need for emergency food assistance is often as urgent as their need for housing.

Like many cities, San Diego is a place where the well educated and highly skilled prosper while one in three children live in poverty.

St. Vincent de Paul Village, one of the largest and best-known shelters in the country, is only minutes from San Diego's upscale Gas Light District, where well-dressed tourists and residents eat expensive meals at lovely restaurants, but it is also a world away.

St. Vincent's rises like a giant hacienda out of the grim industrial section of town. The perimeter of the huge yellow-brick building takes up an entire city block. The main two-door entrance is topped by a bell tower reminiscent of the old California missions. In the year 2000, St. Vincent de Paul Village had an annual budget of $9.5 million. It employed 180 people and had more than 500 volunteers. Each night, about 850 men, women and children slept at St. Vincent's and, each day, more than 2,000 hungry people were fed there. All this is relatively recent.

The Village began as a small breakfast feeding program for the homeless in 1982, when the late Bishop Maher of the Diocese of San Diego decided to respond to the growing needs of the homeless. A short time later, he asked Father Joe Carroll, a native of New York, to spearhead the new project. Father Joe had worked at jobs that ranged from bookstore manager to teacher before becoming an ordained Roman Catholic priest at the age of thirty-three. During his first eight years in the priesthood, he had developed a reputation for being a man who made things happen. Between 1982 and 1987, true to his reputation, Father Joe raised $11.5 million for St. Vincent's.

When he began fund-raising, he had three major objectives: the first was to create a facility that would last forever; the second was to make it a beautiful building that would enhance the self-esteem of the people it served, and the third was to provide comprehensive services. Father Joe designed what he called a campus or a "one stop shopping center" so that the homeless could get the food, shelter, health care, child care, education, counseling, public assistance, jobs and permanent housing they needed. His unique concept became an internationally recognized model, but Father Joe still wasn't satisfied. He said he would not rest until all the homeless in downtown San Diego who wanted a bed had one. At that time there were over four thousand homeless people in San Diego. So, even feeding two thousand people a day and providing beds for eight hundred left him with a long way to go.

"The lunch line at St. Vincent's begins forming at nine A.M. each morning and stretches around the block by ten. We feed five hundred to six hundred people an hour, every day, seven days a week," explained John Moore, the heavyset, cheerful retired military officer who serves as the director of volunteers. "Families always come first, and then the disabled, but the mass of people waiting for food includes the homeless and the working poor and the military families. Some come only occasionally but we can usually pick out a hundred or a hundred fifty regulars, people who come every day. We ask no questions because we don't want to make them feel uncomfortable about being here. We know that many of them are not homeless, at least not yet. So I always tell them, 'Save your money to pay your rent and your other bills and come here to eat with us. That way you won't become homeless.'

"We also provide medical help to anyone without insurance," Moore explained as we walked through the mission's kitchen, filled with gleaming pots, cooks learning their trade and volunteers practicing their skills. It was noon now and the dining room was rapidly filling up. Hundreds of women and children were already sitting at long, narrow tables, so close together that they were almost elbow to elbow.

About two hundred more people with trays in their hands were walking along the rapidly moving line. A dozen or so of those had the dazed look in their eyes that comes with having been at the bottom too long. It was like nothing I had ever seen before but a lot like what I imagined a Red Cross relief effort might look like in a third world country during a famine or after a natural disaster. It seemed almost impossible to believe that this was actually San Diego. The hall was filled with a loud but indecipherable hum. There were so many people eating and talking at once that it was impossible to hear what anyone was saying.

A pretty, young blonde girl in a pink T-shirt and black shorts caught my eye. She was holding a baby and had been led to the front of the line. Both the mother and baby were stuffing food into their mouths as if they were starving.

"We'd rather be overcrowded like this than turn away someone who needs us in their moment of crisis," John said, speaking loudly and leaning close enough for me to hear. "Our determining factor is whether they are at risk. If there is a child involved like that one over there on the line, we always immediately assume that they are at risk."

As we watched the young woman and the baby, I couldn't help wondering where her own mother and father were, what had gone wrong at home and how she and her little daughter had fallen through all the cracks in all the programs and wound up here.

"People are often starving when they first arrive at our door because they have waited too long to come to us," John said, as if he were reading my thoughts. "They have resisted us too hard. They are also often sick for the same reason. We have four volunteer doctors and nurses who see thirteen hundred to fifteen hundred patients every month. There is no charge to them. The only requirement is that they have no health insurance. We've had the American Medical Association visit us here to see how we do it. That's how amazed they are.

"Our biggest concern," John added as my eyes moved away from the baby and her mother out over the huge crowd, "is how we can help people get back on their feet. It starts with the simple gift of a meal. It's usually the hunger that brings them in, but the urgency of hunger provides us with the opportunity to address the deeper, longer-term series of needs. People usually want help, and after their second or third time eating here, they feel safe enough to start asking questions about our other services.

"Meeting their needs is a huge challenge. We know we can't do it all but we just keep trying. There were five or six thousand people on our streets last winter. They come because it's warm here. They often just don't realize how difficult it is to find work or affordable housing in San Diego. They also don't know how tough it can be to live without shelter even in a warm climate. We respect the fact that it's hard for them to come to us. A lot of people are very proud and they're afraid that if they show up here they will be considered incompetent. Some of them think that they might lose their kids. They are scared to death of that.

"One woman came here for lunch when her baby was only a few days old. She was living out on the street but she didn't tell us that, she just said she wanted food. We accepted that and sent her to the lunch-room. We deliberately don't have any caseworkers in the lunchroom because we don't want to frighten people like her away. We want them to feel comfortable coming here. We want them to know that they can eat with no questions asked and no downstream repercussions. Only when they ask do we tell them that we are a resource center in the fullest sense, a helping hand, not just a handout."

As John talked, the line of hungry people just kept coming and coming in what seemed to be an almost endless procession.

"Do you ever run out of food?" I asked, glancing at the mother and baby again. They were finally about to sit down but a lot of the food on their tray had already disappeared. Some, I noticed, had been stuffed directly into the mother's pockets.

"Yes," John said. "We run out all the time. It's a constant turnover. The food comes in and it goes back out. We never know exactly how much we'll need or even how much we'll get. Even with our regular suppliers like Food Chain, it's hard to predict. Both the supply and the demand are always uncertain. The only thing we know is that we always need more. There is really never enough.

"But then sometimes, just when we're feeling most concerned, something amazing happens. Like last year, Bill Gates was planning a big party for two or three thousand people, and then the weather got bad. When the party was canceled, he donated the food to us. Bill Gates was personally out there along with Father Joe helping to unload the food. Can you imagine that? Bill Gates himself unloading all those crates of food for the hungry." John grinned broadly. "It renewed my faith.

"Father Joe doesn't run the Village like a priest," he explained, turning serious again. "He runs it like a businessman, like Gates himself might. He has to because, just to keep things going, he needs to raise $43,000 every day. We are on a $24-million-a-year non-profit budget. But at the same time, we're independent, at least in our thinking. We've turned down grants, big grants from the government, because Father Joe doesn't want them to control him. We could have grown bigger, quicker, but he wants to remain true to his vision and true to his dream. He's an organized man but he's also a man with a vision. To do what he's done, you need both. If you're not organized, you will simply be overwhelmed by the need that's out there. It would be like taking a bag of bread crumbs and throwing it up in the sky and all of a sudden there would be one hundred birds. You can't just say, 'Come and eat,' without a plan and without resources because you will be overwhelmed. They will want more than you have to give.

"Father Joe's a bubbly guy who gives parties and does a lot of entertaining to raise money so we can keep on expanding. His entire job now is fund-raising. He signs one hundred fifty letters a day. He's turned over the daily operations to others. Some people think that's a shame, but after all, he's just one man, one man who doesn't know the word stop. Folks like me are here because we believe in Father Joe and we believe in his dream. His belief empowers us. Because of it, there is nothing we can't do. We can make the rules, we can bend the rules and we can break the rules. Our vision is to do what we can for everyone who is in need. It is a huge vision but it is also as individual as each person we serve."

• • •

I was still thinking about St. Vincent's the next day at lunchtime as I sat in my car in front of the Presbyterian Crisis Center. The modest, yellow clapboard house on Market Street was about as different from St. Vincent's in appearance as anything I could imagine. The clientele, however, were very similar. There were several mothers with small children, an elderly couple and a father with two teenage daughters sitting on the porch eating oranges.

The place had the look of a cozy cottage that had been misplaced on a busy street in a poor neighborhood. The front porch was filled with white chairs and the low green fence was covered by creeping vines and bounded by a small city lot. The Crisis Center, which began in the late '80s, provides emergency food, clothing, transportation tokens and whatever other emergency assistance they can.

"We sit down with people," explained director Bill Radatz, the warm, articulate pastor who heads the Presbyterian Ministry, "and we say, 'Have you thought things through and figured out why you are in crisis?' We've got some folks who have been coming here every month for years and others who are in an acute state for the first time in their lives. We try not to enable them but, at the same time, we want to meet their needs. Sometimes, it's a delicate balance."

Then Bill stopped talking and leaned back in his chair. "On second thought, I'm not sure I really meant what I just said about it being a delicate balance. I think most of the people we see here really do want to be self-sufficient. We've moved more toward advocacy recently because so many people are just trapped in an economic situation where they can't earn enough to make it no matter what they do. Housing availability in San Diego is down to two percent and some people are spending between fifty and seventy percent of their income on a place to live. We know that they will never work their way out of poverty when that much of their income is spent on shelter.

"To barely get by, and I mean barely, a family of four needs to have someone who earns eleven dollars an hour, forty hours a week plus benefits. So if it's five dollars and seventy-five cents an hour and there are no benefits, no matter how hard they are working, we know they are doomed. Our politicians don't have the political will to help these people by changing the system or even the minimum wage, at least not nearly enough. They'd rather pretend that the people had problems instead of admit that the system did."

Bill stood up, walked to his office door, and closed it for privacy. "The political will is to eliminate welfare, not to eliminate poverty," he said. "It's a very important distinction. They want to cover up the problem, not solve it. On the other hand, it is also true that a few of our clients are not highly motivated enough. I've had people come to me and say that they don't have time to work because getting food takes all day. After breakfast, they have to wait on the lunch line, then after lunch they have to get on the dinner line." He smiled. "I know it sounds like a joke and I personally don't accept it as a reason to give up on working, and yet I also know that there's more than a grain of truth to it."

"Yes," I said, as the memory of two thousand people stretched around several blocks came back. "The lunch line at St. Vincent's starts forming at nine A.M. and it's halfway around the block by ten. It takes three hours just to get lunch."

"You think that's difficult? Take a look at this free-meal announcement," Bill said as he handed me a sheet that listed other free-meal centers in the San Diego area.

I glanced down at the page:

- Breakfast—Lutheran Church, Third and Ash—9:00 A.M. *Fridays only*
- Lunch—Neil Good Day Center, 299 17th Street—1:30 P.M. *Wednesdays only*
- Dinner—Vacant lot, 13th and Broadway— 4:30 P.M. *Thursdays only*

There were a half dozen more meal sites on the list that were scattered throughout the city but many served one meal only, one day a week. I thought about how tough it would be to get to the right place at the right time on the right day for the right meal without any money or transportation, and how difficult the logistics might get if you were also working part- or full-time but didn't earn enough for food. To make it even more complicated there was a note at the bottom of the page that said you must attend church services to receive certain meals at certain sites. In some cases you also had to attend services at one specific address or on one specific day to get a ticket to eat your meal at another site on another day. When I pointed this out to Bill, he nodded and said, "Yes, I know, and some people have to figure out how to get over here to the crisis center first to get a free bus token to take them over there."

When I turned the sheet over, I saw that in order to get a free token, a client had to remember to bring valid identification or a birth certificate. In some cases, they also needed a social security card and appropriate clothing. Even then, the tokens were strictly limited to six per month.

As we talked, Bill led me into the small client waiting room. I immediately spotted the same mother and baby I had seen eating so quickly the day before on the lunch line at St. Vincent's. I smiled at the mother and thought I saw a flash of recognition in her eyes.

"I saw you yesterday at St. Vincent's," I ventured, stooping down to greet the baby, who was sitting in a small, portable plaid stroller with red plastic wheels.

"Yes. I remember you," she said shyly. Her smile was beautiful. Her eyes were pale blue and shining.

Everything about her, even her voice, her pink T-shirt, her short, blonde hair and her perfect teeth made her seem more like a midwestern high school cheerleader than a hungry, homeless mother.

"Do you live around here?" I asked while the baby squeezed my index finger. She laughed, nervously.

"I don't know where I live right now," she said, seeming to take my question literally. "It's like I really don't live anywhere. I mean I don't have a place. That's why I'm here."

"I'm sorry," I said, hoping I hadn't embarrassed her.

"That's OK," she answered, sweetly. "I just said that, I don't know why. I know what you meant. I grew up in Michigan then one of my brothers invited me to move to Arizona. While I was there, I met an ex-Marine. We're still best friends but we got divorced when he moved back to New York to finish college. Things have been pretty bad ever since."

I settled down in the chair next to her, told her about the book I was writing and asked if she'd like to be part of it.

"Wow, me in a book? Sure, that's cool. But why would anyone care about me?" She tilted her head and smiled her beautiful smile again. "My father never did. My stepfather never did. I thought my husband was different till he started hitting me and messing around with other girls, but I think that's because we were too young for a committed relationship."

"Were you abused?" I asked, thinking of Bertha and the statistics on poverty and homelessness.

First, she shrugged and said, "No, not really," then the story poured out. "He beat me up a couple of times but he was always sorry. Now he's gone back to his old girlfriend but I don't think it will work out for the two of them. My mother always said an X is an X for some reason and I believe that. My mom's still in Michigan with my stepfather. I really miss her a lot. I came out here with my mother-in-law. It's kind of a screwed-up situation. See, she's HIV positive because her husband was on drugs. She needed care and she couldn't get it in Arizona, so we came out here together with a hundred fifty dollars after bus fare. We got a room at the Y but then she got real sick and went into the hospital. I ran out of money. My real mom always said I was impulsive and I guess I didn't think this thing through very well.

"I get three hundred fifty dollars a month from my husband whenever he remembers. It goes directly into my checking account.

I think it will come soon but it's not here yet. I only had twenty-nine cents left yesterday and we were really hungry. I mean like really hungry. We hadn't eaten in two days. That's when you saw me. Right after lunch, I applied for welfare. I hate the idea of getting welfare and if I didn't have a baby, I'd rather live on the beach. But the baby needs food and shelter and stuff."

As Tina spoke, I was struck again by the fluctuations in her tone, which wavered between childishness and maturity, depression and cheerfulness, hope and fear.

She picked her baby up. "You can't live on the beach," she cooed. "No. No. It's too hot and you're too little." She kissed the baby then put her back in the stroller.

"So, I told the caseworker that we were homeless and we needed help right away and she gave us this hotel voucher for one night. But what good is a one-night voucher when another night's coming in just a few hours?"

Then Jean, an attractive, well-dressed, middle-aged caseworker, came over to us. "Tina," she said softly, "I've pulled some strings and gotten you and April into St. Vincent's. Be there at the front desk at 4:30. No later." She stroked the baby's hair and continued without waiting for an answer. "They're strict, and if you're late you can lose your place. They'll keep you there for ninety days and then you can apply for transitional housing."

Tina's eyes widened. Her face turned crimson. "Wow. Ninety days, ninety whole days," she said. "That's ninety days I don't have to worry."

She started to laugh with childlike delight then suddenly she was crying.

"I knew something good was going to happen when I walked in here today," she said, hugging Jean. "I could just feel it. Thank you sooo much. How did you do it? How'd you ever get me in?"

"I pulled all the strings," Jean answered gently. "We're small and they're big but they owe us, and every once in a while when I really need a favor, I remind them of that."

Tina was still laughing and crying. "I just know we're gonna be safe there. We were at their food line yesterday. I was so hungry that I was about to faint. The place was jam-packed. It was the longest food line I've ever seen in my whole life and I thought, how am I ever gonna stand here on this line and wait my turn, but guess what? They saw me holding my baby and they came right over and led us to the front of the line, I mean the very front, and then they gave us all this food. They didn't just give us a little. They gave us a lot, a whole lot. I'm not used to eating very much anymore 'cause for a long time I've just been eating a little here and there and giving the rest to my baby, but at St. Vincent's there was so much that I filled up both of my pockets and we ate some for dinner last night and some for breakfast this morning."

She sniffed then laughed again. "Boy, I still can't believe it. No more going hungry for ninety whole days. I've been hungry a lot lately. Even when I got my child support, it was only three hundred fifty dollars, and my rent was two hundred ninety-five dollars including utilities, so that left just fifty-five dollars a month for food and everything else. We haven't had a phone for two years. But I sure learned how to shop. I bought a lot of rice and beans and Bisquick mix. I bought big bags of cereal for two dollars and powdered milk because it is cheaper and it lasts longer. I almost never bought meat." She shook her head incredulously again. "I still can't get over this. I feel like I've just been rescued. I thought about asking the people yesterday at St. Vincent's if we could stay there, but when I saw how many people they had on that line, I said to myself, 'No way. Never. There's no room for us here.'"

Another flood of tears poured down Tina's cheeks. "I'm not sure why I can't stop crying," she said, laughing again. "I'm just so happy. I think it's because this is the start of something good. I think my luck is finally going to change. I can just sort of like feel it."

She wiped her eyes with the bottom of her pink T-shirt then tucked the shirt into her shorts. "I want to go back to college so much." She sniffled. "And I want to major in business and then someday, I want to own a chain of hotels." Tina was talking quickly now and her flawless young face was a brighter pink than her shirt. She looked pretty and buoyant. She raised her shoulders, let them drop again and wrinkled her nose. "Well, maybe it won't be a chain exactly," she said, making the compromise with herself out loud. "But it has to be at least two hotels. If you're rich and you're mean, you will go to the expensive hotel. If you're nice, you can go to the free hotel even if you have money.

"You know," she added reflectively. "In a weird way, it's a funny thing that I'm homeless, me of all people, because ever since I was a little girl and I saw this huge farmhouse one day, my whole focus has been on housing. I couldn't have been more than four but I can still remember exactly how that farmhouse looked. It had three stories and it had to have at least ten bedrooms. I told my momma that I wanted to buy it and paint it blue, not just any blue but cobalt blue with a fluorescent pink door. Then I wanted my whole broken-up family to come and live there all together in that one farmhouse. See, my stepbrothers lived with their mother and I only got to see them once in a while. My stepdad had five kids from before and one little girl with my mom. That's my little sister. I'd kill for her. She was two and a half years younger than me and I always protected her. If she was bad, which was pretty often, my stepdad would whip out his big black belt with the brass buckle, but I'd always run in front of her and say, 'I did it, Dad. I did it. It was me.' So I'd get hit, of course.

"My husband said I was abused. I never thought of it that way. I thought it was just another whopping. Anyhow, it was my idea, my dream that we'd all come together in this one big house and my step-father would have to leave because there would be no whopping allowed. Then we'd be a real family and live happily ever after.

"My real father died when I was very little. I don't remember him. My stepfather works for General Motors. My mom's a school cook."

Some more tears leaked out of Tina's eyes and landed on her shorts.

"I'm sorry I'm so emotional today and I know I'm talking too fast and too much. I'm just so relieved. See, I would never ask my mom to send me any money because I know she would do it and then she'd get in trouble with my stepdad and he'd wop her. I've always taken the fall for her too, for her and for my little sister. I never want her to ask him for anything that will bring a whopping down on her. That's why I never want her to have to send money."

"Why'd you always take the fall, honey?" a very thin, sallow-skinned woman who introduced herself as Melissa asked. "Why do you think it's your place to get punished?"

I had noticed the woman watching and listening to us a few minutes before but I had been too captivated by Tina's breathless speech to think much about it. I looked at her more carefully now. She had a sad face. Her forehead was high and deeply creased. She was much thinner than she was meant to be and her teeth were brown and rotted.

Tina shrugged. "I don't know why I took the fall," she answered, looking confused and a little uncomfortable. "I guess it's just the way I am. But I better get going now so I won't be late for the shelter." She hugged me and invited me to stop by and see her once she was settled.

"My son Shad's a bright boy," Melissa said even before Tina was out the door, "but he was failing in school because he was always hungry. Now, he gets As and Bs because I go to the store almost every day and steal food for him so he can concentrate. We've talked about it together, my son and me. I'm not proud of it but I'm not ashamed either. It's just something I have to do to take care of my boy. I tried all the other options first and they didn't work."

She leaned closer. There was an odor I recognized but couldn't name. I'd smelled it before in urban tenements and in rural shacks but I had never known if it was the smell of illness, of hunger or of simply being unwashed. A wave of nausea swept over me and I felt myself moving back a little.

"I always tell my boy never to steal. If there is anyone getting caught and getting in trouble, I want it to be me."

I looked up and nodded to indicate that I understood the fierce protective instinct.

"I go in with my purse and my backpack, then I get a shopping cart," Melissa explained. "I put the things I'm going to buy into the big part and, in the little part where the baby's supposed to sit, I put the things that I'm going to steal. I keep my purse open and I put some small things in there. I also put some flat items like cheese and lunch meat under my sweatshirt, which has a tight band at the bottom. I wait till I get to an aisle where there are no cameras or people before I take the things from the top part of the cart and put them into my backpack."

Melissa looked at me again to check my reaction.

"There are two tricks to not getting caught," she said, solemnly. "The first is to make sure everyone there thinks you're a regular customer. The second is to always buy a couple of items."

She paused again. "Food is the only thing I have ever stolen. I still steal it because I have no choice. I have to do it or my son and I will both go without eating. There is nothing and nobody that's going to tear us apart. Over the past year, I've done it a lot. This month, we got thirty-seven dollars in food stamps. Thirty-seven dollars spread over four weeks. You know how far that goes? Usually, for me personally, I only take what I consider to be the necessities, but last week I stole some coffee for myself and a candy bar to go with it. I knew I shouldn't have done it because they were luxuries that I didn't have to have. I think I just needed to pamper myself and I gave in to it." Her face colored. "For Shad, it's a different story. He's a growing boy. He has to eat. Last week, I stole meat and a lot of other things he enjoys. When I got home, I dumped out the backpack and the purse I was carrying and I compared everything I bought with everything I had stolen. It was fifty-eight dollars that I stole and ten dollars that I bought. There's just no other way. Fruit is too expensive, even milk. Meat is way too high.

"Yesterday, I bought a couple of potatoes and some macaroni and cheese, the cheap things to go with dinner, but all the rest I stole."

Melissa straightened up and folded her arms defensively across her chest.

"What the hell else am I supposed to do with thirty-seven dollars in food stamps, a growing teenage boy and a boss who doesn't pay me? Whenever I go to the store, I take a little something. Lately, I almost feel like it's our right because I work hard. I've worked hard ever since I was a young girl and it never got me anywhere."

She slumped down in her chair again.

"I prefer to be honest," she said. "I'm really trying to make it without stealing. Today I got three bags of food from the Salvation Army but we get so tired of eating that stuff. I know the poor aren't supposed to care what they eat, but they do just like everyone else, especially the kids. You don't get any fresh meat or even sandwich meat. I've tried everything else and I've resigned myself to the fact that the only way to eat right when you are poor is to take what you can't afford to buy.

"My welfare check was five hundred forty dollars a month. Then, Welfare to Work came along. They hooked me up with a job and my stamps were cut. My job was cleaning empty apartments so they could be rented. It was hard work with mops and brooms, vacuums and scrub buckets, bending over half the day with a bad back. I was supposed to be paid six dollars and twenty-five cents an hour once a month, but that's not how it went. I worked for one month, then on payday my boss told me that I had to work another month. I said, 'Wait a minute. I started May thirteenth and now it's June seventeenth. In my book that's more than a month.' He said, 'No, love. That's not how it works. One month is always withheld.' Meanwhile, welfare thought I'd been paid and they cut all my benefits.

"I brought my boss a paper saying he hadn't paid me and I asked him to sign it so I could keep getting my welfare. 'Not now, love,' he said. 'But they're cutting me off welfare,' I told him. He didn't care. He didn't give a damn. He wasn't signing anything. I couldn't pay my rent so I lost my apartment. I was still working full-time but now I was homeless and hungry. I was desperate and panicked. I was half out of my mind when I finally came to the crisis center with my son. They put us up in a cheap motel, and that's where we are now.

"A month later my boss finally gave me a hundred dollars just to get me off his back because he knew it was illegal. He said, 'This is all I have now. Call me in a couple of days, love, and I'll have some more.' I called his cell phone, his pager, his home phone. He had caller ID, and when he saw it was me, he wouldn't answer.

"I had no choice but to steal food," she said, sighing deeply. "If I waited for him to pay me, hell would freeze over and my son would starve. Five or six days later, I called from a pay phone. He didn't recognize it and he answered, saying, 'Hello. How can I help you?' I said, 'This is Melissa.' He said, 'Who?' Then the phone clicked dead, so I went to the supermarket and took our dinner. I'm trying to get our benefits back but in the meantime . . ." Melissa shrugged, then said a little nervously, "There's only one thing worrying me. I've heard that stealing is a felony and that in California if you have three felony convictions you can get a life sentence. It's called the three-strikes law. Can you imagine that, a life sentence for feeding your kids? Thank God I've never been caught, because if you get caught stealing food even once, you're no longer eligible for food stamps or any kind of aid.

"It's ironic, isn't it? You steal food because your children are hungry and you don't have enough food stamps to feed them. You get caught and you lose the few food stamps you had, so naturally you need to steal again. Pretty soon, you've eaten it all up, you're hungry. After all, people have to eat. Then what happens? It's your third offense, so they can put you in jail for life where they have to feed you and house you until you die. They put your kid in foster care where they have to pay a stranger to house him and feed him. They break up your family. They take away your freedom. They spend a fortune punishing you, so why not just give you and your kid the food you need to stay alive in the first place?"

•   •   •

"Be careful," Anna said as she stepped back and closed the door of room 67 in the Palms Residential Hotel. "We've got fleas. I have a vacuum cleaner. It's the only thing I kept after we lost everything else. My husband kept his electric guitar and I kept my vacuum cleaner. I try to vacuum the fleas up in it but it doesn't seem to help much. In fact, I'm beginning to think they breed in there and then crawl back out at night just to bug me. No pun intended."

She laughed. It sounded forced, as if she'd told the joke before.

"No, I mean seriously, if you wanna sit down you might want to try that wooden chair over there in the corner. At least you can see what you're getting into."

She chuckled again, then pushed up the sleeve of her sweater to show me that her arm was covered with little red bites.

"The kids get it even worse 'cause their skin's so tender. Show the lady your bites, Alicia," Anna instructed. "Go on, honey," she added, gently. "Don't be afraid. Show her."

Alicia came toward me on her tiptoes and tilted her angelic face up toward me. I leaned forward and she pressed her nose against mine and rubbed it. "That's an Eskimo kiss," she squealed, smiling. Her blonde ponytail, bright blue eyes and turned-up nose made her look like something out of a kid's fashion magazine.

"I'm three," she announced as she lifted her shirt and presented her belly. "I've got more bites than he does," she added coquettishly, pointing toward her brother, Zac. She put her hand on a spot and said, "This one itches the most."

Then as if the sight of her own stomach had suddenly reminded her, she began to wail.

"I didn't have anything to eat."

Anna took one of the free oranges from the crisis center out of her purse.

"I'll fix this for you."

"I want one too," her brother screamed. "Daddy said I get the next orange. He told me. He promised."

Zac's face puckered up and turned red. "If I can't eat then I'll break Daddy's guitar."

He eyed the electric guitar propped up against the wall behind the filthy couch and began to move toward it. Anna leaped up and grabbed him by the arm.

"Oh, no you don't, buster."

"I'm hungry," Zac wailed again.

Then suddenly, Anna began to cry.

"What's wrong, Mommy? Why are you crying?" Alicia asked as her little face contorted with worry. "Please don't cry, Mommy. I love you, Mommy. Will you stop crying if I give Zac the orange?"

Anna wiped her eyes and stood up straight except for her shoulders, which seemed to have been permanently bent by the weight of her spirit. She was tall, thin and boyish-looking in her tight jeans. Her hair was cut short on top and the sides were brushed back. She ran her fingers through it, then closed her eyes.

"No, honey," she finally said. "You'll share the orange with your brother.

"We've been homeless for almost two weeks," Anna explained after she'd divided the orange and counted the sections. "We used to live in Colorado. My husband runs heavy equipment. You do real good there in the summer, like twenty-eight dollars an hour, but in the winter, you starve in Colorado because the ground freezes and the work basically stops. We figured we'd be better off if we came to California, where the weather is always warm. What we didn't know was that the International Union of Operating Engineers out here takes two and a half years to break into. They have three lists. You start with the C list and work your way up. Until you make the A list, you just work when they call you and go where they send you. Like one time, they said there was work in San Clemente, so we headed out there. The only information we had was that my husband should report for work on the corner of two streets. They named the streets but we didn't have an exact address. While we were driving down there, the battery on our car blew, causing a fire that burned a bunch

of the wires out. After we finally got that fixed, which took most of
our money, the starter went. By this time, we had no money left to fix
it. We didn't even have money for gas. It was a 1974 Subaru that we
bought for one hundred dollars. The car wouldn't move so we slept in
it for a few days and lived on two boxes of day-old donuts that we had
in the trunk. When they were gone, we had nothing left. But even if
we had food, we couldn't all live in a car that wouldn't move for very
long so we went to the Presbyterian Crisis Center.

"My kids are three and five. The center gave us some food and
put us up here in the Palms Hotel for two weeks. This place was a
grand old hotel once. You can still tell by the beautiful mahogany
woodwork in the lobby and the winding staircase, but it's a fleabag
roach trap now. Bad as it is, I'm just praying that we can stay when
the two weeks are up. If my husband keeps working and we can pay
the rent, they told us at the front desk that we can live here. I mean
downstairs where it's cheaper and smaller. It's, um, you're not going
to believe this, one hundred eighty-five dollars a week for the smaller
room. We know it's robbery but we're trapped. It's this or the streets.
We can't get enough money together to rent anywhere else, not with
security deposits and everything. The bathrooms are down the hall.
There's one men's and one ladies' for the whole floor and we have
one stove, one sink and one kitchen counter for everyone to share.
That's about fifteen or twenty families. The kids are not allowed out
of the room without an adult, and believe me, it's hard to keep them
penned up in here."

I nodded; that was already very clear from the gestures, gri-
maces, quarrels and sense of competition between the children. I
looked around at the shabby, airless room and wondered how much
smaller the ones downstairs could be. There was a double bed
toward the front, twin beds behind it, a refrigerator and a sofa
against the wall and a small ceiling fan to the right of the double bed.

"There are no screens," Anna said when she noticed me looking,
"and we're up on the third floor but we can't open the windows no
matter how hot it gets.

"The crisis center is giving us as much food as they can but the kids are always fighting over it. We used to get welfare but, of course, every time my husband works a couple of days it gets canceled and then we have to apply all over again. We just got a letter last week saying that they had canceled all our food stamps because he had worked three days. Now we have to go through a fraud investigation so they can see if we've ripped them off.

"They want to know how much our car is worth. They don't care that it doesn't run. What really bothers me . . ." The words broke off. Her eyes watered and immediately swelled up. She put her face in her hands. I started searching in my purse for a Kleenex.

"Thanks," she said, wiping the tears then blowing her nose. "What really bothers me is to have to go down there and ask for a bag of food. We've never done this before. We've never lived this way. We waited as long as we could. We waited until we were down so low we could hardly crawl up. My husband hates to take the food stamps and the food as much as I do because it's embarrassing and it's humiliating, especially for a proud, macho, hard-working guy like him.

"We had a house until a year ago January. It was a big place with four bedrooms, but the owner decided he wanted to sell it, so we had to leave. We moved into a camper. Randy was still working then. When the work stopped, we lost the camper. I went to welfare and got some motel vouchers. I actually visited about forty motels asking if they'd take us. But only three of them were willing to voucher out to low-income families. In the end, we took the cheapest place. It was two hundred thirty-five dollars a week, no cooking, no water, no private bathroom, just a toilet and sink down the hall for everyone to share. This was in Colorado. Our last week there was the worst we ever had. Alicia was still a baby. My milk had dried up. We were fighting like hell to get free formula for her. It was winter so no one was hiring. It kills me to see my kids suffering. My husband could walk out on me and I'd be OK, but when my kids are hungry . . ."

She began to cry again then stepped on a roach that ran across the floor in front of us.

"I love my kids. My life just revolves around them."

Alicia came over and put her arms around her mother. Zac followed, grabbed her by the waist and pushed her away. A fight broke out.

"Stop it," Anna shouted. "You're both driving me crazy."

She reached for the only toy in the place, a small battery-operated plastic potted plant that played music as the flowers moved up and down.

"It's mine," Alicia screeched as Zac grabbed it. "It's mine," she repeated more forcefully. "I found it in the trash."

She scratched his arm. He kicked her leg. They both wailed, their beautiful oversized blue eyes filling with tears at the same moment.

Anna grabbed the plastic plant and pulled out the batteries then put it on top of the empty refrigerator. Zac took a chair, carried it over to the refrigerator, carefully positioned it beneath the plastic plant and climbed up.

"He's my difficult one," Anna said, sighing as she stood up again and lifted him off the chair. "They're acting up because they're hungry. If I just had some food, I could calm them down."

Her face turned red. Her body slumped forward. A wet streak of grief flooded down her cheeks again and rested on her lips.

"My husband doesn't get paid till Friday but they canceled our stamps because he worked those three days. We've got nothing till then, I mean absolutely nothing."

I looked at Anna, then at Zac and Alicia. I remembered my own children at their ages. It was only Tuesday. I had just been to the MAC machine and had taken one hundred dollars, which I had figured would last for the rest of my expenses in San Diego if I was careful. I debated silently for a minute, then realized that there was no debate. I felt my heart beating a little faster as I leaned forward and reached for my purse.

•   •   •

From affluent San Diego to the exclusive northwest suburbs of Chicago in the year of the millennium, the story was much the same. Hidden among the urban development, the suburban sprawl and the economic boom times was the quiet desperation of the hidden poor and their children. At the very bottom of that heap were a rapidly growing number of homeless families like Anna's.

According to the Urban Institute in Washington, D.C., about 2.3 million people, including up to 1.35 million children, were likely to be homeless at some point in the course of 2001. That number was up about 65 percent since 1996.

The U.S. Conference of Mayors estimates that one-parent families, especially those headed by women, represent approximately three-fourths of homeless families in America.

The Coalition for the Homeless in Pennsylvania reported that young families are much more likely to be homeless than older ones. Seventy-five percent of the homeless parents they interviewed (both married and single) were under the age of thirty. Their children, of course, were also very young, often under the age of five. While many people believe that most homeless families have wandered in from other areas looking for jobs the way Anna's family did, the majority have actually been longtime residents of the cities that now shelter or fail to shelter them.

Fortunately, homelessness is usually a temporary condition. The main factors determining how temporary are the resources available to help the homeless get out of trouble, primarily the job market and the availability of low-cost housing. While most families seem to find their way out of homelessness within about three months, the emotional impact it has on them is almost always permanent. Many of these families refuse to stay in traditional shelters. Some women, who are running from abusive men, are afraid of being found there by their husbands. Others have been so frightened by stories of violence, drugs, theft or disease that they actually feel safer sleeping in their cars or in empty buildings. Still others refuse to go because many shelters separate fathers from mothers and children, adding another huge source of grief and insecurity to families who are already living on the edge.

Yet, except for the small percentage of homeless men, women and children we see in the doorways or on the steam vents and grates of our cities, the huge number of homeless families have become more and more invisible in the last decade. They are kept off the beaten track and hidden from our view so effectively that it often takes a specific and determined effort to find them or even to find their shelters.

I met Beth Neighbors, the interim director of a homeless shelter network known as PADS, in a white cinder-block building on a run-down stretch of the Northwest Highway just past Route 53 outside of Chicago. I had been told to start looking for a sign in the window that read, "Northwest Suburban Public Action to Deliver Shelter" right after I passed an empty building on the left-hand side of the highway. Still, I missed it and had to circle back. The sign was difficult to see and even harder to interpret. Maybe it should have read, "Homeless? Hungry? Stop here." Or maybe, like the Statue of Liberty, it should have displayed a pair of outstretched arms holding some food. Just the same, about six hundred desperate people manage to decode the sign and find the place every month. They are people in crisis, people who are absolutely frantic for food, for shelter, for clothing and for jobs.

Beth Neighbors has a master's in psychology and spent six years as a therapist before becoming an administrator. She's friendly but businesslike and tough, especially when she talks about the poor.

"Right from the beginning, I wanted to work with these issues but it's not all tolerance and compassion," she told me.

"We want people to make a difference in their own lives. One person's small success might actually be bigger than another's large one. It all depends on where they are coming from and what they are capable of." She shuffled some papers on her desk, then said, "Sometimes, we have to make tough decisions here and say, 'We aren't helping you. This isn't the right environment for you because we are enabling you.' A large variety of people come to us. Some are very engaged in what we try to do for them and some practically have to be dragged into the services. Others come once or twice then try to avoid us. That's because we make them see themselves. They are used to being invisible both to themselves and to others."

Her words reminded me of something Michael Harrington had observed almost forty years earlier. In *The Other America*, published in 1962, he wrote, "The millions who are poor in the United States tend to become increasingly invisible. Here is a great mass of people yet it takes an effort of the intellect and will even to see them."

"A lot of the people who come here are invisible," Beth explained, "because they look like everyone else. The only difference is that some have lost their jobs. Some have left an abusive partner, others are working full-time but still can't afford the high cost of housing and food. The lower end of the job market in Chicago's suburbs just doesn't support the cost of living. A two-bedroom apartment runs about seventeen hundred dollars in this neighborhood. Minimum-wage workers just can't make it around here even if they have two or three jobs. If they work at McDonald's in the daytime, Wendy's at night and do a third shift on weekends at, say, Wal-Mart, they might just get by. But then they will never get to see the children they work so hard to house and feed.

"If there's an affordable apartment left in this area, there's so much competition to get it that it's almost impossible to be the chosen one. Interviewing for a place to live around here is like interviewing for a job, only harder. If your credit is bad or your wages are low, you can forget it because they've got half a dozen or more other applicants on their list. So people lose hope. If you think about it, that's not surprising.

"Of course, I have to say that some of these people were depressed before they came here," Beth continued. "And that may have contributed to their downfall. Some may have been substance abusers, but depression and substance abuse are true of the general population too.

"I don't think I have ever come across a family, whether it's the elite, high-income family or the poor struggling family, that doesn't have a member with some form of chronic depression or bipolar personality or substance abuse. This is a national problem, not one that only affects poor people. The difference is that the high-income family can afford to get treatment and stay behind closed doors until they are functional again. The low-income family can't afford treatment so they get worse and worse. Finally, they lose their jobs and houses and go hungry.

"There is also the old chicken-and-egg question. Is a chemical problem making them depressed or are they depressed because they can't earn a living and feed their families? It's often hard to say which came first. Chaos and stress are known to increase depression and substance abuse—poverty, homelessness and hunger cause the most extreme kinds of chaos and stress. But I challenge anyone to say that alcoholism and depression don't also exist for the gentleman who owns the racetrack or the president of a large company. The difference, like I said, is that they can send themselves away to the Betty Ford Clinic and come out without anyone knowing it, or they can be taking their depression medicine or their bipolar medicine and still maintain a functional life because they have a physician managing their care and places to go to talk about their problems.

"This is where I get on my soapbox," she continued, sounding almost strident. "There are a lot of tough issues that go along with being hungry and poor. But depression and substance abuse are predominantly human issues regardless of your station in life."

"I'm glad you're talking about this," I said as I made a quick mental scan of depression and substance abuse in some of the more prominent families I knew. "You're making a point that's rarely made."

I thought about how quickly our lives can change and how easily people can be peeled apart, especially if they are poor and have fewer resources both economically and emotionally.

"Over and over, I hear from the hungry and the homeless that they can't go home to their families," Beth said. "Their parents and relatives are rejecting them. They don't want them anymore, but these people struggling with the stress of hunger and poverty are no different than others would be if they had the same issues to cope with."

There was silence for a minute then Beth shook her head and said sadly, "I only wish we could judge people the way we judge money. If someone gave a person a fifty-dollar bill, then crumpled it up and threw it on the ground and asked them if they still wanted it, they'd say yes. But if you take a human being and dirty them up a little, all of a sudden they don't have any value. No one wants them anymore because they are a little crumpled."

"What happens to them when they come here?" I asked, looking around Beth's office and wondering what else was in the large, barren-looking building. "Do you shelter people here?"

"Oh, no," Beth said. "We only feed them. This is the administrative center for PADS. We have a soup kitchen on the other side of the building but we actually run twenty-three shelter sites in the northwest suburbs of Chicago."

"Where?" I asked, impressed that there were so many local shelters involved in such an affluent suburban community.

"In the basements and rec rooms of churches," she answered.

What happened next surprised and disappointed me. Beth got up and handed me a list of emergency shelter sites, the same list that she gives to the hungry and homeless. As soon as I saw it, I was reminded of the list of meal sites that I had been given by Bill Radatz at the Presbyterian Crisis Center in San Diego. Only this time, instead of providing a single meal, each church provided a place for the homeless to sleep one night a week.

I scanned the list several times, knowing that I was uncomfortable with it but not quite knowing why. By the third time, it had all become clear. The churches took turns serving as shelters, which seemed logical enough at a glance. Most offered shelter and food on whatever night they chose and a few, like the Christ Lutheran Church in Palatine, which was a Sunday-night-only shelter, also said "shower" next to it. The First United Methodist Church, on the other hand, said "washer and dryer" but that was only on Tuesday nights. I also noticed that different churches had different "guest line-up times" for food. For a minute, that too seemed logical enough, but then I tried to imagine what it would feel like not only to be homeless and hungry and broke, but to have to get my children to a different church basement without money or a car every single night of the week and stand on a different soup line at a different time. I visualized my kids, hungry and tired with trusting eyes and dirty faces and clothes at the end of each day, and thought about how it would be for them to have no stable place to sleep at night, not even a stable shelter. I wondered how it would feel to only shower on Sunday night and only be able to wash the outfits we had been sleeping and living in on Tuesday night while sharing one washer and dryer with the entire crowd. I knew that these were "emergency" shelters but I also knew that sometimes these emergencies lasted for months.

And what about schools and school buses and a place for the kids to do their homework? Then as I thought about what it would feel like to walk or hitchhike to a shelter, eat whatever they gave us, sleep wherever they put us and know that we had to be up and out by seven the next morning with no place to go and still no money, an overwhelming sense of hopelessness crept over me.

"We're different from Suburban PADS," Elaine Michelini, the petite, soft-spoken senior case manager for WINGS explained. "PADS is designed for short-term emergencies. They give people a place on the floor and something to eat. We are much smaller and harder to get into but we provide complete, long-term transitional services for up to two years.

"We're a nonprofit shelter where women can stay while they heal and learn to manage their lives. They live together in single- or multiple-family homes that have been donated to us in residential neighborhoods. We have ten houses and apartments in different locations, including Barrington, Des Plaines, Hoffman Estates, Niles and Park Ridge. We screen for mentally ill women or for women who are currently being stalked by men because we know our limits. We are not equipped to deal with serious emotional problems and we are not a safe house.

"There are several different definitions of homelessness floating around," Elaine explained. "But here we define it as having lost your own home due to extreme personal hardship. That means people don't have to be out on the street. If a family is living with a friend or relative or if they are living in a car or in a shelter we will consider taking them in here. They can stay with us while they are going to school or working and taking care of themselves and their children. Our biggest problem is supply and demand. We get about two hundred calls a month and have only forty beds. That may not sound so bad at first, but think about how many calls we get in the two years that we keep each of those forty people. I often wonder where all the women go that we can't take here. Each one is on the brink of crisis or disaster. Some of them have low skill levels but most are high school graduates. Some are even college graduates. We had one young girl here who was about to be evicted. She already had an undergraduate degree in social work. She was pregnant and had many student loans. She spent two years with us. While she was here she had her baby, started working on her master's degree in social work and got accepted into a Ph.D. program.

"We have rules that some people might consider strict; for example, women have to take their children's curfew because we don't want kids left here alone. We insist that women work full-time unless they are also in school. Once they are working, they pay fifteen percent of their salary in rent and save the rest. We're tough on them but we encourage less dependency that way and the women get stronger. Our goal is to heal their past wounds and develop new skills rather than just put food in their mouths and a roof over their heads.

"Our second executive director, Katherine Ross, was once homeless herself. She experienced the process of recovery firsthand and built a philosophy around what she learned. It was under her direction that WINGS became a two-year program with stage-one and stage-two housing. In stage two, women live on their own instead of here with the others in a shelter. They live in one of seven apartments but still have support from us. Katherine implemented the two-year transition after learning that it often takes that long to recover from emotional injuries and develop new vocational and parenting skills."

When we had finished talking, Elaine took me to a two-story yellow-brick house in a suburban Chicago neighborhood. It was one of the stage-one houses that had recently been donated to WINGS.

One of the newer residents was standing at the kitchen counter making tea.

"Wow, you look gorgeous," Elaine boomed as soon as she walked in and saw Carol wearing a white blouse, a black three-quarter-length skirt, black stockings and high heels. "I'm not used to seeing you all dressed up."

Carol smiled shyly as Elaine introduced me. Her lips were full, her teeth were very white and her skin was the color of ebony. I held out my hand. She took it, looking a little scared, and I held on for a moment.

"I been out looking for a job," she said. "That's why I'm dressed like this."

"Yes," I said, "Elaine told me."

Then I thanked her for agreeing to talk to me and explained that, even though there were more than six thousand homeless people in the northwestern suburbs of Chicago, it had taken me three days of long-distance phone calls to find someone who was willing to tell me her story. She smiled again and seemed a little more comfortable.

"A lot of people feel ashamed to talk about it," she said. "But I don't because one of the things I learned here at WINGS is that many people lose their homes and it don't mean they're bad."

Once we were settled in a little room off the kitchen, she asked what I wanted to know.

"Whatever you're comfortable telling me, and if there are things you'd rather not say, don't," I answered.

Carol straightened her skirt, pulling it down below her knees, and thought for a while.

"I'd been living with my boyfriend at his grandma's house ever since I was fifteen," she said, finally. "There was about ten of us living in this three-bedroom town house. When I was seventeen, I had my first baby. I dropped out of school and married him about six months later. It was my junior year and I hated leaving school. The real problem, the one that started the whole thing, was that I hadn't been connecting with my parents so I was looking for love somewhere else.

"Even when I was real young, my parents just didn't spend any basic time with me. I wanted support and love from Dan's family because I hadn't gotten it from my own. But I was carrying a lot of past hurt that made it hard for me to accept love even from them. Anyhow, we stayed at Dan's grandmother's house for a few years before we finally got our own place. It took both of us workin' just to pay the rent. I had a job at McDonald's. So did he. We always did everything together. When he switched to child-care work at a group home, I did too.

"But as I got older, I knew deep inside that my goals was changing and that we was drifting apart. I was scared about that because it seemed like a double whammy. I had grown up feeling the same kind of distance from my parents that I was now startin' to feel with him. A lot of things had gotten real cluttered and confused in my head. We was also having financial problems. We lost our apartment because we lost our jobs 'cause of a problem with the union. When we went back to his grandmother's house, a lot of the people living there was doin' drugs and fighting constantly.

"All the time, the past hurts from my own childhood kept reflectin' itself back. I knew I needed to heal myself and I needed to get my daughter out of an unsafe environment. Finally, I found us a little 'partment that I thought we could afford.

"But by this time, Dan had stopped working altogether. We was fighting a lot and I was starting to wonder, 'Do I still love this boy? Can we make this marriage work? Should we stay together for the child?'

"I had a job as a cashier at a little mini-mart but I wasn't earning enough to support us. Little by little, I began taking food from there so we could eat. Dan was spendin' all his time at the church. Religion had taken over his life. He called it religion, I called it a cult. He spent from day to night at this church. When I found out that he was giving them money, the money I made at the mini-mart, that did it. I wasn't trusting him no more. I began to hide my money to try to pay the rent. When it wasn't enough for the utility bills, I got a second job, but I couldn't do it alone. I just couldn't keep it up. By this time, we was living on nothing but the bread and lunch meat that I stole from the mini-mart. I wanted to stop. I went to a food pantry and asked them for food but they would only let me come once a week and it wasn't enough.

"Saying grace over the lunch meat I stole really bothered me. I could hardly swallow it. I'd get cramps and feel like I had to throw up. I felt so guilty that one night I told the owner what I been doing. Luckily, he felt bad for me and he began giving me the lunch meat that was past the date. He also gave me more hours so I could afford to buy some food. He understood that my condition was desperate so he forgave me.

"I have always worked in places where I could get free food on purpose. At McDonald's, they just gave it to us. At the group home, I cooked for the residents and brought my daughter along so she could eat. This mini-mart was the first place I had ever worked where I was stealin' the food.

"After I left my husband, I got a job at a restaurant and market called Catfish Warehouse. I knew the owner and she knew I had just separated so she offered me food along with the job. At that time I was working two jobs again.

"I was so tired I was barely keeping my eyes open. I was falling asleep coming home. I almost ran off the road trying to drive my daughter to school. Then, after I dropped her off, I'd have the other job to go to.

"At about that time, I met a man. I was lonely and broke. He was kind and had an apartment so me and my daughter began living with him and, for a while, that made things easier. He really was a good guy but he was goin' through his own problems. He was ten years older than me and he had three kids. Everything was OK until his kids' mother took him to court for child support.

"We had our own place. It was nothing fancy but we had the basics. Then his ex-wife wound up getting almost half of his income. He's a manager and does retail work, he has a degree, he has a career and he's been working for ten years. He earned enough for us to get by but there was no way he could earn enough to support two families.

"By this time I was pregnant and too sick to work. I woke up queasy every day and threw up all morning. With me not working, things got worse and worse. We went to the judge and told him that at this rate we would lose everything but he wouldn't listen. First, our credit went bad then we lost our 'lectric, after that, the car got repossessed. Then we had nothing to eat. Finally, right after the baby was born, we got evicted. We had to be out of our apartment by the next day. I had just had my son a few weeks before. He wasn't even a month old. It was winter and it was cold, bitter cold, and we was out on the street. Every word we said, we saw those little white puffs coming out of our mouths because it was February and that's how cold it was. I wrapped the baby up the best I could but he was crying and wailing. We knew we couldn't stay out on the street with the kids. We had two choices, the hospital or the police station; we chose the hospital. We waited for three hours in the intake service room. We held hands and took turns holding the baby."

Carol leaned toward me and whispered, "You know what they did? They sent me to a shelter just for women. Dan's shelter was across town and just for men. I was in shock. I didn't know that shelters separated families. They don't care if you need your partner and they don't care if your kids need their daddy. They have their rules and all they know is men and women are kept separate. It's even that way here at WINGS. It's just for women and children, not for families, so me and my baby's father never did get back together. When I became homeless, having my family broken up was my first shock, but it got worse. It was very overcrowded in this shelter. I had one baby on my hip and one in my hand. I couldn't hold on to them tight enough. There are some really scary shelters out there and this turned out to be one of them.

"Some women are strong enough to deal with homelessness and others are not. Some just lose it, and when the mothers lose it, the kids do, too. Poverty is not a good feeling, and some of these people don't have nothing at all. They stay on the street in the daytime because they are forced to go outside, then they come back into the shelter at night. It isn't like a hotel, where you can reserve a room when you need one. When they are full, they are full. If you're lucky, they squeeze you in and let you sleep on the floor. When I got there, they had no cots, they had no cribs, they had no baby beds. We got offered a choice between the floor or the sofa. We took the sofa, but during the night, when we was asleep, rats began coming out of the cushions, big gray rats with long gray tails. They started to crawl on us and it woke us up. I was terrified. My daughter was terrified. We was both screaming. I didn't know where to go or what to do. Finally, I found two wood chairs and put them together. I gathered my children and I held them in my arms real tight and I cried all night, that's all I could do.

"It was a big open space with bunk beds but some people had tried to put sheets around their beds for privacy. They had everything there, drugs, prostitution, fighting, hallucinations—you name it. The bathrooms had five stalls but the toilets didn't flush. I saw two little kids who came in there so hungry that they were eatin' out of those toilets."

A moan rose up from deep inside her, then Carol gagged.

"It was the bottom. That place was definitely the rock bottom, the place where hell meets earth. A lot of these people didn't have

their right minds anymore. They lost them when they lost everything else. Don't get me wrong. I have to give it to the shelter. It
wasn't their fault. They did whatever they could for the people, but
they were up against their own troubles. They had two floors and
they had a soup kitchen and it wasn't nearly enough. The single
ladies slept in the bottom part on them little pads on the floor, and
they had to be out of there by seven o'clock every single morning,
snow, rain, wind, no matter how cold it was.

"Upstairs is where the women and children stayed. They was all
cramped together but they could stay inside all day. I stayed three
days listening to those screaming kids and watching all that pain. I
stayed as long as I could, then when I couldn't take it anymore, I
went back to square one at the hospital. I sat there and I begged
them to get me into the Salvation Army. They tried but they
couldn't. Their hands was tied because the Salvation Army was full.
I had discovered that a shelter, a good shelter, is almost impossible to
find because the government and charity is so overflowed with need.
My last shreds of pride was gone. I began calling everyone I knew. I
was just begging and pleading with them to let me stay at their
house.

"Finally my sister said we could stay with her for a while. Then,
when I was with her, I found out about the WINGS program. They
was strict, they asked a lot of questions and they made me wait. They
gave me tests to take but finally, when they had room, they took me
in. They told me that what happened to me can happen to anyone.
They told me it wasn't my fault. That was their greatest gift to me
because, for a long, long time, I had put all the blame on myself.
They also said that what you plant is what you harvest. I thought
about that and I understood it. Kids is fragile just like seeds, if you
don't feed them, they die. So now I'm trying to give my kids a little
more water and a little more food because I don't want them growing up empty. I'm trying to give them some sunshine too so they can
finally bloom."

Chapter 6

Hunger, the Immigrants and the Refugees

"They shall not hunger or thirst; neither shall the heat nor the sun smite them; for he that hath mercy on them, shall lead them, even by the springs of the water shall he guide them. And I will make all my mountains a way and my highways shall be exalted."

ISAIAH, 49: 8–11

Dreams of the Dispossessed

"What you want to know?" Chea asked, sitting on the edge of her chair as her dark eyes darted nervously around the room. "I'm American citizen. I pay taxes."

"Yes, I know that. I'm not from immigration. I'm writing a book about hungry families in America."

Chea's face relaxed. She smiled gently. "And my children are hungry. Often we are as hungry in America as I was in the camps. That's why I agreed to talk to you. But sometimes when people ask me questions, I get scared even if I know who they are. It's like an automatic response. There are some things I just can't forget and others . . ." She hesitated. "Others I can't remember."

Then Chea explained that, even though her sister told her many times, she cannot remember the six months of intense bombing of her homeland by the United States Air Force. Nor can she recall the day when she was nine years old that the Khmer Rouge, led by Pol Pot, forced her family from their home at gunpoint. She cannot even remember why the black-clad soldiers with the AK-47s ordered everyone from her village to pack up their belongings and leave for the remote countryside. She does not know why they obeyed or why they bundled up their rice and cookwear then hid their gold and jewelry and hurriedly left. Most of all, she cannot or dares not remember what happened to her mother. Chea knows only that her own heart still beats wildly in her chest whenever she recalls her mother's shy smile and good-night kisses now buried forever in that village.

And, although her sister tells her that she was there and saw it with her own eyes, Chea cannot remember her father slumped over the kitchen table with his chest rising and falling in grief as he called out her mother's name then gathered his children together and left their home in the light of the quartered moon.

But Chea clearly remembers the fact, the cold statistical fact, that she was one of the 600,000 Cambodians who fled to the Thailand border. She also knows that thousands were already starving and that some, who were too weak for the journey, tried to return to their homes only to find that everything in their village had been destroyed. She has been told that some of those who returned were killed outright, while others were slowly starved, worked to death or brutally tortured. Thousands of children, like her, were sent to the mountains to cut down trees and plant corn as slave laborers. Her father explained that, because the Khmer Rouge wanted to create a Marxist, agrarian society, anyone who could read or write and anyone who was suspected of being an intellectual, in fact anyone with more than a second- or third-grade education, even anyone who wore glasses, was killed. Schools were closed and turned into prisons and large-scale centers of torture.

Chea has also heard that, in all, about 1.7 million people, or somewhere between 35 percent and 50 percent of the population, died. She knows that some people lived chained together for months at a time and others were buried alive, but she does not remember seeing them.

For thousands, forgetfulness or even hysterical blindness was the only escape from memories too haunting or too brutal to bear. Chea thinks, perhaps, that is why she still does not recall the long journey to Thailand, walking for days over mountains and through jungles with very little to eat or drink and walking over buried mines that could explode at any time and often did right in front of her terrified eyes.

Chea may be wise in her pointed forgetfulness for, even today, more than twenty years later, most Khmer stagger under the weight of recalled torture and many struggle with depression and flashbacks.

"All I remember," Chea told me as we sat in the small office where she now works, is that "Someone put us in camp where they rape you and kill you if you make mistake. We sleep in tiny room in long row of rooms but we not have enough food to eat, just some small rations, usually one little cup watered-down rice. My sister could not go to search for food because she was older than me. If she was caught she would be raped or killed. If my father or brothers were caught, they would be instantly killed.

"I was ten years old but so small and thin from malnutrition they thought I was only five, too young and too skinny to rape, so I was the one who would sneak out of camp to search for food for family. My dad would sometime tell me, 'Chea, don't go, it's not worth it, it's too dangerous.' He heard about what happened to children who stole food, like eight-year-old boy dragged down from mango tree and shot to death. But someone had to do it or we all die and I knew it was safer for child like me than someone my sister's age.

"So, when it was night, I climb fence," Chea said, talking slowly and keeping her dark eyes focused on the light that came in through the window. "Sometimes, I go into fields and find mushrooms or bamboo shoots. Sometimes, I go to small river and catch little fish, then dry myself with my hair. Sometimes, I pull young leaves from low trees and eat them then rest for a while, but I always go when dark and come back when dark."

Chea turned her head slowly away from the light, then explained to me that in 1978 things suddenly became much worse. Killings increased for no reason and there was even less food than before. People were told there were too many prisoners and the Khmer Rouge wanted to be rid of them. They started taking people, forty thousand in all, to the top of a mountain. They forced them to walk at gunpoint down a very steep ravine. If people refused, they were instantly shot or killed by knives or by palms that were dry and had sharp blades. If they went, they walked in terror because they knew there were land mines buried all the way down the mountain.

"If you didn't die from guns or land mines and you didn't starve, you'd be killed by soldiers when you got to bottom," Chea said, then she stopped talking and coughed. Her forehead was covered with small beads of sweat.

In 1978, some of the luckier Cambodians entered the new refugee camps that had been set up on the border of Cambodia and Thailand by the United Nations High Commission for Refugees but, even in these new camps, life was a desperate experience. In addition to the continuing civil war, there were regular raids and bombing attacks. Rape, robbery, extortion and starvation were also everyday events. Yet refugees like Chea and her family had no choice but to stay and wait for resettlement to America, the promised land, or some other country. Often it took months and sometimes even years.

"We thought America would be answer to all our prayers but when we finally arrived, we found out no one wanted us here. We were unwelcome. We were poor. Even though we are American citizens now, we are still often hungry and we are still outsiders."

Chea had not only come to a country that did not welcome her, she had arrived with all the problems she brought from years of torture. There is an idea in America that all Southeast Asians are well adjusted, well educated and ready to succeed. Americans tend to think of them as model immigrants, people who excel in science and math. But the truth is, some excel and others do not.

Doctors, lawyers and other professionals are assimilated with relative ease, but millions of the most educated Cambodians had already been killed or had died of starvation in their own country. Many of those that survived and came here were not only uneducated, they also struggled with the aftermath of war and with cultural differences, like American social values, unfamiliar foods and even different approaches to pregnancy.

"We are involved with prenatal care," explained Kallyane Sok, program coordinator for health care at the Southeast Asian Mutual Assistance Coalition. "We face huge difficulties based on fear. The parents or grandparents of the young Asian women are often afraid of American-style prenatal care. When they hear about vitamins and food supplements, they are terrified. They think the baby might be born too large. Sometimes, with education, we can see their attitudes changing, but the changes occur very slowly. We try to get young women to call us during their first trimester and to come in and get immunizations after their babies are born. We introduce them to doctors but they are used to having another housewife deliver their babies, not a male doctor. A strange man delivering their baby or looking at their private places makes them embarrassed and ashamed.

"They also eat differently. They don't eat cheese or drink milk every day, so when the doctor gives them the prenatal diet to follow or the WIC supplements it is all very foreign to them.

"We know that they struggle and we know that they don't want to tell us they are struggling. Of course, we also know that if they are on welfare, they can't be eating well because the welfare department provides as little as possible. We know that these families are often living ten people in two rooms. We know that if they have twenty thousand dollars a year for five people, they frequently rent a place for three hundred dollars a month and have ten people live in it. They can live like that more easily than Americans can because what they lived with at home was even harder. In addition to hunger and poverty, when they were at home, they also had the Communists torturing them. Here in America, sixty-one percent of Cambodian refugees still live in poverty. Their lives are miserable by American standards but they are better than they were so they tend to think it is good enough. Our program tries to help them get off of welfare and get out of poverty. We train them for jobs. We try every day to reach them, but if we reach one or two we are grateful.

"Over there, in Cambodia," Kallyane Sok added, "the government does not care at all. The rural people are so poor. They often have no clothes to wear and no food to eat yet they work very hard. When they come here, we tell them about the stigma of welfare. We discourage them from depending on it. We say that it is not a good model for their children. We encourage them to do whatever work they can. We tell them they can do housework because they don't have to speak English to do that."

"It's better here. Yes. It's better, but even here life is much harder than we imagined," Chea explained. "When I came here, we were poor. We ate mostly rice but I went to school for first time in my life. I was so happy because I wanted to learn but American kids threw gum in my hair. They spit at me. They threw fruit and juice at me in lunchroom. Sometimes, teachers would just let it go. All my clothes were dirty every night. I wanted to read and write but my father finally said, 'No, Chea. You have suffered enough. We can't stay here. It is too difficult here.' He took us out of school and we went to California, but they beat us up there, too.

"Finally, I gave up school," she said. "I worked in factory with sewing machines, making clothes. I met my husband and I got married. I had three kids, then my husband left me. We were always struggling for food and money before but now it was worse. I had no money. I had no car. I had no job. I had no husband. I had nothing. I was not going to let my kids be hungry and starving or be dumb like me. I wanted my kids to have food and an education, to read, to write. I did not want welfare. I felt it wasn't right but, for one year, one terrible year, I took it.

"But the money welfare gave me was not enough because landlord make rent very high for Asian people. We pay or they kick us out, so finally I sold food stamps at grocery store and gave money to landlord. I was afraid because I heard Asian people are not treated well when homeless. They are looked down on. They are kicked out of shelters. It is bad when you are American but it is much worse when you are Asian. After I paid rent and other bills, I had fifteen dollars left for food, just enough to buy rice for month. At that time, I could get one fifty-pound bag rice for fifteen dollars and we lived only on rice, so in the end, for a while, we had same food, maybe a little less, maybe a little more in America than in camps. Then I began having trouble with my kids. They wanted to be American.

They wanted to eat like American kids. They didn't want to listen to me. For me, this is still big problem," Chea said as she rubbed her damp eyes. "I want my daughter to finish school, not run with boys, so I am strict. I am strict because Asian people should not hang out in street."

Chea was the first person ever to tell me that she had sold her food stamps. Perhaps it was because she was the only one used to surviving on a cup of rice each day or perhaps it was because the American landlord deliberately took advantage of her. I knew that technically she was breaking the law but I don't think she knew it. All she knew was that, trapped between food and shelter here in America, she had once again reverted to the starvation rations of the prison camps.

Despite all that Chea had gone through and all that she had forgotten about her home and her early childhood, it was clear that the traditional Khmer values were still important to her. It was also clear that her attempt to hold on to them in a radically different environment was creating pain and tension that compounded the struggle with poverty and hunger. In the years she cannot remember, she might have been prepared by her mother and father for the life of a poor peasant in a Cambodian village, but she certainly was never prepared for poverty in an urban American city like Philadelphia.

"I work full-time now. I pay taxes but still I don't earn enough to pay bills and buy food. We run short every month so still I buy only one fifty-pound bag rice a month. The price has gone up to twenty dollars but since I work full-time now, sometimes for flavor I also buy pork leg for six or seven dollars. The meat lasts two weeks, then I use the bone for soup. Sometimes, I buy fish sauce that costs only ninety-nine cents a bottle. We use only when we do stir-fry once, maybe twice a week. The rest of time, we boil rice. In summer, we go fishing. We freeze fish. For winter, we buy a fishing license for seventeen dollars." She smiled with pride. "We have learned these little tricks of America. We live very carefully. I never let go my money. We spend maybe fifty or sixty dollars a month for food for five people. That's only ten dollars a month or two dollars and fifty cents a week for each person. So food costs us around fifty cents a day for each person. Of course, we eat no fruit and we eat almost no vegetable. We cannot afford it, mostly just rice like in the camps and something to flavor it. But, even eating this way, I still can't make it." Chea shook her head sadly.

"The more I try save, the more bill is going up. Now, it's gas for the heat. I owe twelve hundred ninety-five dollars for the heat because I have not been able to pay very much all winter, only the minimum. Yes, even here in America, it is a hard life for me and my children. Even here, it is a struggle and even now, as American citizens, my kids still hungry." She thought for a moment then added, "They are still hungry but at least they are free."

Difficult as life was for Chea, many legal immigrants now have access to even less "safety net" assistance than she did. One of the severest provisions of the 1996 federal welfare law was to make a huge proportion of legal immigrants ineligible for federal food stamp benefits. In 1997, an estimated 940,000 of the 1.4 million immigrants receiving food stamps lost their eligibility. By September 1998, seventeen states had initiated state-funded programs to provide food assistance to some of them, but these state-funded programs only replaced benefits for about 25 percent of those who had lost them.

Even though many children in legal immigrant families did not lose their food stamps, restrictions on their parents' eligibility often deterred the entire household from participating.

Many of these families are now facing extreme hunger and food insecurity. A study conducted in 1998 by Physicians for Human Rights revealed that of the 630 Asian and Latino household members surveyed, 79 percent were food insecure and more than one in three households reported suffering from moderate or severe hunger due to a lack of resources.

California Food Policy Advocates found similar circumstances among the children of legal immigrants in Los Angeles and San

Francisco. Where food stamps had been cut, children were one-third more likely to experience food insecurity and severe hunger than in immigrant households where stamps had not been cut.

Life is often even more difficult and dangerous for those who are here without documentation. Each year countless thousands of immigrants leave their homelands in search of a better life and enter America without permission. They work at whatever they can find. Many who come from Mexico end up doing migrant work and following the seasons for very low wages. They live in trailers, garages, tool sheds, caves, fields and parking lots. They harvest our crops, but they often have little to eat.

Nineteen seventy-one was an unusually cold winter in Florida. The crops were frozen and the migrant farm workers were without food or work. Caridad Asensio, who had been forced to flee her own homeland in Cuba twenty years earlier, had volunteered to help. She had grown up in a professional and well-off Cuban family. Her husband worked for IBM. She knew little of hunger, poverty or migrant life. But as soon as she brought food and blankets to the families, she realized that they didn't want charity, they wanted work. They also desperately needed food, homes and health care. Their children were hungry and they were being turned away from school because they could not get the required physical exams and vaccinations.

From the beginning, it was the plight of the children that moved Caridad most. She couldn't stop thinking about the things she wanted them to have and the things they didn't have. "They had no meat, they had no milk, they had no Pampers. Many of them were starving and dehydrated. Their mothers did the best they could. They cooked rice and fed the babies rice water because it was all they had."

Now, thirty years later, Caridad, a large-boned, handsome woman with delicate features and close-cropped white hair, was talking to me as we sat in her office at the Caridad Clinic, a state-of-the-art,

7,600-square-foot, $2.5 million complex on 6.8 acres of land. Today, the clinic is staffed by over five hundred volunteers that treat more than eleven thousand migrant families each year.

"I built this place from only a dream. I started it with nothing," Caridad, who is now seventy, told me. "I did it because I don't believe in giving up.

"I'm no one special. I am just a refugee. Everyone who comes to America comes with a dream. It makes no difference if they are refugees from Cuba like me, refugees from Cambodia or immigrants from Mexico, from Guatemala or someplace else. Everyone in America, except the Indians, first came here from someplace else. They came because they dream. They came because they believe that America is a haven.

"It broke my heart to see these kids. I wish I could speak better English so I could tell you," she said, struggling for the words. "But I'll try to explain. I'll do my best. I'm not a political person and I don't believe in fighting. I believe from love, comes everything."

I looked around the office with its poster-sized portrait of a double-wide trailer where Caridad first began her work.

"Do you ever wake up in the morning and marvel at what you've done?" I asked.

"Yes," she said. "Every day. I have breast cancer now," she added in the direct and open way she says all things. "And that has made me think more deeply and feel more grateful. I had surgery and chemotherapy and radiation two and a half years ago. I am doing well now but sometimes, I feel so tired, I think I will have to retire. Then I ask myself what would I do if I retire, sit at home and watch the television? How am I going to leave all this behind? There is still so much to be done and the children still need me. So every day, I ask God please to guide me and give me the strength to keep working. I have Alli now," she said, referring to her young assistant. "And she helps me a lot. She was volunteering here when I heard what I had. I decided I better hurry up and train someone because I wanted to be sure someone would continue all my special programs, like my adopt-a-family program, my scholarship program and my Christmas program, and I wanted to be sure someone would expand the clinic and build my education center in case . . ." Her voice trailed off. "Come," she said. "I'll show you around."

Caridad moved slowly and with obvious difficulty. But as we walked through the clinic with its specialized centers for pharmacy, dermatology, gynecology, pediatrics and pulmonary disease, her pride was obvious. There was even a dental center, an on-site laboratory, a computer room and a classroom converted from the dental waiting room.

"Food, housing, health and education," she said, counting on the fingers of her right hand. "Those were my dreams when I started. Of all the parts of my dream, the education part is the only one left. I still want to build a school for the children on this ground. We have one hundred and twenty-six volunteer teachers right now but we only have space in this building for twenty-two children. After lunch, we use the soup kitchen next door for the extra children. Many of the kids are so behind when they come here that in the fifth grade, they still can't read or write. We work with them, we teach them and, do you know what?" Caridad said, smiling. "They catch up."

As we walked, Caridad told me how two Delray Beach teachers, Connie Berry and Denise Saberson, had helped her create the Migrant Association of South Florida. Once she had established a nonprofit corporation, fund-raising quickly became one of her strengths. The Catholic Diocese of Palm Beach leased her property for one dollar a year and the First Presbyterian Church of Delray Beach donated ten thousand dollars for the double-wide trailer that housed the first clinic.

Next, Caridad convinced the owners of local trailer parks to donate old mobile homes to poor migrant families that had no stable shelter.

"The families had to keep the trailers in good condition for a year before they received the deeds in exchange for whatever sum they could afford to pay. That money was then placed in a fund to help move and fix up other trailers. That way, at least some of the migrant families and their children would have a home to come back to."

In the years that followed, Caridad has used her strong love for children to connect the vastly different segments of society in south Florida and make both the rich and the poor feel they were getting something wonderful from the transaction. In 1995, she received an anonymous donation of $100,000, which allowed her to begin planning for the larger clinic. Shortly after the land was purchased, she received another $250,000 donation.

The money continued to flow in. Today, the miraculous new health clinic stands beside a new soup kitchen where hundreds of other volunteers provide daily food to the poverty-stricken and undernourished families who grow, pick, sort and harvest our food. The adjoining but independently run soup kitchen is open daily to provide lunch for anyone who wants to come, no questions asked. Emergency food bags are also available three days a week.

It was eleven in the morning when we arrived and the place was already full. There were a few African Americans and a few Caucasians and several senior citizens but mostly it was the migrant population. I sat down next to a young woman with a six-week-old baby and two small daughters. As we ate together, she told me in broken English that her husband, a migrant worker, had been killed in an accident six months earlier. She said she came to the soup kitchen with the children whenever she could get a ride so that they could have something to eat.

Our conversation was interrupted when a small woman in her seventies who volunteers at the kitchen on Wednesdays arrived to show me around.

"Anybody can eat here and anybody can take home bags of food," she explained. "But we don't like to give the crews bags because even if they have families, most of them have no kitchens and no refrigerators and a lot of our food is either perishable or it needs to be cooked. Our standard bags are not great. We give out fresh produce, beans, rice and extra cartons of things that we have in the freezer, but all I have to do is hear a sad story and I give people whatever else I can. I try to load them up and keep them supplied as long as they need it. Then if they stop coming back, I just pray that it's because they've moved up and no longer need the food.

"We don't take federal funding and we don't advertise. But we have a lot of wealthy donors in the Florida area. Somehow, they all seem to know that we are here and they give very generously. We usually have enough food so that people can choose from about three or four possibilities. Most of the volunteers are retired like me. I was a librarian in my other life. I live in a condominium. I'm grateful for what I have and I'm happy to help. To tell you the truth, it's the highlight of my week. Up to four hundred people eat here every day. Eighteen volunteers staff the soup kitchen. But each day of the week, we have a totally different group. That way, a lot of people get a chance to help and no one has to give up too much of their time. We were also on the site of Caridad's old clinic, the trailer, but we were much smaller then too. When she got the new land, she got extra for us, so everyone who visits the clinic can also eat lunch. We operate as a team because we all know that without good food there can't be good health.

"The doctors and clinic staff also come here to eat. Everyone has the same food and everyone eats together at the same tables. We have no borders here. We are all friends."

After lunch, Caridad and her assistant, Alli, took me for a ride down West Boynton Beach Boulevard toward the farms.

"Mega-farmers own the land and their managers hire thousands of workers," Caridad said as we drove. "The migrants here are not just picking the crops, they are growing the crops and taking care of them too. They are really good farmers. The only difference is they are farmers who work the land that other men own.

"Quick, hurry up, Loretta. Close your eyes. I don't want you to be scared," Caridad said, half joking as we turned off the highway and bumped our way across a canal on a rickety homemade bridge of boards. We passed a No Trespassing sign then turned onto a dirt road where acres of large, ripe tomatoes grew on one side of the narrow road and acres of red and green peppers grew on the other. We stopped, got out of the car and picked a few to eat as we drove. Then Caridad pointed to about a dozen small, run-down old trailers. Some had flowers growing in front. One had lace curtains. There were dogs and small children everywhere.

"At least they have some degree of comfort here," Caridad said, pointing at the trailers. "Even though they are still very poor, they are happy. Mother, father and children, they are always together, and as long as they have something to eat on the table, they are happy. Some people don't understand how they can be so poor and also so happy. One family had been living in a little shed with five children. When we gave them a small trailer, they thought it was a palace. They thought they were in heaven. Many of these people, they live nowhere. They have nothing. It's another life." Caridad's face saddened. "A life no one knows."

As we turned back onto the main road, our conversation was interrupted by about twenty young men who suddenly jumped in front of our car then raced across the street.

"They run like that whenever there is a crew leader," Caridad said as she jammed on the brakes. "See, over there," she added, pointing to a small grove under some trees. "See. There he is. That is the crew leader. He is choosing men for a job. They all want to be picked. They all are desperate to work and earn money for their families. That's why they came here. This is *El Norte*. This is the dream they grew up believing in. They risked their lives to come here and they will risk their lives again every day, if they have to, just to stay. You have no idea what being in America means to these people.

"When the immigration truck comes through, I watch them. Sometimes twenty people at one time, sometimes more than twenty, even the children jump. They jump into the canals with their shoes and clothes and everything on. They go underwater and grab on to

reeds. They put one end in their mouth like this," Caridad said, trying to demonstrate as she drove, "and the other end, it comes up
above the water so they can breathe. They stay there like that until
they get a signal that the immigration truck has passed. They only
come up when they think they are safe from the deportation again."

As Caridad talked, we turned down another lane and stopped at
a large open wooden structure with a tin roof where about forty
Mexican women were standing shoulder to shoulder at a conveyor
belt.

"This is a packing plant," Caridad said. "They are sorting the
green from the red cherry tomatoes. They do this by hand before the
tomatoes are put in the cardboard shipping crates that take them to
the supermarkets."

We got out of the car and approached the group. "These
women, these girls, they stand there like that ten, twelve hours a day,
sometimes more for almost nothing." Caridad was whispering now
so that the heavyset crew leader standing nearby wouldn't overhear.

As the conveyor belt turned, some of the women looked shyly in
my direction. I noticed a pretty young girl with thick black hair that
came down below her waist. We smiled at each other. I moved closer.
I wanted to talk to her and sensed she was also eager but the crew
leader approached. He spoke to Caridad in Spanish and gestured
angrily.

"He says we are not allowed to be here," Caridad explained,
translating. "He says we have to go. He is upset, he is also angry so I
told him that we would go."

I nodded and waved good-bye to the girl I could not speak to.
All the women and girls smiled back and waved as I reluctantly
returned to Caridad's car. One thing I had learned in my years of
journalism was not to openly challenge angry strangers whose rules
I did not know or understand. Staying safe was still a priority. It was
something I had promised my son I would always try to do.

"They perform a service no one else will perform," Caridad said
as we drove off. "But they are not treated right, he knows it. That is

why he does not want you there. He doesn't want you to see."

As we drove down the road toward another camp, we passed an opulent new development filled with huge, newly constructed estates.

"They are two-million-dollar homes," Caridad told me as we turned down a narrow dirt lane across the street and just down the road from the estates. There, hidden from the view of the casual traveler, were eight tiny broken-down shacks and one small, run-down trailer. A beautiful, dark-eyed child ran gleefully toward us. She wrapped her arms around Caridad's legs to greet her then sat on her feet laughing with joy. Inside, the child's mother sat on a stained, torn, dilapidated couch holding a little boy and singing softly.

"For many years, they had had no electricity and no telephone lines here but now they do. The lines were finally brought in when they built the estates and the country club," Caridad explained as we entered the trailer. It was narrow and dark with a torn linoleum floor and soiled walls.

Caridad spoke with the mother in Spanish and then introduced me. The woman smiled and offered me the couch as she explained in Spanish that her husband was in the fields picking tomatoes. After a few more minutes of talking, I asked how much her husband was paid for his work.

"Five dollars an hour," she answered proudly in Spanish but Caridad explained to me in English that the salary was only paid for eight hours a day maximum and, in order to keep the jobs, the men often worked twelve or more hours each day.

"What about this trailer?" I asked.

"It is free," the woman said in Spanish.

"No," Caridad explained in English. "The rent is deducted from the paycheck before the worker gets paid.

"And food. Do you have enough?" I asked.

"*Si*," the woman said, smiling. "We have rice. We have beans. Sometimes we have tomatoes. It is enough."

"Are you satisfied with your life in America?" I asked, still talking in English through Caridad, who was still translating. There was a long pause. The woman appeared to be confused by my question.

"Would you like to have more money or more food or a better house?" I said, putting it a different way.

The woman still seemed puzzled, almost bewildered. I thought perhaps the translation was difficult but I was wrong. She was simply formulating her answer.

"No," she said, finally gazing at me with dark liquid eyes that sparkled. "Why should we expect more? In Mexico, we have no work, we have no food, we have no soup kitchen, we have no health clinic and we have no Caridad. We are happy to be here. This is enough. This is more than enough. We are blessed beyond words."

The little girl climbed up onto her mother's lap and kissed her, then climbed down again and kissed Caridad and touched her hair.

"It is a special community," Caridad said as we drove back down the road past the opulent country club and the mega-estates. "It is a community of people who never complain. Maybe they don't have anything except rice and beans for two weeks but they will still tell you they have enough. Like I told you before, they live in a little shack and they think it is a castle. But I see the need. I see the need. . . ."

Dr. James Leone, a retired physician who volunteers at the Caridad Clinic, also sees the need. He told me that he is treating severely undernourished and anemic migrant children, children with hemoglobin counts so low that they are just above the transfusion level.

"The problem here is especially serious," Dr. Leone explained. "Because many of the families we see are undocumented immigrants from Mexico. They have no green cards so they are not eligible for WIC, for food stamps or any other federal program. They are so poor that all that many of them eat is rice and beans. The kids grow up on this. They can get free milk here at the clinic and because the babies are so hungry, they often use too much of it. Sixteen ounces is usually enough. No child should drink more than thirty-two ounces of milk a day, but because it's all they can get these kids often drink much more. They go to sleep with the milk in their mouths so they end up with milk anemia or nursing bottle disease on top of everything else. That leaves them with brown, rotting front teeth. Too much milk also causes iron to be lost through the intestines and makes it difficult for the body to use the iron that is left. We explain this to them but sometimes, with the children so hungry, it is difficult for them to believe us. If milk is good, they think more milk is better. Yet, we know that if we took it away, they would be even worse off. We try to advise them and put them on vitamins but it's not enough.

"We also see a lot of asthmatic children who are made sick from the farm dust and sprays. In addition, we see something here that we used to call the 'ghetto allergy.' It's caused by decaying cockroaches that have been sprayed. The kids breathe the dust and next thing you know, you don't just have malnourished kids, you have asthmatic, allergic, malnourished kids."

Despite the problems that Dr. Leone sees at the Caridad Clinic, it is clear to him that these are the lucky families. Most of the migrant families in the United States and even in other parts of Florida have no access to free health care, educational support, housing assistance, soup kitchens or the love of Caridad Asensio.

As of March 2000, the U.S. Senate was facing complex new immigration legislation introduced by Ted Kennedy called the Latino and Immigrant Fairness Act. The act would make it possible for about 300,000 undocumented immigrants to receive permanent residency and, perhaps, food stamps and WIC if they have already lived in the United States for fourteen years. Under the existing Immigration Reform and Control Act, passed in 1986, immigrants must have lived in the country since 1972 in order to be eligible for residency.

But even if the new legislation goes through, it would only affect about 5 percent of the estimated 6 million undocumented immigrants who are currently living in the United States and are desperately in need of help. The unfortunate reality is that even permanent residency might not make much difference since many of the legal immigrants who pay taxes on their meager wages are also blocked from receiving food stamps. Even now, after a 1998 law fixed a mistake in the 1996 Welfare Reform Act, the revision only applied to immigrants who were legal as of August 22, 1996. Among those who aren't citizens, hunger is reported by California food policy advocates to be "severe and spreading."

According to Dianne Hanzlicek, director of volunteers at the Community Food Bank in Fresno, the largest food-producing county in the world, an astonishing one in four people are hungry.

But despite all the difficulties, the number of immigrants living in the United States has tripled since 1970. If current levels of immigration remain in place, about 10 million more will settle in this country during the next decade.

Even in the moments it takes to read this page, hundreds of immigrants are risking their lives to come here in search of work, in search of food and in search of dreams that often don't come true. Ten years ago, the risks they took were not as great as they are today. For the most part, those who came from Mexico simply curled up in car trunks and sneaked over the border.

But as Luis Alberto Urrea points out in his stunning book *Across the Wire*, the Border Patrol today has more than doubled. Urrea says that now the helicopters swoop and circle all night with their brightly focused lights raking the ground. Borderland locals have become so used to the sight that they hardly notice people being herded like cattle on the dusty slopes. They hardly react to the sight of trucks speeding in and out of the landscape and to the shadows of uniformed men patrolling with flashlights and guns and dogs. They barely blink at the spotlights and the people running, getting caught or being herded onto buses by armed guards. To them, it has all become almost commonplace.

In his haunting narrative, Urrea writes, "Imagine the poverty, violence, natural disasters or political fear driving you away from everything you know. Imagine how bad things get to make you leave behind your family, your friends, your lovers, your home, as humble as it might be. . . . Then you come hundreds or thousands of miles across territory utterly unknown to you (chances are you have never traveled further than one hundred miles in your life). You have walked, run, hidden in the backs of trucks, spent part of your precious money on bus fare."

Urrea also writes, "If you have daughters or mothers or wives with you or if you are a woman, you've become watchful and tense because rape and gang rape are so common in this darkness as to be utterly unremarkable."

Today, many immigrants who are desperate to avoid the wall of agents, floodlights, video surveillance cameras and violent crime are pushed toward more desolate and desperate terrain along the border's 1,952 miles. They often struggle through deadly heat, burning sands and the rapid currents of rivers like the Rio Grande.

If they are lucky enough not to be among the roughly five hundred scooped up each night by the Border Patrol or robbed by the "coyotes" who promise to help them across the border, they still have to fear life on the other side. Many have heard the widely circulated but undocumented rumors that, if they are caught when they arrive in America, the patrol will kill, beat or rape them, but they do know, for a fact, that if they are discovered, they will be taken to compounds, put on buses and sent right back across the border. Yet, they still keep coming. Even talk of our recent sluggish economy doesn't slow them. From October 2000 to March 2001 in the border town of Naco alone, 56,819 were rounded up and sent back. This figure was up 11 percent from the same period the year before.

If they somehow manage to survive all that and arrive in America, they are still just aliens . . . despised illegal immigrants on the run in a foreign land whose language they cannot speak. Yet, somehow they have to manage to start life over, to figure out a way to eat, to sleep, to get shelter and to find work. For many, arriving in America is not a dream come true. It is only the end of one difficult journey and the start of another.

•   •   •

•   •   •

Selena was standing on the steps of a second-floor rear apartment in a pale yellow house made of cinder blocks. She was hiding in the shadow of the sunlight and holding Jorgé, her four-year-old son, who had almost died three times.

The first time Jorgé almost died was when Selena was four months pregnant and the doctors in Mexico told her to have an abortion because "something" was wrong. The second time was when the same doctors warned her that two-year-old Jorgé needed an operation that her husband said they could not afford. The third time Jorgé almost died was when Selena escaped to America to save him.

Selena had to carry Jorgé as she swam across the Rio Grande. It was dark. The current was fierce, the dogs were barking and the Border Patrol helicopters were shining their lights as they rose and dipped, up and down, up and down over the river. But Jorgé didn't die and now as Selena held him and waited for me, she stayed in the shadows, not because she didn't like the sunshine but because she was still not sure that an immigration truck was not following my car.

Jorgé kept his thin brown legs wrapped around Selena's waist and held his good arm tight around her neck. She greeted me with a silent nod and a smile and I followed her into a room with a white linoleum floor, so clean that they could easily have eaten from it, if only they had food.

We sat down at a round table with a green flowering plant as its centerpiece. Selena found the plant in the trash outside and had nursed it back to health because in the struggle for her son's life, she had developed a quiet reverence for life in all its forms.

She had grown up in the clatter and poverty of Mexico City, one of seven children who had to share three pairs of shoes. The shoes were too big for some of the children and too small for others, but that didn't stop them from fighting for their turn whenever they wanted to go someplace.

Her father was a farm worker and her mother took in ironing, but there was so little work in the city and so little food in their house that Selena's mother used to say only God could save them. Selena thought about what her mother said and decided that it would be difficult for God to save them if they had already died of starvation. Finally, she took matters into her own hands and began selling Chiclets and pleading for pennies from the American tourists with the white skin and the fancy clothes. When Selena's mother found out that her daughter was begging in the streets, she cried and prayed for guidance. Soon afterward, the family moved to the country, where they hoped her father could get more farm work. But, in fact, things were not much better.

Now, as Selena spoke to me, Jorgé tilted his chin all the way up and, for a minute, he smiled at his mother, but the effort tired him so he let his head fall back down again onto Selena's shoulder.

"He is a good child, a sweet child, very affectionate," Selena explained, "but he sleeps a great deal of the time and he can't keep solid food down. He can't walk very well and he has no strength in his left arm."

Jorgé's eyelids fluttered softly against his cheeks like the wings of butterflies, then closed. His face was calm and wistful and his almond-shaped eyes were larger and darker and perhaps sadder than any I had ever seen before. His short dark hair barely covered a circular scar on the right side of his head.

"He has hydrocephalus," Selena said simply. "It affects the left side of his brain and his vision is very poor."

Our conversation stopped when her older son, Juan, a boy of about ten, came into the small room carrying his backpack. Although I was a total stranger, he greeted me with a handshake and a kiss on each cheek. Then, without being told, he walked into the bedroom that he shared with Jorgé and carefully hung up his white, ironed school shirt. Jorgé squirmed out of his mother's arms and tottered after his brother with worshiping eyes. His gait was unsteady and his body tipped from side to side as he lurched haltingly on wire-thin legs.

"In Mexico, they said he would die without the operation. They said there was nothing more they could do. I begged my husband to find the money. I quarreled with him. We were married ten years. He is a plumber and a good man who never abused me but he could not earn enough to save our son. After the final quarrel, he kissed me. I still remember that kiss above all the others because I knew that it would be the last one.

"When I told my closest sister that I had to come to America because I could not let Jorgé die, she said, 'You are crazy. You will never make it across the border. You will all die. You will be killed and the children will be killed.' But I knew I had to risk it. I did not tell my husband I was leaving but I said good-bye to all my brothers and my sisters and to my priest. My priest made a prayer for me that God would light my way and guide me across the waters.

"When I left, I had only one bottle of water, one bottle of milk and some crackers. I walked for two days carrying the baby just to get to northern Mexico. During those days, I drank only the water and saved the milk and crackers for the children. When a man finally gave us a ride to Juarez, all we had left were the clothes on our backs and a little money. My older son said that he was hungry and tired and scared and I said, 'Don't be scared. I am with you and don't think about the hunger. We will soon have food.'

"In Juarez, we slept under a pile of weeds that covered our bodies and I hoped we would not be found or robbed. I hoped I would not be raped. I was afraid to close my eyes because I had heard so many stories about the women being raped and being robbed by the coyotes and the Border Patrol. I had heard that the dogs would tear off our flesh and eat it if they caught us. I had also heard we could drown in the river if the current became too rough.

"I knew that there was another route into America through the dark tunnels and sewers that went under the ground, but you had to crawl for hours and often there were rats, sometimes hundreds of rats that could bite you in these tunnels. My children are afraid of rats and I had no flashlight. Besides, I knew I could not crawl carrying the baby. So, for all of these reasons I decided that the river was the only way.

"When it was still dark, I think about five in the morning, I began to hear the helicopters and dogs of the Border Patrol. I woke up my older son. We still had not eaten and we had nothing to drink for a day and a half, but I knew we were near the big river, the Rio Grande. My son wanted to eat but I told him that the dogs were nearby and we could not risk the daylight or the search for food.

"I held his face between my hands and I told him that now was the time for us to swim across the river into America. When I saw the fear in his eyes, I said, 'God will be our guide.' Then I said, "Juan, you will see that in America, all the rivers turn from muddy black to a beautiful shade of green and even the flowers have hearts of gold.' Still, he did not smile, he only trembled, so I told him more sternly that we had no choice and that he had to be very brave because our salvation depended on it.

"Then we started walking down a hill toward the river. I was carrying Jorgé. I stumbled and fell and small stones cut my knees. I put my hand over Jorgé's mouth and prayed that he would not cry. The dogs were already barking and I knew there was no turning back. Soon the muddy water was up to my neck. I held on to Jorgé and told my older son, Juan, to start swimming. He is a good swimmer but the current soon became rapid. I was holding the baby and, when I looked over, I saw that the current was carrying Juan away. I reached for him, I called to him but he was too far away. I prayed and prayed and finally he caught onto a log. I drifted toward him and I grabbed his shirt and then he began to follow me again. We went on that way for what seemed like a long, long time. When we finally reached the other side, I thought we should run, but we were so tired and so weak that we could hardly walk.

"A man offered us a ride. He said, 'Where are you going?' I said,

'Wherever.' He took us to a bus station. I went into the bathroom to wash and when I came out the immigration was there. I cried and I said, 'Please don't send us back. My baby needs to go to a hospital. My baby is very sick and he will die in Mexico.' Just then the baby began to throw up. I think that the immigration took pity on Jorgé because they gave us a hamburger and let us go.

"'You see,' I said to my oldest son, 'what did I tell you? In America, not only the flowers have hearts of gold.' Then I gave each child half of the hamburger. I did not want to buy food yet because I did not know how much the bus ticket would cost. After buying the bus ticket, I had three dollars left so I bought bread and soda for the trip. This time I also ate and the food was quickly gone.

"The bus went to Houston then to Louisiana then to Tampa. I did not know if I was on the right bus and I was afraid to ask. I was trying to get to Lake Worth, Florida, to live with my mother and father. They came three years ago after all the children were grown because there was still no work at home for my father.

"By the time we got to Houston, we were all very hungry again. The children were crying and, this time, I was crying too because I knew that there was no more money to buy food. Altogether, we did not eat for three days."

While Selena was speaking, her mother came into the room. She was a gentle, tired-looking woman in her fifties who stood quietly against the wall and listened. Her skin was lined and uneven in color. There was something in her eyes that looked like she had never been young, but there was also something else, something that seemed like quiet satisfaction and pleasure.

"You must be very proud of your daughter and grandchildren," I said, looking for some way to connect and to express my own admiration.

"*Si,*" the mother said, smiling softly. "And I am proud of her," Selena responded. "My mother and father have struggled for everything. This is a country with a kind heart but, even here, we are poor and there is not enough food for us. We have no food stamps, we have no WIC and we have no welfare, but we are not complaining. What could we expect? We were not born here, we were not invited here, we have come here to save my son and to live and to work because we heard that here, if you work hard enough, you can create a good life from nothing at all.

"You see this furniture? My mother and my father, they found most of it outside in the trash. My father, he works delivering electric parts for two hundred dollars a week. My mother, she does housecleaning when she can find the work. The rent here is six hundred fifty dollars. The electricity used to be fifty dollars but now, every month, it goes higher. The telephone is another thirty dollars but we need the phone for my son's emergencies and for the immigration. When the immigration truck comes through, the neighbors, they call each other and we hide. That leaves sixty dollars a month, if we are lucky, plus whatever my mother can earn for five of us to eat and get clothing and everything else we need. So, just as in Mexico, we are often hungry, but at least here we can go to the soup kitchen and they have a food bank in West Palm. On Friday, they give us a big bag to take home for the weekend. We go to the soup kitchen almost every day and that is how we live. My biggest fear now is that the immigration will find me when I go out to get food. I am afraid that they will send me to prison or send me home. If it were up to me, I think I would hide in the house all the time. But my mother says, 'Selena, you are young. You must go out, you cannot live your life in the shadows.'

"At night, when I sleep, sometimes I dream that in America there is no immigration truck and there is enough work for everyone so we can buy all the food and all the medicine we need. In my dream, I can pay for Jorgé's operation and my husband is also here. After work, he is playing ball with Jorgé because now Jorgé can walk and run and jump. Then, when I wake up, sometimes I cry because my husband does not know where I am. I miss him but I am afraid that if he finds us he will try to take us back. I have left my husband to save my son. I will do anything for my children.

"The other day Jorgé had a seizure. In Mexico, I know that he would have died by now. But here, I dialed 911 and they came. For life-and-death emergencies, they will not turn him away. They will take him to the hospital and, thank God, so far at least, they have been able to save him."

Selena wiped her cheeks and then she smiled radiantly.

"You see," she said, "there is no other country like America."

Chapter 7

A Story without an End

"It was only possible for me to do it," he said, "because it was necessary. I either had to write the book or be reduced to despair."

HERMAN HESSE,
The Journey to the East

The Ghosts of Yesterday

In writing this book, I have often traveled alone in uncharted territory. I have zigzagged through dirty streets, lonely towns and unfamiliar cities. I have climbed the steps of tenements, heard the glass of broken windows cracking under my feet and held the hands of hungry children on flea-infested beds. I have knocked on countless unfamiliar doors, seeking the eyes of strangers in the opening cracks, hoping they would see beyond the uncertainty in my eyes and read the friendship.

I am by nature a timid person with a poor sense of direction and a fear of the unfamiliar. Sometimes, when I got lost and the tiny screen on the red cell phone that linked me to my home and family read "no service," I wondered why I had come and why I felt so compelled to take on this massive self-imposed task, all alone, for the second time in twenty-five years.

I didn't have a research grant, a large advance, a team of physicians, a nonprofit organization or an assistant to help me. I had never even learned to type and so I still wrote and rewrote my manuscripts by hand on yellow legal pads.

I knew that I had taken on this work partly because I felt more richness in the empty homes of poor strangers than I did at lavish cocktail parties where I stood making small talk on the heels of too-tight shoes, feeling the weight of my small evening bag like a heavy backpack after weeks on the open road.

But I also knew that it was because, in these homes, I would always find children whose eyes still sparkled with hope, innocent children, peeking around the safety of their mothers' skirts to stare at me before venturing out, eager children whose hands and hearts still opened in the anticipation that life would be full, silent children fluent only in the language of dreams. I knew that I was there because I found, in the eyes and hands and hearts of these children, the core of all that was profound and meaningful in my life.

As I listened to the dreams of mothers who had sometimes lost everything but the skin that covered their bones and their children's good-night kisses, I found truths that empowered me. Sometimes, I found myself drawn into unfamiliar places, places I had never expected to go, yet I was never really afraid. Somehow, I always felt more like a refugee who had finally found shelter than a pilgrim who wandered alone, because I knew that these were the places I left home for and found my true home in. It was as if this path had been marked out for me a long, long time ago; as if it had been imprinted in the chambers of my heart that day when I was six years old and had traveled through the poor, still-segregated South.

Though I hadn't seen her since, I sometimes felt as if a small barefoot girl I met that day at the edge of a dusty road with tears that made paths on her cheeks was still leading me.

We had stopped in search of a bathroom but the sign on the door where the little girl stood read, "Colored Only." When she held up an empty water bottle and asked us for food, my mother gently led me away. As we drove on, I saw more children. They tumbled out of broken shacks and stood in doorways that had no doors. Some had thin arms and legs but bellies so swollen with hunger that they looked like the bellies of grown women who would soon have babies of their own.

I cried at the accumulated grief of the ragged hungry children. I cried at my own helplessness and I cried because my mother and father, who I still believed could solve any problem, had said that this one was too big for us. I cried with inconsolable, broken sobs. I cried until I had ruined my parents' afternoon. I cried until they finally stopped at a small Woolworth's and gave me a dollar to spend in hope of distracting me. I wandered down the aisles still crying until I spotted a small doll with ebony skin, a pink dress, cropped hair and glowing eyes. I named the doll Lettie. For me, she was the future and the beginning of time.

When my father's car drove past the muddy poverty of the Mississippi Delta toward the beautiful gulf coast, I eventually stopped crying. But, though I did not know it, my life had been defined in that moment, that one moment that came and went and stayed with me forever. The coals of my heart had been lit by a girl I never knew and by a desire to understand why some children seemed destined to remain hungry and poor.

In the decades that followed, the questions that haunted me were asked again and again by politicians, scholars, hunger task forces and groups of physicians. But to this day, none of them have found and implemented an answer that solved the problem. There has always been a dream in America, a dream that anyone willing to work hard enough could succeed. Americans love the story of the poor boy who grew up in a log cabin and became the president of the United States. But the reality is that, most of the time, family legacy plays a larger role in our lives than the work ethic.

George Bush Senior knew that the presidency was a real possibility for his sons the same way the poor know that hunger is a real possibility for theirs. Just as the children of doctors and lawyers build their hopes on their parents' successes, so the children of the poor often have their paths marked out for them by their parents' poverty and by the hunger and malnutrition they experience as a result.

Dr. Debbie Frank, a Boston pediatrician who has been running the Failure to Thrive program at the Grow Clinic at Boston Medical Center since November 1984, says that all of the children she sees in her practice are poor and malnourished. They get sent to her because the primary-care physicians find them "too scary" to deal with.

In her seventeen years at the clinic, the biggest shift she has observed is in the increasing number of hungry and malnourished children from working families. That is because access to food stamps and other benefits always depends on the last month's income, and families with uncertain income who run out of food can't wait until the next month. They need the help immediately because without it they will soon become so desperate that they will eat anything they can find, beg or steal.

Since malnutrition impairs the immune system, especially the ability to fight off viruses and gastrointestinal impairment, the malnourished kids she sees get sick a lot more often than well-nourished ones. Like all sick children, they frequently throw up, lose their appetite and lose weight. The difference is that when these kids get over their illness, there's nothing extra in the house to feed them and help them gain back the weight they've lost. So, each time the cycle repeats, the child loses more weight. Since malnourished children acquire illnesses faster, with each weight loss they become more susceptible and less able to quickly recover from the next episode.

As Dr. Frank puts it, "Child hunger is a health issue, a very serious one. My kids don't have AIDS but they function as if they did. The difference is that their immune systems were fine until they became malnourished. Now, they just continue to decline and decline. That downward spiral is what I worry about most in the short term, but in the long term, I worry about their cognitive mental development. The first thing malnourished children do is cut down on discretionary activity like talking, reading and interacting. They sleep more, they play less and they connect less.

"By the time most kids get to me, they have become so listless and tired that they have slept through many opportunities for learning. Even before their growth has been noticeably compromised, the high cognitive cost of hunger has been felt. Since learning is cumulative, just think how much learning is lost over many years of hunger."

Some of the effects of malnourishment are silent and almost invisible to the average person. Like yo-yo dieters, poor children who have experienced hunger frequently gorge when they have access to food. They also tend to fill up on fried foods and soda because they are cheap, and the fat and the bubbles make them feel full. But the kids Debbie Frank sees don't even get enough french fries or soda.

"The impoverished Asian population gets a lot of thin soup," she explained. "The African-American population often eats oatmeal and the Spanish population subsists mostly on rice and beans." Dr. Frank keeps a food pantry right there at the clinic. "I have to," she said. "What's the point of telling them what their child needs to eat and watching them burst into tears because they don't have the money or the food stamps to get it? Malnourished kids don't just need to eat, they need to eat one and a half times the food the average kid consumes in order to make up for the nutritional deprivation they've already experienced.

"When I got involved here in the mid-1980s, I thought it was a short-term thing, but the hunger I've seen in America is like a famine that sometimes recedes but never goes away. That's because it's not an act of God, it's an act of legislature. It increases whenever our public programs decrease. We see a lot of kids here who are hungry now because of the 1996 Welfare to Work changes. We see others that are victims of the Family Cap policy. That's the program that will not increase payments to a family when another child is born. As a result, when families grow in size, each kid gets even less to eat. We don't punish the parents, we punish the kids. Since '96 our federal policies have really become punitive policies because on top of the federal cuts, we've had such high housing costs and such high fuel costs that the need for emergency food has been driven up even further.

"Politicians and legislators seem to be in very serious denial about the fact that they are voting on policies and choosing programs that starve children.

"Even if a family got all the food benefits from WIC, welfare and food stamps combined, they'd still only be getting two-thirds of what a growing child needs to be healthy, and that's if they weren't already undernourished. It's like me giving a kid half a dose of penicillin and expecting him to get well.

"It's not that these programs aren't useful," Dr. Frank added. "It's that there isn't enough food provided by them. Just like with medicine, you have to give the right dose. Politicians and legislators have to be realistic. They have to understand that, even if they say the cuts are for the able-bodied family members, the children will also eat less because the food in these families is shared. Poor families aren't going to let Uncle Harry starve because he can't find work and his stamps have been cut off. Little as they have, the poor are often kinder and more generous to each other than the larger population is to them.

"One pregnant mother I saw here recently looked hungry so I said, 'Have you eaten today?' She said, 'Not yet, but don't worry, my son Johnnie will bring some of his free lunch home to me in his pockets.' The spirit of sharing is wonderful, but because these families lack an adequate supply of food to share, the whole family often ends up chronically malnourished."

In economic terms, we have always known that in a land of plenty, hunger and malnutrition make no sense. The 14.5 million American children who experienced food insecurity, hunger or starvation in the year 2000 had a profound impact on the entire nation. As the Children's Defense Fund put it, "All segments of society share in paying the costs of children's poverty just as they would all share in the gains if child poverty were eliminated. In fact, the American labor force is projected to lose as much as $130 billion in future productive capacity (an amount more than twice the size of the U.S. annual trade deficit with Japan) for every year that 14.5 million American children continue to live in poverty."

"I don't see it as very different here than it is in third world countries," Larry Brown said the first time we met. "The impact is still morbidity and mortality. The latest research on cognitive function shows us that there is really no mild undernutrition.

"What we found in our field studies was often similar to what I saw in third world countries. What we do in this country is not really very different from taking people who are desperate into a refugee camp and then threatening them under the guise of helping them. I've been in those refugee camps and I've seen the faces of people who are lost and terrified. I've also been in our welfare offices and our food stamp offices. At the slight risk of a little hyperbole, I saw the same kind of faces, the same kind of people and the same kind of fear. I saw them being treated in the same kind of mean-spirited, threatening, intimidating way.

"I've seen hunger in the third world and I've seen hunger in America and I've seen very similar outcomes. In America there are not as many lives being crippled and perhaps not as deeply but it is clearly a continuum and not a dichotomy. Where is the line to be drawn between a child in a third world country who has chronic hunger and a child in America who doesn't get enough to eat? Both kids' minds are being sapped. Both kids are never going to live up to their potential. Both have their health compromised and both have to have altered senses about the adult world and about what love and care mean.

"When I was in the Peace Corps in India, I learned that I couldn't ride in on a white horse and fix things. I saw that the people didn't need charity, they needed justice. The same is true here. Since 1982 or 1983 domestic hunger has been my work. I've never been able to give it up because I've never really succeeded. Oh, I've had some successes. There were five billion dollars in add-backs to the twelve billion dollars that the Reagan administration cut from the budget and I could tell people these success stories, but the fundamental fact is I've been a failure because hunger still exists."

Brown's eyes narrowed. "I work with about two hundred food banks now, and as far as I'm concerned they are at the right hand of God. They have their finger in the dike. I see all of them as saints but I see the need for their charity as the failure of a nation.

"The problems are so easy for the federal government to solve that if the president and Congress really wanted to they could do so in six months. It's a failure of will and a failure of political leadership that they haven't done so.

"The official, unspoken policy position is that the American government doesn't have enough money or food to solve its social problems or feed its hungry children. The reality is, we have a trillion-dollar surplus building up."

Back in 1997, the Center on Hunger and Poverty received a request from Second Harvest to analyze the impact that the Contract With America with its food stamp cuts would have on hunger. The center was asked to determine whether Second Harvest and other emergency groups could fill the gap and feed all the hungry people the cuts would create.

"The analyses will be pleasing to no one," the center wrote after the study had been completed. "Food Stamp cuts, part of the changes in welfare policy . . . are the largest cutbacks in any federal food program in the nation's history; moreover, there is no basis to conclude that either Second Harvest or all emergency food providers combined can begin to make up for the magnitude of food that will be withdrawn from low-income families. These changes in food policy are certain to result in more Americans going hungry."

The analysis pointed out that the loss of food stamps was equivalent to 20.63 billion meals, or enough food to feed all the people in Texas three meals a day for an entire year. The loss was four times the 5.82 billion pounds of food that the forty-two thousand agencies of the Second Harvest network were likely to be able to distribute over that period.

The study concluded that even if they could double the amount of food they provided, the entire emergency food network could still only manage to supply less than one-third of the food that would be needed to make up for the shortfall.

On April 19, 2000, Food Chain, which still specialized in distributing excess perishable food from restaurants, hotels and caterers, merged with Second Harvest which, by that time, had established nearly two hundred food banks throughout the United States.

Together, during the course of a year, they distributed a billion pounds of food to about 26 million people, including 8 million children. But it still wasn't nearly enough.

What is needed is a change in vision, a change that acts on the American belief that every child in this country has the right to food, a change that converts that belief into a workable plan.

One such plan was actually handed to us back in 1990. At that time, growing anguish about hungry children had caused the Center on Hunger and Poverty to convene a group of concerned experts at Tufts University in Medford, Massachusetts. Over several months, the group drafted a document that became known as the Medford Declaration. The committee was made up of the members of several national hunger organizations, including World Hunger Year and the Food Research and Action Center. The document they created was reviewed by corporate chairpersons, foundation presidents and community leaders. It was revised six times based on their comments.

The committee believed that we had the knowledge, the programs and the resources to end hunger in "a matter of months."

The program itself required two steps. The first step was to see that food was made available to the hungry on an adequate and consistent basis by expanding existing public food programs so that, when they were combined with the "heroic efforts" of voluntary food providers, the food needs of hungry and starving Americans could finally be met in an adequate way.

They suggested that until federal programs were expanded to that level, we could meet the emergency food needs of our families by moving surplus food into the communities in much the same way that we ship goods to feed our military personnel overseas or respond to starvation in third world countries.

The second, more long-term step, was to attack the causes of hunger by increasing the earning power, independence and self-reliance of poverty-stricken American families.

The middle class is used to receiving help in ways that the poor have largely been denied. They have received loans, mortgages, retirement accounts and tax breaks that have helped them build equity capital and other assets.

With the poor, the government has done just the opposite. They have insisted that the poor have nothing left at all, no house, no car of any value, no savings and no income that is large enough to lift them out of poverty before they can receive even short-term help with food.

The Medford Declaration sought to change that. It got substantial press coverage when it was released but did not have the long-term impact that its founders had hoped for. They saturated Congress and the press with thousands of copies of the two-sided red, white and blue declaration but found that it was very hard for a single document to drive public opinion and create far-reaching, permanent change. While there have been other plans to end hunger since then, most have followed the same basic principles.

The concepts behind the Medford Declaration are as usable and as sound today as they were in 1990. If we had the will, it could still become a standard by which this nation expresses its values, its goals and its commitment to end hunger and starvation among American children and their parents.

But our legislators not only failed to respond to the Medford Declaration of 1990, they introduced the massive cuts of 1996, which are still in the process of being implemented. As a result, over 100 million more children have needlessly gone hungry.

If I have grown less optimistic than I was when *Starving in the Shadow of Plenty* was published, it is because, in researching this book, I have traced the battle against hunger all the way back to 1967 and I have recently watched what happens when a government of great power diminishes its commitment to its families, especially its children, by withdrawing the equivalent of almost 24 billion pounds of food.

Ending poverty and hunger means more than just ending welfare and asking charity to do the impossible by picking up the shortfall caused by massive food stamp cuts. It means training people to do meaningful work at fair wages and it means caring enough to make sure that their families don't starve during the process. It means providing food stamps and food aid to the children and adults who need them without intimidation or humiliation. It means adequate pay to all working people, including immigrants and military families. It means a minimum wage that can actually support and feed families.

On the iron gates of the Nazi concentration camps, there was a sign that read, *Arbeit macht frei* (Work will make you free). But work only makes people free when they are not imprisoned by the circumstances of their lives and when they are justly compensated for it. Setting people free from poverty and starvation is not only economically wise and morally just, it is at the very heart of America's value system. It is also within our grasp.

During the mid to late '60s, when the Johnson administration declared its war on poverty, the number of poor children in the country actually decreased by 45 percent from 17.6 million to 9.7 million. During the next two decades, however, the number of children in poverty increased again by over 37 percent.

That is because, once again, at the start of the '80s, the Reagan administration decided to reduce the role of the government's food aid and poverty measures. Some domestic programs were eliminated entirely while funding for others was reduced.

"In the quiet of American conscience," George W. Bush said during his inauguration speech twenty years later, "we know that deep, persistent poverty is unworthy of our nation's promise and whatever our views of its cause, we can agree, children at risk are not at fault."

The word "hunger" was never mentioned. The reference to America's vulnerable children was as close as George W. Bush came to publicly acknowledging that hunger still ran rampant, starving the souls and the bodies of 12.1 million of America's children in the year that he took office. Perhaps that is because he genuinely did not know or perhaps it is because acknowledging America's starving children would require responding to them swiftly, urgently and as a top priority.

But he made another reference to the future of those children and to all our futures when he said, "We have a place, all of us, in a long story, a story we continue but whose end we will not see."

President Bush's remark made me think of another story, a small personal story, just a fragment really but a fragment that contains the larger, sadder American story.

As I drove home from my last trip to the Mississippi Delta, I found myself on a long dusty road near Greenwood, Mississippi. I passed several shacks. The area looked strangely familiar but I had grown so used to rural poverty that I didn't really make a connection until I saw a small, thin, barefoot child dancing like a sunbeam off in the distance with a plastic water bottle in her hand. I followed behind her and watched, fascinated, as she turned into a run-down gas station.

I stopped my car at the side of the road, jumped out and ran up a dusty path as the image of another small girl with charcoal eyes burned through all the years.

The child looked at me and put her hands on her belly. Her fingers opened wide and splayed across it like stars. I turned for a moment and glanced behind me, half expecting to feel my mother's hand on my shoulder gently pulling me away or see my father's old maroon Chevy parked there in the dust. But my father had died sixteen years earlier and my mother was in the care center of a life care community.

There was only my small, rented Geo Metro with one unopened bag of pretzels and a can of Coke inside. I quickly grabbed them and handed them to the little girl in hope of forgiveness and as a silent offering for all I could not say. As I looked at her and watched her reaction, I saw how one small act of kindness, just one, had made her opaque eyes turn to diamonds. She pointed to a door that no longer read, "Colored Only" and offered me the bathroom first.

"No, thank you," I said. "I stopped because I saw you." I hesitated, searching for the right words. "You remind me of someone. I know this is impossible," I finally said, "but I think I might have seen your mother, no, I guess it would have been your grandmother, here a long, long time ago."

I wanted to say more, much more, but I didn't know where to start.

She opened the pretzels and offered me one.

"You might have," she said kindly, almost as if she sensed my need. She looked at me more closely, then reached out her hand and gently touched my fingers with hers. "She used to come here all the time to get fresh drinking water just like I do. We all live right down there," she added, pointing toward a group of shacks off in the distance, where whole families still sat in doorways that had no doors.

"Nothing's changed around here," I whispered.

"No," the child said softly. "Nothing's really changed."

The Last Word

All of the interviews in this book took place before September 11, 2001. In the winter that followed the terrorist attacks, 800,000 more Americans lost their jobs, and hunger in America increased dramatically. On the brighter side, in January 2002, enlisted military families received a small pay increase, but it was still not enough to lift them out of poverty or to provide adequate food for their families.

The 7.5 percent military pay increase just amounted to about $75 a month before taxes. For most newly enlisted personnel, that brought basic pay at the E1 level to $1,022.70 a month. An E2 earned $1,105.50. There was also a housing allowance increase that, according to statistics released by the Department of Defense, raised off-base housing subsidies to $429.60 a month for E1s and E2s with dependents and to $450.90 for E3s with more than three years of service. The result, according to Pat Kellenbarger, director of Military Parish Visitors in San Diego, was positive but short-lived. For the first time, many of the families had a housing allowance that came into the ballpark of what they needed for rent and utilities. But as soon as current leases ended, Pat predicted that most landlords would raise the rents proportionately. As far as food goes, Pat said, sadly, "There is still not enough money to feed these families. In fact, we have more military families lining up for free groceries than ever. San Diego has also sent more units to Afghanistan than any other part of the country. They've taken our best and bravest but, because of COMMARTS, the wives and children have lost their husband's food allowance. A little over seven dollars a day has been taken out of their monthly paycheck. After thirty days, one hundred of the two hundred seventeen dollars they lost are put back in the form of separation pay but that still leaves a discrepancy larger, considerably larger, than the pay raise for the newer recruits."

The military increase President Bush mentioned in his 2002 State of the Union address is being proposed for 2003. As of this writing, the amount had not been announced. But whatever the boost, Pat Kellenbarger thinks it is not likely to match the constantly rising cost of living. "For example," she said, "we just got a fifteen percent surcharge put onto our utility bills. It looks like there's more money in the paychecks but the ripple-down effect is so small that our enlisted soldiers will still be struggling just to feed their families. No," she said with sorrow in her voice, "I don't expect to go out of business any time soon."

The shifting political mood since September 11 has also affected millions of immigrants. When Mexican president Vincente Fox came to the White House just six days before the attacks, he and his new wife, Martha, were greeted in the Grand Foyer by strolling violinists and twelve-foot trees with blooming white flowers. There was tequila sauce on the dessert and fireworks on the back lawn.

Bush said he had chosen Fox to be the first state visitor of his administration in recognition of the fact that "the United States has no more important relationship in the world than the one we have with Mexico." It looked as if America was finally going to admit that its economy counted heavily on Mexican workers. It appeared that those undocumented men and women whose labors contribute $154 billion to our gross national product each year would finally be allowed to come out of hiding.

But since the attacks, all support has crumbled. Though none of those people was suspected of terrorism, analysts say it would be political suicide for Bush to revisit the issue of legalizing Mexican immigrants. They have suffered incalculable damage. They have become the secondary victims of those who cannot distinguish between the people who seek the American dream and the people who want to destroy it.

As the *New York Times* pointed out in an article on December 27, 2001, the food lines in New York now began forming just after sunrise. Men, women and children often stood quietly shivering in their thrift-store parkas, too tired and too hungry to say much. They were waiting for boxes of raisins, cans of salmon, instant mashed potatoes, or whatever else was available. Although an entire system existed to feed these people, with donations sinking and need increasing, that system was in danger of collapse. In New York City alone, one and a half million people now counted on food pantries. Sixty percent of them were seeking emergency food for the first time. But many who lined up hungry at sunrise received only a numbered ticket that allowed them to return at dusk for something to eat.

The director of one New York church reported that before September 11, when three hundred people arrived for food on a single day, he thought it was a lot. Now he expected to see more than a thousand each day.

The story was the same all over the country.

A director of the Philadelphia Food Bank and its eight hundred member agencies said that they did a fund-raiser in January 2002, then added, "That's unheard of for us, but the response to our usual fund-raising efforts was down nearly seventy percent. Our supermarket donation campaign, 'Check Out Hunger,' so successful for the last ten years, was also suddenly down fifty percent. No doubt it was the result of people giving so generously to the September 11 relief funds."

At the same time that the newly unemployed continued to create an unprecedented level of need, cutbacks, hiring freezes, and fierce new competition made it harder than ever for people to find jobs. A surge of evictions spread across America. Suddenly, in New York, Philadelphia, Boston, Cleveland, Milwaukee, and other cities, social workers and tenant advocates reported frantic calls from men and women desperately searching for ways to shelter their children while getting out of leases they could no longer afford. By February 2002, evictions had surged to an all-time high, so had pleas for emergency food.

In Cleveland, the Catholic Charities basic-needs hotline logged 82 percent more calls than they had the year before with most of the increases coming since September 11.

The Cleveland Justice Center was packed with so many land-lords and tenants pleading eviction cases that on a typical day they filled every bench and lined both sides of the courtroom.

In the winter of 2002, the swelling counts of homeless people reached into every urban area. There were 29,800 in New York City alone and more than half of them were children. Shelter directors were setting up cots in the hallways and mats on the floor with only an inch between them, and still they were turning people away.

In Boston, the crisis was so severe that they were sending families to suburban hotels thirty miles outside of the city. In Minneapolis, some of the shelter directors were holding nightly lotteries to see who would win beds or mattresses on the floor.

President Bush's primary response to the burgeoning crisis that followed September 11 was to call for another $48 billion for the Pentagon and refuse to revisit the issue of tax cuts that primarily benefited the rich.

As Mathew Miller of the *Philadelphia Inquirer* perceptively pointed out, no one could really demand a tax increase or challenge a wartime President by saying he wanted too much for defense in a time of real national danger. But those priorities effectively ruled out funding the unmet social needs of Americans for perhaps another generation.

It should be acknowledged that soon after the war in Afghanistan began, President Bush took to the airways and, in an admirable and compassionate gesture, he spoke openly of hunger and homelessness. His speech was effective. The need was dire, and his power to lead was obvious. Within two weeks, more than 1.5 million children had each sent a dollar to help feed the hungry children . . . *of Afghanistan.*

Appendixes

"I still have the audacity to believe that people everywhere can have three meals a day. . . . I still believe that what self-centered men have torn down, other centered men can build up. . . . I still believe that we shall overcome."

MARTIN LUTHER KING, JR.,
Nobel Prize acceptance speech

Appendix A   The Medford Declaration

The Medford Declaration is reprinted with the permission of World Hunger Year.

THE MEDFORD DECLARATION
TO END HUNGER IN THE U.S.

We can end hunger in America, and we can end it now.

Three decades ago a new President challenged our nation with two goals: to reach the moon and to end domestic hunger. We have reached only one of these goals. It is time to achieve the other.

Hunger has no place in the new world tomorrow brings. It is a form of economic suicide. Hunger is also inconsistent with our conscience. If anything is un-American, it is hunger.

We believe Americans have reached a consensus on ending hunger. We come to this consensus from many points of view.

Many of us are moved by the belief that the United States is losing its economic leadership, and that we must invest more in our children and families to insure national productivity in a more competitive world. Others are moved by enlightened self-interest, pointing out that we either pay now or pay later for preventable problems.

Still other citizens address domestic hunger out of strong moral or religious convictions. And many in the fields of education and health are moved by the crippling impact of hunger on the health and learning capacity of our children.

From many walks of life, we are one people—a people who agree that we can eradicate hunger in our country. A people who believe we must do so.

Abolishing hunger at home will require two steps.

In the short term we must use existing channels to see that food is available to the hungry on an adequate and consistent basis. If we fully utilize existing public programs in conjunction with the heroic efforts of voluntary food providers in local communities—we can end hunger very soon.

But we must move as a nation to end the causes of hunger as well. Many things can be done to increase the purchasing power of American households, and to fulfill the desire for independence and self-reliance which so characterizes our people.

We can achieve this two-step goal before the start of the new century.

We can begin with children . . . and we can virtually eliminate domestic hunger by 1995.

Programs exist to insure that all Americans have enough to eat by 1995. Within months we can meet emergency needs by moving surplus foodstuffs into the communities of the nation as quickly as we ship goods to feed our military personnel overseas. Within two years we can fully use existing federal food programs to prevent hunger.

We must begin with children. We can reach every needy child with the school lunch and breakfast program. We can start with the six million poor youngsters who often begin their school day with no food. We can fully use the highly effective WIC program to help insure that poor mothers do not give birth to undernourished babies—protecting four million more youngsters who presently are at risk.

We can expand the benefits of food stamps which help unemployed households make it through economically difficult times. And we can insure that no elderly citizen goes without the nutrients provided by Meals on Wheels and congregate feeding.

These steps alone can virtually wipe out domestic hunger by mid-decade.

We can achieve economic self-reliance for most American households by the year 2000.

Promoting adequate purchasing power is the way to achieve the goal of a hunger-free United States. This nation will have defeated chronic hunger when its people achieve "food security"—regular access to an adequate diet through normal means.

A variety of steps can be taken this decade to accomplish this end: market-based employment and training programs to build skills and expand jobs; making sure child care is available so parents can work; expanding concepts such as earned income tax credits and children's allowances so that the tax system strengthens families. The goal is to increase the purchasing power of employed heads-of-households so that work raises families out of poverty.

The current window of world peace now gives us the opportunity to abolish domestic hunger. We can increase the competitiveness of our work force and protect the vital energies of our young. And we can assist emerging democracies of the world with pride because all Americans will enjoy the most basic fruit of our own democracy—freedom and family security.

We stand at a special moment in history. Perhaps for the first time, our desire to end hunger is converging with the opportunity to do so. We have moved from ability to consensus. We now need the political leadership to achieve the longheld goal of an America free of hunger.

Appendix B   Organizations

This list was graciously supplied by World Hunger Year. Anyone who wants to become involved in the volunteer effort to fight hunger can contact these organizations for more information. World Hunger Year, America's Second Harvest and the Food Research and Action Center can provide Web site lists of specific local organizations that are broken down by state.

ORGANIZATIONS

WORLD HUNGER YEAR (WHY)
505 8th Avenue (21st floor)
New York, NY 10018
(212) 629-8850
www.worldhungeryear.org

World Hunger Year is committed to telling the story of hunger to the public, the media and policy makers. They document grassroots organizations around the country so that their successful programs can be replicated by others searching for long-term solutions to poverty. WHY has seven programs:

Reinvesting in America
USDA National Hunger Clearinghouse
WHY International
Kids Can Make a Difference
Artists Against Hunger and Poverty
Harry Chapin Media Awards
Harry Chapin Self-Reliance Awards

AMERICA'S SECOND HARVEST
35 E. Wacker Drive
Suite 2000
Chicago, IL 60601
(312) 263-2303
www.secondharvest.org

America's Second Harvest is the nation's largest domestic hunger-relief organization.

BREAD FOR THE WORLD
1100 Wayne Avenue
Suite 1000
Silver Spring, MD 20910
(301) 608-2400
www.bread.org

Bread for the World has educational activities and resources for learning about hunger.

CONGRESSIONAL HUNGER CENTER
525 A Street NE
Washington, DC 20002
(202) 547-7022
www.hungercenter.org

The purpose of CHC is to ensure that the issues of domestic and international hunger remain at the forefront of national debate.

INSTITUTE FOR FOOD AND
DEVELOPMENT POLICY
398 60th Street
Oakland, CA 94618
(510) 654-4400
www.foodfirst.org
Email: foodfirst@foodfirst.org

This is a hunger research and educational center. It is a member-supported, nonprofit "people's" think tank and education-for-action center. Their work highlights root causes and value-based solutions to hunger and poverty around the world.

KIDS CAN MAKE A DIFFERENCE®
P.O. Box 54
Kittery Point, ME 03905
(207) 439-9588
www.kids.maine.org

This is a program of WORLD HUNGER YEAR that provides
educational programs for middle and high school students and
focuses on the root causes of hunger and poverty, the people most
affected, solutions, and how students can help.

NATIONAL STUDENT CAMPAIGN AGAINST HUNGER
AND HOMELESSNESS
233 N. Pleasant Street
Suite 32
Amherst, MA 01002
(800) NO-HUNGR
www.nscahh.org

The National Student Campaign Against Hunger and
Homelessness is the largest student network fighting hunger and
homelessness in the county, with more than six hundred
participating campuses in forty-five states.

OXFAM
26 West Street
Boston, MA 02111
(800) 597-FAST
www.oxfamamerica.org

Oxfam America invests privately raised funds and technical
expertise in the local organizations around the world that hold
promise in their efforts to help poor people move out of poverty.

RESULTS
236 Massachusetts Avenue NE
Suite 300
Washington, DC 20002-4980
(202) 543-9340
www.action.org

Results: Ending Hunger and Poverty is a nonprofit, grassroots citizens' lobby that identifies sustainable solutions to the problems of hunger and poverty. Results identifies the most cost-effective programs that positively impact the lives of the poorest of the poor, and then advocates for increased funding and replication of these programs.

SHARE OUR STRENGTH (SOS)
733 15th Street NW
Suite 640
Washington, DC 20005
(202) 393-2925
www.strength.org

The nation's leading antihunger organization, SOS works toward ending hunger and poverty in the U.S. and abroad by supporting food assistance programs, treating malnutrition and other consequences of hunger and promoting economic independence among people in need.

FOOD RESEARCH AND ACTION CENTER (FRAC)
1875 Connecticut Avenue NW
Suite 540
Washington DC 20009
(202) 986-2200
www.frac.org

FRAC is a leading national organization working to improve public policies to eradicate hunger and undernutrition in the United States.

Notes

Preface

page

3 marasmus *Living Hungry in America,* Dr. J. Larry Brown and H. F. Pfizer, Macmillan, pp. 191–92.

4 Harvard Physicians Task Force Ibid., p. 193.

4 USDA *Hunger in the United States,* Ashley Sullivan, Food Security Institute, Center on Hunger and Poverty, 2000, p. 1.

13 denied the validity *Living Hungry in America,* p. 163.

14 1995 study *From Welfare to Work,* Felice David Perlmutter, Oxford University Press, p. 6.

15 Pollett *The Link Between Nutrition and Cognitive Development in Children,* Center on Hunger, Poverty, and Nutrition Policy, 1998, p. 3.

17 welfare to work *Unraveling the Safety Net and Welfare Reform,* Policy Research Action Group, Center for Urban Research and Learning, 1997.

18 tribute to Congress *Philadelphia Inquirer,* May 21, 2001, p. 1.

18 *Welfare to What? Early Findings on Family Hardship and Well-Being,* Children's Defense Fund, National Coalition for the Homeless, 1998.

Introduction

24 **safety net** Statements made in interviews in the *Washington Post*, December 4, 1983, and July 8, 1983, respectively. They are quoted here from *Hunger in America: The Growing Epidemic*, Physicians Task Force, p. 139.

24 **newly poor** Ibid., p. 135.

Chapter 1: Hunger and the Middle Class

49 *No Shame in My Game*, Katherine S. Newman, First Vintage Books Edition, April 2000, p. 43, copyright © 1999 by Russell Sage Foundation.

49 *Falling from Grace*, p. 203, quoting from Census Bureau report, pp. 60–187, *Who Receives Child Support*, May 1995.

51 **suburbs** *All Our Families: New Policies for a New Century*, National Center for Policy Analysis Idea House, the Berkeley Family Forum, New York, Oxford University Press, 1998.

Chapter 2: Hunger and the Always Poor

61 *Falling by the Wayside: Children in Rural America*, Arloc Sherman, Children's Defense Fund, 1992, p. 42.

61 "... fifteen minutes late." Ibid., p. 58.

76 **domestic abuse** *Trapped by Poverty, Trapped by Abuse*, by Jody Raphael, ex-director of the Taylor Institute, and Richard M. Tolman, Ph.D., Assistant Professor, School of Social Work, University of Michigan, April 1997, p. 4 of executive summary.

77 **often seek employment** Ibid.

77 **Ford Foundation** Floor statements by U.S. Senator Paul D. Wellstone, December 26, 2000, introducing the National Domestic Violence Hotline Enhancement Act.

78 Child Protective Services and Domestic Violence, Janet E. Findlater and Susan Kelley, *The Future of Children, Domestic Violence and Children*, vol. 9, no. 3, winter 1999, p. 1.

78 **living with poverty and hunger** *New Mobility* magazine, 1995.

Chapter 3: Hunger and the Military

85 **Military pay varies** "Feeling the Pinch of a Military Salary: For Some Families, Pay Doesn't Cover the Basics," Steve Vogel, *Washington Post*, July 20, 1999, p. 2.

96 **53 percent of fighting forces are married** *Making the Corps*, Thomas E. Ricks, Simon and Schuster, 1998, pp. 19–25.

99 **Danny Holley** Associated Press, reported in *Democrat and Chronicle*, Rochester, N.Y., August 30, 1984.

99 **military-civilian gap** "Life in the Military, Fallen on Hard Times," *USA Today*, May 18, 1999, front-page story by Carol Morello.

100 **public assistance** Ibid., p. 1.

100 **Marine Community Service** Ibid., p. 2.

Chapter 4: Hunger and the Working Poor

135 **cut off food stamps** *Hunger in America*, p. 153–57.

138 *The Link Between Nutrition and Cognitive Development in Children*, Center on Hunger, Poverty and Nutrition Policy, 1998, p. 5.

139 **School Breakfast Program** Ibid., p. 9.

137 **poverty level** *From Welfare to Work: Corporate Initiatives and Welfare Reform*, Felice Davidson Perlmutter, Oxford University Press, 1997, p. 14.

148 *One World, Ready or Not*, p. 417.

Chapter 5: Hunger and the Homeless

151 **homeless families** *Homeless Families, Failed Policies and Young Victims*, Children's Defense Fund, Child, Youth and Family Futures Clearing House, 1991, p. 2.

173 The Urban Institute press release, February 1, 2000, p. 1.

173 **Seventy-five percent** *Homeless Families*, p. 3.

175 *The Other America, Poverty in the United States*, Michael Harrington, New York, Collier Books, Macmillan Publishing Co., 1993, p. 2.

Chapter 6: Hunger, the Immigrants and the Refugees

196 California Food Policy Advocates *Paradox of Our Times: Hunger in a Strong Economy*, Center on Hunger and Poverty, 2000, pp. 20–21.

207 Paraphrased from *Across the Wire*, Luis Alberto Urrea, pp. 11–12.

208 "If you have daughters . . ." Ibid., p. 15.

208 "coyotes" *Time* magazine, "The Coyote's Game," June 11, 2001, p. 58.

Chapter 7: A Story without an End

226 analyze the impact *Analysis of the Capacity of the Second Harvest Network to Cover the Federal Food Stamp Shortfall from 1997–2002*, pp. 2–5.

229 children in poverty *Two Americas, Alternative futures for child poverty in the U.S.*, Center on Hunger and Poverty, p. 9.

The Last Word

235 food lines in New York *New York Times*, December 27, 2001, "Hungry, Cold and Stuck on Line," Alan Fever, p. D1.